SPEAKING ILL OF THE DEAD:

Jerks in Connecticut History

Ray Bendici

gpp

Guilford, Connecticut

Text design: Sheryl P. Kober
Project editor: Lauren Brancato
Layout artist: Mary Ballachino

Library of Congress Cataloging-in-Publication Data is available on file.

ISBN 978-0-7627-7215-5

Printed in the United States of America

10 9 8 7 6 5 4 3 2

Contents

Acknowledgments v
Introduction vi

CHAPTER 1: Benedict Arnold:
            From Hero to Traitor to Scourge 1

CHAPTER 2: George Metesky:
            Angry Jerk with a Short Fuse 17

CHAPTER 3: Lydia Sherman: Connecticut's Own
            Black Widow 33

CHAPTER 4: Julius Schacknow:
            Self-Made Prophet, Savior, and God 48

CHAPTER 5: Uncas:
            Last (and Likely Worst) of the Mohicans 61

CHAPTER 6: Rev. Samuel A. Peters:
            Exiled Loyalist and "Victim of Pseudomania" . . .77

CHAPTER 7: Anastase A. Vonsiatsky:
            Fascist Jerk in the Time of Hitler 92

CHAPTER 8: Amy Archer-Gilligan: The True Story behind
            Arsenic and Old Lace 107

CHAPTER 9: P. T. Barnum:
            Prince of the Humbugs .121

CHAPTER 10: Philip Musica:
            Multiple Identities, One Jerk 135

CHAPTER 11: Samuel Colt:
            The Jerk Who Won the West 150

CONTENTS

CHAPTER 12:   Hannah Hovey:
              The Wicked Witch of Monroe 164

CHAPTER 13:   Rev. Herbert H. Hayden:
              Minister Turned Murderer 175

CHAPTER 14:   Salvatore "Midge Renault" Annunziato:
              A "Made" Jerk 189

CHAPTER 15:   William Stuart:
              The (Allegedly) Most Celebrated Jerk in
              Connecticut History 204

Bibliography 219
Index 226
About the Author 232

Acknowledgments

A collection of biographies is only as good as its sources, and although I am truly indebted to every author listed in the bibliography, there are a few writers to whom I am particularly grateful for their meticulous and dedicated research efforts (and I strongly recommend reading their terrific works): Sheldon S. Cohen, *Connecticut's Loyalist Gadfly: The Reverend Samuel Andrew Peters;* Michael M. Greenburg, *The Mad Bomber of New York: The Extraordinary True Story of the Manhunt that Paralyzed a City*; Christopher Hoffman, "Midge Renault and the Heyday of the Mob," the *New Haven Independent;* Michael Leroy Oberg, *Uncas: First of the Mohegans;* and M. William Phelps, *The Devil's Rooming House: The True Story of America's Deadliest Female Serial Killer.*

I would also like to thank Charles Monagan, my mentor at *Connecticut Magazine,* who helped me with my jerk brainstorming, in particular the stories of the Mad Bomber and Brother Julius (the latter of whom he personally covered); Jim Benson, who made me aware of the case of Lydia Sherman; Meredith Rufino, the editor who originally offered me this opportunity; and Lauren Brancato, my faithful project editor who shepherded the manuscript to its completed state.

I also would like to thank a few people who went out of their way to be of great assistance in providing images for this book, including Mary Witkowski of the Bridgeport History Center at Bridgeport Public Library, Carol Ganz and the Archives staff at the Connecticut State Library, and Angel Diggs of the *New Haven Register.* I also owe a huge debt of gratitude to my talented friend Greg Shea, who bailed me out with his amazing original portrait of Lydia Sherman.

As always, I appreciate the love and support of my wife, Sue, and my sons, Zane and Kade, who put up with my jerkiness even when I'm not trying to write a book.

Finally, I would like to acknowledge the descendants of the compelling people who are profiled in this book. As my children can attest, it's not always easy living in the shadow of a jerk, but it can be fun to share the stories.

Introduction

So let's make this clear right from the outset: I'm a jerk.

Although who better to assemble a cast of obnoxious characters from Connecticut's long history—it takes one to know one, right? Also consider that I'm publicly willing to single out other people who are no longer alive to defend themselves and call them "jerks." If that's not the work of a true jerk, what is?

But hey, I'm in compelling company, as you will discover while reading through this book. As renowned British politician Chris Patten has said, "In a democracy, everybody has a right to be represented, including the jerks." This is our—I mean, their—opportunity for their stories to be told.

"An annoyingly stupid or foolish person," is the dictionary definition of a "jerk," but that seems a bit limited in scope. In order to make this book an entertaining and varied read, and to provide a good cross section of Connecticut history, I stretched the definition a bit to include some people whose "jerkiness" could be debated, and others who might be classified as "lovable jerks." In addition to a few sensational murderers—okay, three, but you'll see each one is markedly different in how they went about their crimes—consider this smorgasbord: a colorful counterfeiter, a Native American sachem, an accused witch, a legendary showman, a vindictive minister, an iconic manufacturer, a transplanted Russian count, a wise guy mobster, a corporate con man, a mad bomber, the nation's most infamous traitor, and God. (Well, a self-proclaimed god, anyway.) A literal rogue's gallery.

Although Connecticut has been referred to as "Corrupticut" on occasion, I decided to stay away from political jerks, mainly because there were just too many from which to choose! [*Insert rimshot*]

The good news is that even though the characters in this auspicious little group are all "bad" boys and girls, people seem to enjoy hearing these kinds of stories. Any time I told someone that

I was undertaking this project, they almost invariably could come up with a jerk or two to include; unfortunately many of those suggested are still alive, although if someone puts together a second edition a few decades from now, I will have a good starting list for them. (Former governor John Rowland, who was busted for corruption while in office, forced to resign in disgrace, and then went to prison, would be the popular choice for cover boy!) After dedicating many nights, weekends, and days to this project, my poor, neglected family would probably insist that I be added to the group, too.

In this book, you will also discover that Connecticut has a long history of jerks—in fact, you might even say it's part of the landscape.

Literally.

Although Uncas, the Mohegan sachem who was born here before European explorers set foot in the land that was known as "Quinnehtukqut" ("by the long tidal river"), is the earliest jerk chronicled in this book (chapter 5), there is the legend of a mountainous jerk who preceded him by a few millennia. According to the Quinnipiac tribe of Native Americans who inhabited the south central region of the state, the story of Sleeping Giant—a distinctive traprock ridge in what is now Hamden—is the story of Hobbomock, a giant who contained the spirits of the souls of the dead, and whom they believe still sleeps under the earth.

As it turns out, Hobbomock was not an especially kind or jolly behemoth, and was prone to throwing temper tantrums, doing things that pleased only him, and making life miserable for everyone else. Once, he got so angry and stamped his feet so violently in a river, it caused a flood that destroyed many villages and created much distress among the mortals. He was also fond of oysters, so the story goes, and quite often gorged himself on every one that could be found, making sure to leave none for anyone else.

He was an enormous jerk, really.

Keitan, the creator-god, eventually took pity on the long-suffering mortals and decided to deal with Hobbomock. But as Hobbomock was a divine creature, Keitan could not kill him, so he waited for the right opportunity to act. One day, after Hobbo-mock went on a particularly zealous oyster-eating binge (think of your Uncle Joe showing up for Thanksgiving with his "eating pants" on), the giant grew weary and fell asleep. Keitan, seizing the moment, cast a spell on him so that he would never awaken again. Over time, the earth and trees have come to cover the slumbering Hobbomock, peace has returned to the area, and all have been spared the giant's wrath.

Although Hobbomock may have literally been the biggest jerk in state history, there have been others whose notorious exploits seem to dwarf his. Hopefully, you will enjoy learning about their stories as much as I did while researching them. I truly found each one to be fascinating, and learned more about the history of this great state than I ever imagined I might.

I should also mention that a book like this only provides thumbnail biographies and barely scratches the surface of some of these great stories. If you can't get enough of any of these jerks—and who can, really?—I heartily encourage you to check out some of the excellent, detailed biographies in the bibliography for extended reading.

Actor Christian Bale has said, "If everyone really knew what a jerk I am in real life, I wouldn't be so adored in the slightest." You may not adore many of the people in this book by the time you're done reading—although I wish I could spend an evening at a pub with the incorrigible ne'er-do-well Bill Stuart, who was an amazing storyteller—but you will know more about some of the greatest jerks in Connecticut history. Enjoy!

CHAPTER 1
Benedict Arnold:
From Hero to Traitor to Scourge

When your name literally becomes one of the top two accepted substitutes for the word "traitor" (Judas being the other), it's a good bet that you are one of the greatest jerks in all of history.

Such is the case with Benedict Arnold, native son of Connecticut who spectacularly betrayed his fledgling country at its hour of need, and in doing so, cemented his bad reputation for the ages. What he then did to the state of his birth following that treacherous event, although lesser known, was equally as reprehensible.

Arnold is also one of the more misunderstood figures in the story of the United States' birth. Although his name is now synonymous with great treachery, he would have been remembered as one of the biggest heroes of the American Revolution if it were not for his tremendous pride, overinflated ego, short temper, and thin skin, all of which ultimately led to his downfall. He has been described as bold, reckless, and ruthless, and capable of doing anything to get what he wanted. He's also known as one of the most inspiring and fearless soldiers to ever take up arms on behalf of his homeland.

In short, he was a complicated and extraordinary man.

Benedict Arnold was born in Norwich on January 11, 1741, the second of six children, to Benedict Arnold III and Hannah Waterman King. At the time of Benedict's birth, the Arnolds were fairly well off; Hannah had inherited significant wealth after the death of her first husband, and the senior Benedict was able to parlay that money into a successful merchant and shipbuilding business. Young Benedict's early life was one of privilege; at age ten he began his education at a private school in Canterbury with plans to eventually attend Yale.

Copy of engraving of Benedict Arnold
by H. B. Hall after John Trumbull, published 1879

In 1753, while he was at school, however, yellow fever struck Norwich. Nearly all the Arnold children succumbed to it, which especially devastated the Arnold family patriarch, who was also in the midst of a rough business patch. The combined events took their toll, and it wasn't too long before the senior Benedict was seeking comfort in profuse amounts of alcohol. The family fortune was soon diminished, and young Benedict was forced to return home.

Despite the loss of her wealth, Hannah Arnold still had connections and was able to arrange an apprenticeship for fourteen-year-old Benedict in Norwich with her cousins Daniel and Joshua Lathrop, who ran a successful apothecary business. Benedict was a good student, but his impetuous nature would soon get the better of him. In 1757 at the age of sixteen, he joined the local militia to fight in the French and Indian War in upstate New York, but by the time he got there, the fighting was done. He returned to Norwich disappointed, but over the next few years, the scrappy and able-bodied Arnold twice sneaked off to join the army. Both times he was brought home.

Nonetheless, Arnold threw himself into the apothecary business, which was necessary—his mother died in 1759, and with his father still struggling with the bottle, it fell to him to support what was left of the family. Two years later the elder Arnold was dead, so Benedict moved to New Haven, where with seed money from the Lathrops, he opened his own business.

By all accounts, Arnold was industrious, and before long had gained success as a pharmacist and a bookseller. He soon brought his sister Hannah (the last living member of his immediate family) to New Haven and taught her how to run his business, which now included trade with the West Indies. Arnold then began to travel and often found himself at sea, usually at the helm of one of his own ships, gaining experience that would eventually play a vital part in his military career.

Although business was going well, there were stories that Arnold was hardly the prototypical entrepreneur. He was purportedly involved in at least one duel while at sea, and the Sugar Act of 1764 and Stamp Act of 1765 both hampered trade throughout the colonies enough that Arnold was among the merchants who turned to smuggling to keep profits afloat. Joining forces with other frustrated colonists, he became a vocal member of the Sons of Liberty, and was soon involved with rebellious activities such as paying unwelcome "visits" to Loyalist jerks like Rev. Samuel A. Peters (see chapter 6).

It was during this time that the handsome twenty-six-year-old took a wife, getting married in February 1767 to Margaret Mansfield. Over the next few years, which were rife with marital discord, the couple welcomed three sons. During the same period, Arnold's business struggled, and he was faced with growing debt.

The winds of revolution were gathering strength, however, and before the official outbreak of hostilities, Arnold gained the rank of captain in the Governor's Second Company of Guards. As soon as word reached New Haven that the first shots of war had been fired at Lexington in April 1775, he assembled his troops and marched off to join the cause.

When he arrived in Massachusetts, the siege of Boston was in progress, but eager for battle, Arnold suggested to the Massachusetts Committee of Safety that he lead an attack on Fort Ticonderoga in New York, a key British outpost that was known to be vulnerable. After two weeks, he was given permission, and took his men west, no doubt with visions of long-sought military glory.

When he arrived in western Vermont, he was met by Colonel Commandant Ethan Allen and his renowned Green Mountain Boys. Allen had heard about Arnold's idea to capture Fort Ticonderoga but hadn't bothered to wait for official permission. More concerned with fighting the British than his countrymen (at this point), Arnold reluctantly deferred to Allen, and together, they captured the fort. Arnold then went on to take a few smaller nearby British outposts.

The happy glow of success didn't last long, however. Arnold continued to squabble with Allen, which grew into a conflict with another commanding officer and Connecticut native, Colonel James Easton. Easton had been part of Ticonderoga's capture, and afterward, when dispatched to report it to the Commission of Safety, downplayed Arnold's key role in the victory. Arnold took exception and challenged Easton to a duel; Easton deferred, but Arnold struck him anyway. This instigated a Committee of Safety investigation, and when questioned, Arnold huffily resigned his commission and discharged his men, whom Easton quickly recruited, which only further angered the future traitor.

While on his way back from Ticonderoga to sort things out, Arnold also learned that his wife Margaret had suddenly died.

Some men might've just thrown in the towel and retired home to bemoan their misfortune, but Arnold, full of brashness and bravado, was not one to quit so easily. By August 1775, he was again headed north, this time commissioned as a colonel thanks to the support of George Washington, who was in desperate need of competent and skilled leaders, which Arnold had proven to be. He had been given one thousand fifty men and the daunting task of invading Canada, specifically attacking Quebec. In order to gain an element of surprise, he took his troops on a rugged circuitous route that went through the wilds of Maine. Along the way two hundred died and another three hundred deserted.

Still, Arnold willed his men through—a success in itself for which he was commended—and was soon joined by forces commanded by Colonel Richard Montgomery. The two tried to take Quebec but the results were disastrous: Montgomery was killed and Arnold was shot in the leg, an injury that would dog him for the rest of his life. Despite his wounds, Arnold tried to rally his troops, but the British were too strong and he was forced to retreat to Montreal. Eventually, the superior enemy would drive him from Canada altogether, but not before the stubborn Arnold was able to dramatically thwart their progress.

History books don't always mention the battles that go on behind the lines, and Arnold was often entangled in interpersonal tiffs, which only further muddled his reputation. Like at Ticonderoga, while waging the Canadian campaign and simultaneously creating what would become the American Navy, Arnold bickered with his fellow officers. For all the military acumen he demonstrated in battle, he showed no aptitude in dealing with those on his own side when conflict arose. One military official accused him of improperly plundering stores while in Montreal; another called for a court-martial when he felt Arnold's strategies didn't properly match his own. Others were simply rankled by his insufferable demeanor.

Like many quintessential jerks, Arnold wasn't one to graciously endure criticism, either—challenging dissenters to duels was often his preferred method of problem solving. He rarely apologized for his words or actions, and quite often didn't hesitate to tell others exactly what he thought of their lesser opinions. As a result, when on the losing side of battles, he was often blamed for the outcome and conversely, when his actions led to victory, which they often did, his role was diminished in reports.

Although being recognized by many high-ranking officers for his valor and leadership, Arnold reached a breaking point when in February 1777 the Continental Congress promoted five junior officers over him. Enraged, he set out for Philadelphia to address the situation.

Being a man of action, however, Arnold couldn't stand idly by whenever there was a scrap to be had. After learning of a British attack on Danbury while on a brief visit in New Haven, he immediately rode to the scene to lead the local forces in a counterattack that would become known as the Battle of Ridgefield. During the fight, his horse was shot out from under him and landed on his bad leg, further aggravating his old wound. While pinned under his horse, he was also nearly captured, but managed to fend off his attackers and escape. Even after having a second horse shot out from under him during the engagement, Arnold was able to lead his Connecticut countrymen in repelling the British, inflicting heavy enemy losses.

His most bitter enemies in the Continental Congress couldn't deny his part in the victory, and begrudgingly promoted Arnold to major general, which was a step up, but not to the level that he felt was commensurate with his performance. Rather than indulge in petty behind-the-scenes politics, he believed his on-the-battlefield successes should speak for themselves. Commander-in-Chief George Washington tried to intercede on Arnold's behalf, submitting a letter to the Continental Congress stating, "It is needless to say anything of this gentleman's military character. It is universally known that he has always distinguished himself as a judicious, brave officer of great activity, enterprise and perseverance." The letter was ignored.

After the failure of Washington's recommendation, Arnold decided that he'd had enough of political games. Timing is everything, however, and on July 11, 1777, just as Arnold was going to deliver his formal resignation, word came that Fort Ticonderoga had fallen back into British control. Again, despite the perceived insult from the Continental Congress, Arnold could not help himself when Washington offered him an opportunity to return to battle. Bad feelings were put aside (temporarily) and, still miffed, Arnold quickly made his way back to upstate New York.

Once there, Arnold found himself in the middle of another personality clash, this time between Continental Army generals Horatio Gates and Philip Schuyler. He threw his support behind Schuyler, which did not particularly endear himself to Gates and would soon cause him more angst.

Arnold's first task was to retake nearby Fort Stanwix, for which he was given nine hundred men. The British had far superior numbers, but through a cunning ruse, Arnold made them believe that his force was the larger. Not wanting to risk a major defeat, the Redcoats quickly withdrew. Arnold took the fort with no resistance, and mission accomplished, returned to the main force.

However, the army gathered was now under the full command of Gates, and the assertive Arnold regularly clashed with the conservative general, a situation that came to a head at the end of October 1777 in Saratoga. During the Battle of Freeman's Farm, Arnold had favored taking the attack to the British, under the command of General John Burgoyne, while Gates had wanted to strike a more defensive stance. During the early part of the multi-day engagement, Arnold discovered that Gates was not only countermanding Arnold's orders, but was also sending reports to the Continental Congress discrediting Arnold's contributions. He confronted Gates through a series of angry letters, which, of course, were not well received. Gates immediately relieved Arnold of his command for insubordination.

Incensed, Arnold was ready to leave Saratoga, but his fellow officers recognized that his battlefield leadership was desperately needed with "Granny" Gates in charge, and signed a petition requesting he stay. Arnold relented and remained, which would become a momentous decision.

Pride wounded and beside himself, Arnold fumed in his tent as the Battle of Bemis Heights began to unfold. Forbidden to participate, he tried to keep abreast of the fight, but watching was near maddening. Finally, unable to stand idly by any longer while the skirmish continued all around him—he could see Gates sitting in his own tent, quietly minding the action from the sidelines—Arnold burst forth from his tent, leapt on his black stallion, Warren, and thundered into the fight.

Keep in mind that Arnold's traitorous actions were still in the future—at this point, the sight of the fiery patriot ignoring what seemed like timid orders, calling any brave men who would follow him into the fray, and then riding right into the fury of the British assault, was stirring. Sometimes being a jerk can be a benefit, and this was one of those moments. Ignoring the fact that he had no official command, the troops fell in behind the impassioned Arnold as he led a bold strike at the heart of the British lines.

It worked. Spurred on by Arnold at the head of the charge atop his faithful steed, sword aloft and bellowing orders while bullets and cannonballs whizzed past, the American forces rallied and began to turn back the Redcoats.

Victory at hand, Arnold crashed through the enemy line and personally took the fight to the British. His mount was shot out from under him, but undeterred, Arnold continued his frenzied attack. A bullet soon felled him, however, striking his troubled leg. Badly wounded yet still exhorting his men on, he finally yielded so that he could be dragged off the battlefield.

Even though Arnold had fallen, the now-inspired Americans did not, and the day's victory was the beginning of the end for the British in upstate New York. Ten days after Arnold's stunning act of bravery in the Battle of Saratoga, Burgoyne surrendered, a key turning point in the war—France decided to lend much-needed support to the fledgling country and its revolution against the English crown.

Because of Arnold's undisputed courage at Saratoga, however, the Continental Congress had no choice but to award Arnold the full promotion and recognition that he had previously been seeking. If at that point he had simply gone home fully vindicated and spent the rest of the war healing from his wounds—which had essentially crippled him—he'd be remembered as one of the great heroes in American history.

Being a jerk, however, Benedict Arnold couldn't leave well enough alone.

He spent the fierce winter of 1777–78 recovering, and maybe because of the long, cold days and constant pain, the warm radiance of his success soon dimmed. Here he was, a war hero who had been repeatedly injured while fighting for his country, yet those who called themselves his compatriots had insulted him with their constant political backstabbing. After all he had done? After all he had sacrificed? How dare they treat him like that!

Despite being hailed by the American army when he visited Valley Forge in May 1778, and even signing the first recorded Oath of Allegiance in American history, Arnold still held a huge grudge against the Continental Congress and those he felt had slighted him. The seeds for betrayal had been sown.

A month later, the British withdrew from Philadelphia, and as a reward for his loyalty and service, Washington made Arnold the military commander of the city. It should have been an opportunity for him to continue to serve but yet enjoy a position that afforded him authority, respect, and less conflict—both with the British and the Americans. Instead, it turned out to be the impetus to Arnold's undoing.

It was during this period while enjoying some quiet time and letting his leg mend, he also found an opportunity to heal his heart. Nineteen-year-old Peggy Shippen, the daughter of Judge Edward Shippen, a Loyalist sympathizer, caught Arnold's eye, and despite their twenty-year age difference, she became his second wife in April 1779. The union allowed Arnold to move in the upper circles of Philadelphia society, and he enthusiastically embraced the lifestyle that went with it.

The problem was that the couple was soon living above their means, and Arnold, ever the merchant and businessman, started using his commissioned authority to try to make up the difference. As the military commander of the city, he was able to arrange lucrative deals and direct business toward his own nonmilitary enterprises. After he had been permanently wounded in the service of his country, he felt he was owed at least that much.

The other issue that came with his new social status is that Arnold now found himself regularly socializing with Peggy's friends, many of whom were British sympathizers. It seems as though his new wife and a few other young Loyalist ladies of Philadelphia had also regularly (and secretly) consorted with English officers. Among them was Major John Andre, who would play a pivotal role in the resentful Arnold's downfall.

His growing indebtedness and new acquaintances made for a dangerous mix, and by May 1779, Arnold had set in motion plans to ally himself with the British. Working through a secret network that involved Loyalists and British spies, he proposed a plan where he would gain control of West Point, a key military post in New York, and then give it over with three thousand American troops in exchange for £10,000 sterling and a commission in the English army.

Meanwhile, word got out about Arnold's business dealings, which had become shadier as he became more indebted. Once again, he was court-martialed and once again, had to plead his case before the Continental Congress. This time, however, he was found guilty, albeit on two minor counts. Washington was forced to publicly rebuke him for the charges, and Arnold, characteristically disgusted with the politics of it all, resigned his position as military commander of Philadelphia in April 1780.

For the next few months, Arnold went about his plan, secretly negotiating with the British. He was passing messages regularly through his wife and her circle of Loyalist contacts, encoding what appeared to be business letters with messages detailing American troop movement and force deployment. He was also getting his affairs in order, selling his Connecticut home, and moving his financial assets to English banks. As his scheme got closer to fruition, he raised his asking price to £20,000—equal to about $1 million today—to which the British agreed.

Even though he was a jerk, Arnold was no dummy. He was able to deceive everyone, including Washington, who had wanted Arnold to rejoin the war effort and take command of active fighting forces. The cagey traitor-to-be used his damaged leg as an excuse to decline the offer and suggested being given command of West Point instead. After Arnold's countless displays of bravery, patriotism, and personal sacrifice, how could the unsuspecting Washington refuse?

On August 3, 1780, Benedict Arnold gained official command of West Point, New York, including military control of the entire Hudson Valley. He immediately went about setting the stage for the strategic stronghold to be taken easily by the British. Without being obvious about it—the plan was to "throw" an engagement with the English and make it seem as though they overpowered the Americans, and he could thus give up with minimal fighting and bloodshed—he spread his forces thinly across the region and tried to get rid of as many supplies as possible to make a siege more effective. Arnold's reputation for using his military position for personal profit played perfectly into the deception, as many of those around him thought he was simply cashing in yet again as they saw vital items disappearing without good reason.

Plans and prices agreed upon, Arnold met with Major Andre near West Point on September 21 to iron out the final details of betrayal. Everything set, Andre went to return to New York City, but the ship that had been his transport, the HMS *Vulture,* had been attacked by the Americans and forced back down the Hudson River. Consequently, Andre had to make his return trip by land, so Arnold provided traveling papers that would allow him safe passage through American lines.

Two days later, Andre was captured near Tarrytown. When he was searched, Arnold's pass was found along with the military plans for West Point and an encoded letter from Arnold with details of the plot. Not realizing exactly what Andre was carrying, the Americans holding the British major almost sent him back to Arnold, who was the region's commanding officer. At the last minute, it was decided only word of Andre's capture was to be sent to Arnold. Arnold was also informed that the documents recovered from the British spy, most of which had been written in Arnold's hand, were being sent directly to George Washington, who—unfortunately for Arnold but fortunately for the Americans—happened to be in the area on military business.

One can only imagine the look on Benedict Arnold's face the morning of September 24, 1780, when he received word that not only had Andre been captured, but also that the nearby Washington was in possession of all the documents needed to ensure that—war hero or not—Arnold would soon be swinging from the end of a rope for attempting to betray his country.

A man of honor might have immediately surrendered himself, but as he had repeatedly demonstrated, Arnold was no man of honor. He did what any good jerk would do when his deceitful plot was exposed: He ran!

As fast as his gimpy leg could carry him, Arnold made for the Hudson River, knowing that Washington would soon be coming to apprehend him. Although he may have been cursing his luck for his machinations coming to light, he was still able to catch one last break as the HMS *Vulture* had returned looking for Andre. Arnold quickly got aboard and managed to get away just before Washington's troops arrived.

Safely with the British, Arnold was made a brigadier general and paid over £6,000 for the failed surrender of West Point. For his part in facilitating Arnold's plan, Major Andre was hanged.

Once again, if Arnold's story had ended here, he'd still be regarded as one of the biggest jerks in American history. But it's his lesser-known actions after changing sides that pushes him to the top of the list of Connecticut jerks.

It is a long-standing tradition that when caught in any sort of crime or social faux pas, a public figure will orchestrate a public *mea culpa*. Arnold, of course, didn't apologize following his aborted attempt at delivering one of the most vital military strongholds directly into the hands of the enemy during a time of war—a little more egregious than say, accidentally releasing a sex tape—but did try to explain the reasons behind his actions. In October 1780, he published "To the Inhabitants of America," an open letter in newspapers across British-held New York City, in which he cited his opposition to the American alliance with France, as well as the political corruption that he felt pervaded the Continental Congress, for his betrayal.

Leaving out the part about being given a lot of money to do it, he also implied that he thought his actions were best for his fellow countrymen. From the letter:

> *I affect no disguise, and therefore frankly declare, that in these principles I had determined to retain my arms and command for an opportunity to surrender them to Great Britain; and in concerting the measures for a purpose, in my opinion, as grateful as it would have been beneficial to my country; I was only solicitous to accomplish an event of decisive importance, and to prevent as much as possible, in the execution of it, the effusion of blood.*

So noble! Of course, the problem was that Arnold chose to end his letter with a suggestion for those who still questioned his intentions.

> . . . with respect to that herd of censurers, whose enmity to me originates in their hatred to the principles by which I am now led to devote my life to the re-union of the British empire, as the best and only means to dry up the streams of misery that have deluged this country, they may be assured, that conscious of the rectitude of my intentions; I shall treat their malice and calumnies with contempt and neglect.

In other words, "If you chose not to accept my explanation, then [*insert your own verb*] off!"

Arnold was given command of one thousand six hundred men that he led to multiple raids throughout Virginia, destroying supply stores and munitions factories. He spent much of the next few months fighting with and running from American troops, who now had direct orders from old ally and former ardent supporter George Washington to immediately hang the traitor if he were ever captured.

Not surprisingly, it wasn't too long before Arnold found there was just as much interpersonal politics on the other side, and was clashing with British officers, including Lord Charles Cornwallis, the general of the English forces in the region. By June 1781, Arnold, with his aggressive strategies, had seemingly worn out his welcome among the English in Virginia, and returned to New York. Not ready to give up the fight, he approached General Henry Clinton, the commander-in-chief of the British army, with myriad battle plans and strategies, including one particularly dastardly attack plan.

Although Clinton didn't care for the majority of Arnold's ideas, he did agree to let him carry out the specific raid he suggested. So, in September 1781, Brigadier General Benedict Arnold of His

Majesty's army set out with a fleet of ships and a force of over one thousand seven hundred men on a mission to attack Connecticut.

All too familiar with the lay of the land, Norwich's native son directed his troops into the harbor of New London, a key American port for supporting privateers who had imposed significant losses on British merchants. Meeting almost no resistance, the invading force wasted no time in wreaking havoc, destroying a huge stock of supplies, and causing a tremendous amount of destruction to the town. They then set the wharf and a few buildings on fire, but the blaze soon raged out of control and when the smoke cleared, over one hundred fifty homes, shops, and warehouses—the majority of New London—was in ashes.

Arnold's forces then turned their sights across the Thames River on Fort Griswold in Groton. With only one hundred fifty men and boys to defend the fort, the Americans under the command of Colonel William Ledyard fought furiously, inflicting heavy damage on the British, but were eventually overrun. Some accounts state that when Ledyard tried to surrender, the invaders ran him through with his own sword and then massacred every defender they could find. Despite exactly how it went down, the end result was the same—the fort was taken by the British and the Americans suffered significant casualties, with over eighty dead and the rest made prisoners. As Arnold's forces were withdrawing, they also tried to destroy Fort Griswold once and for all, but the attempt was thwarted.

Still, by the time the British sailed out of the harbor, New London had been burned to the ground, Fort Griswold was knee-deep in American blood, and dozens of Connecticut men, women, and children were dead or homeless, all thanks to prodigal son Benedict Arnold.

Now that's the work of a true jerk.

The destruction of New London was one of the final English victories of the American Revolution. A month later, Cornwallis would surrender in Yorktown, essentially ending hostilities. After the war, Arnold tried to stay in the British military, but the same inabilities that had made him numerous political enemies in America—his abrasive personality, arrogance, and questionable interpersonal skills—did the same for him in England. When coupled with his defection, which was not looked on favorably by the British either, it effectively ended his service career.

In the ensuing years, Arnold, his wife Peggy, and their children would move back and forth between London, England, and Saint John in New Brunswick, Canada. The infamous traitor tried his hand at different endeavors, including a return to trading with the West Indies, but was constantly in debt and in court. He also endured numerous personal attacks and even engaged in the occasional duel—some habits die hard.

Some jerks die hard, also. Gout ravaged his bad leg, causing him years of pain and torment. After a while, he developed edema, also known as "dropsy," which eventually proved to be fatal. He died on June 14, 1801, in England, at the age of sixty, and was buried in London. When his will was read, it was found to provide for a "John Sage," who turned out to be an illegitimate son that Arnold had sired while in Canada—one last deception on everyone, including his long-suffering wife, Peggy.

A few months later, Arnold's obituary appeared in newspapers in America. The August 1 edition of the *Columbian Centinel,* of Massachusetts, reported his death with one line: "Died—In England, Brigadier-General Benedict Arnold; notorious throughout the world."

Yeah, a notorious jerk.

CHAPTER 2
George Metesky:
Angry Jerk with a Short Fuse

When life hands some people lemons, they make lemonade. If they're jerks, however, they might make bombs . . . and then use them to terrorize millions of New Yorkers over a sixteen-year span.

When George Metesky was born on November 2, 1903, chances are his mother Anna didn't realize that she had given birth to a child who would ultimately be known to history as the "Mad Bomber." (Then again, what parent *would* have that kind of aspiration for their child?) Generally polite and quiet, it would take an unfortunate accident in adulthood to unleash the jerk within. Once that inner jerk was freed, however, it would lead Metesky to wage one of the most public campaigns of misguided vengeance in twentieth-century American annals, one that would inspire the likes of "Unabomber" Ted Kaczynski and the infamous Zodiac Killer.

Of course, Metesky didn't start his campaign of terror from the cradle. He had a fairly unremarkable childhood; his Lithuanian parents George and Anna Milauskas (who had immigrated to Waterbury via Poland, and changed their surname to Metesky after arrival in the United States) worked hard to take care of him, his brother John, and his sisters, Mae and Anna. He dropped out of high school in 1918, and following World War I, joined the Marines in 1920. He served a two-year hitch and was discharged, but re-enlisted in 1925 and was assigned to the US Consulate in Shanghai. He served there without incident as a specialist electrician, no doubt gaining the mechanical expertise that would aid his later criminal actions.

Upon his second honorable discharge in 1929, Metesky came home to Waterbury and moved into the family home at 17 Fourth

New York Police arrest accused mad bomber George Metesky
© BETTMANN/CORBIS

Street with his still-single sisters Mae and Anna, who worked in nearby mills. Now twenty-six, he was soon able to parlay the technical skills he had honed in the military into employment with United Electric & Power Company, a subsidiary of the mighty Consolidated Edison Corporation based in New York City. He embarked upon a career as a mechanic for the company, working around the metropolitan area, and from reports, was a reliable, meticulous, and skilled employee.

At home, Metesky lived a quiet life. Aside from the occasional courteous greeting, he wasn't one for chitchat and didn't interact much with his Waterbury neighbors. At that point, to them he was just another face in the immigrant-heavy neighborhood, a well-dressed man who kept to himself.

All was well, but like many stories involving a jerk, there's a "fateful day." In this case, it was almost a bit like the creation of a comic book super villain—eerily similar to Batman's arch nemesis the Joker—where an injurious industrial accident was the catalyst for a life spent wreaking havoc on an unsuspecting public.

On September 5, 1931, Metesky was doing routine maintenance at the enormous Hell Gate generating plant in the Bronx, one of the largest generating stations in the city. While working amid the complex machinery, cleaning the massive equipment, a nearby boiler backfired, releasing a cloud of hot gas into the vicinity. In the closed space, Metesky was unable to escape the noxious fumes, which quickly overpowered him.

Although he survived, significant damage was done to Metesky's lungs during the accident. While recovering from his injuries, he came down with pneumonia; following that, he developed tuberculosis—and it was this particular malady, which essentially left him disabled, and the circumstances surrounding it, that would be the root cause of the Mad Bomber's future actions.

Metesky claimed that his tuberculosis had been brought on by the accident and subsequent pneumonia, and thus applied for workman's compensation. Con Edison maintained that the formerly capable mechanic had filed his claim beyond their established deadline, and as a result, the utility giant was not obligated to provide workman's compensation. He was given sick pay for twenty-six weeks, and also collected fifty-eight dollars a month for three years via a company life insurance policy. As he could not return to work, Metesky was fired.

Disabled and unemployed, Metesky spent the next few years trying to appeal Con Edison's denial of his workman's compensation. On three separate occasions, he went through the formal appeal process, and each time his claim was denied—unfairly, in Metesky's opinion. He wrote dozens of increasingly angry letters to the company requesting they reverse the decision, but to no avail. By the time that his final appeal was rejected in 1936, the mild-mannered George Metesky was gone, replaced by an exasperated, revenge-minded tyrant.

Con Edison had cruelly taken his health and his career and had left him with nothing, Metesky decided. It was time for them to pay for their "dastardly deeds," as he had told them in one of his final letters. Justice would be done.

Enter the Mad Bomber.

Unlike other disgruntled workers who are terminated from their employment and then promptly return wielding automatic weapons, Metesky was more patient and calculating in seeking his retribution. Over the next four years, he carefully plotted his course of action, crafting a plan that he thought would bring the mighty Con Edison—as well as all of New York City—trembling to its knees.

In other words, the thirty-seven-year-old Metesky launched a new career . . . as a terrorist.

Using the skills and knowledge he had acquired in military service, he built a crude pipe bomb—filled with gunpowder, it had a simple ignition made of sugar and flashlight batteries. Placing it in a small wooden toolbox, he brought it to the Con Edison offices on West 64th Street in Manhattan on November 16, 1940, and entering the busy building unnoticed, quietly placed it on a windowsill and left.

It was discovered two days later, and the bomb squad was called. The device was a dud; around it had been wrapped a note, with a message inscribed in neat block letters: "CON EDISON CROOKS, THIS IS FOR YOU." It was signed "F. P."

Although it was never confirmed, given Metesky's mechanical ability and the presence of the note, which would've been destroyed if the bomb had exploded, this first "unit" (as the Mad Bomber would always refer to an explosive device) was most likely an intentional failure to serve as a warning of what was to come.

Ten months later, a similar bomb was discovered unexploded lying in the middle of 19th Street, only a few blocks away from Con Edison's offices at 4 Irving Place in Manhattan. This one, however, didn't have a note, but was wrapped in a red woolen sock and included a throat lozenge as part of the detonator fuse—traits that would be common to all units left by the Mad Bomber. Its alarm-clock ignition switch hadn't been wound and it was found in the road, leading to speculation that it had been discarded in a hurry.

In late December 1941, three months after the discovery of the second device and shortly after the Japanese attack on Peal Harbor, a letter was received by Manhattan police. Precisely written in all capital block letters, it said:

I WILL MAKE NO MORE BOMB UNITS FOR THE DURATION OF THE WAR—MY PATRIOTIC FEELINGS HAVE MADE ME DECIDE THIS—LATER I WILL BRING THE CON-ED TO JUSTICE. THEY WILL PAY FOR THEIR DASTARDLY DEEDS . . . F. P.

Metesky may have been a jerk, but the former Marine fancied himself a patriot first, putting the needs of the nation before his desire for revenge. For the duration of the war, there were no bombs, although Metesky was hardly sitting on his hands in the interim. Over the next nine years, he kept his cause alive by sending a barrage of angry, cryptic letters to police, newspapers, private citizens, and Con Edison. As it turns out, these letters—all in the distinctive block-letter hand—would eventually prove to be Metesky's undoing.

But that was still years away. The war ended, and once it was a good distance behind the country, it was time for the Mad Bomber to step back on the stage. On March 29, 1951, Metesky renewed his public reign of terror, this time with an actual bang!

For the first time, one of the Mad Bomber's units exploded in a public place—Grand Central Station, in the heart of New York City. The bomb had been placed in an urn used to extinguish cigarettes, on the terminal's lower level near the renowned Oyster Bar restaurant. Although it jarred many commuters, no one was hurt.

Metesky would later confess that this was part of his master plan—to cause fear, confusion, and damage, but not to injure anyone. To this end, he would often provide clues to the authorities and the press as to where his bombs were located before they would detonate (again, like a bad comic book villain), giving ample warning. No one would die at the hand of the Mad Bomber.

Then again, Metesky was still planting dangerous explosive devices in very crowded urban areas. As is often the case with great jerks, hypocrisy is a common theme: Fifteen people would be injured—some severely—as a result of the Mad Bomber's "dastardly deeds."

The bomb at Grand Central Station was the opening salvo of Metesky's renewed spree. A little less than a month later, on April 24, one of his units exploded in a phone booth in the basement of the New York Public Library—no one was injured and it did little harm. In August, Grand Central was the target again (only a phone booth was damaged and little else), followed by another attack on the morning of September 12 at the Irving Place offices of Con Edison, which also destroyed another phone booth.

Between the letters and the similarity of the bombs, the police realized that the attacks were related. In the decade that Metesky had refrained from his task, he had honed his craft, creating more sophisticated and dangerous bombs—all his pipe-encased units were not much bigger than a D-sized battery.

Being a jerk, he decided that merely leaving explosive devices to cause random damage wasn't always enough, so he sent what appeared to be a letter bomb to the offices of Con Edison. After an initial panic, it turned out to be an intentional dud, filled with sugar.

Metesky ratcheted up the public rhetoric, sending a handwritten letter to the *New York Herald Tribune* on October 22 using all capital block letters, demonstrating that such expression, even long before Internet message boards, has been an idiosyncrasy of angry folk. In the letter, he promised to continue his bombing campaign until "THE CON EDISON IS BROUGHT TO JUSTICE FOR THEIR DASTARDLY ACTS." He also added that he felt that his efforts would "CAUSE OTHERS TO CRY OUT FOR JUSTICE FOR ME."

As if striking fear in the hearts of innocent people by arbitrarily blowing things up is a great way to get them on your side!

Also, like an egomaniacal super villain (or a mentally ill person who secretly wanted to get caught), Metesky made authorities aware of two more units before they detonated—one at the Paramount Theater in Times Square and another at a Pennsylvania Station phone booth; the police found a bomb at the former but nothing at the latter (this unit wouldn't be found for two years, when the phone booth was removed for servicing). In late November, another device exploded, this time destroying a coin-operated locker at the subway station on 14th Street.

Shortly afterward, Metesky sent another letter to the *New York Herald Tribune,* in which he apologized for his bombastic binge, promising again that "THE CON EDISON" would regret their "DASTARDLY DEEDS," and that he would be placing more units under theater seats. "F. P." also claimed that "IT CANNOT BE HELPED," and, perhaps a bit obviously, "I AM NOT WELL."

The calendar turned to 1952 and the attacks slowed down somewhat: A March bomb wrecked a Port Authority Bus Terminal phone booth, while in June and December, units exploded in the seats of the Loew's theater on Lexington Avenue. The December event was noteworthy because it was the first time that someone was hurt as a result of the Mad Bomber's handiwork. Sadly, this helped spread the bomber's public notoriety, although the authorities subsequently requested that newspapers no longer print any of Metesky's missives.

Despite the police's efforts to keep the presence of the Mad Bomber quiet, Metesky's actions over the next two years would foil that. In 1953, he blew up seats in Radio City Music Hall and the Capitol Theater, and set off another one again near the Oyster Bar at Grand Central; in addition, a dud unit was found at Penn Station. None of these injured anyone.

The same couldn't be said for the Mad Bomber's 1954 efforts. On March 16, a bomb planted behind a men's room sink on the lower level of Grand Central exploded, injuring three individuals, although none seriously. A bomb detonated in a Port Authority Bus Terminal phone booth injured no one, but a unit that exploded on November 7 at Radio City Musical Hall was among Metesky's most damaging. With a crowd of over six thousand watching the film *White Christmas,* Metesky's bomb went off in the fourteenth row of the theater, hurting four people. The cushioning of the seats, the bodies in the audience and the sound from the film were enough to muffle the noise from the explosion so that it was barely noticed by the crowd in attendance. The injured were removed and the film continued uninterrupted, but the repercussions were felt throughout the city.

Metesky's dangerously misguided efforts also continued unabated through 1955. Over the course of the year, bombs went off in the Sutter Avenue subway station in Brooklyn, Penn Station (twice), the Paramount Theater, and Grand Central Station; fortunately, no one was injured in any of the incidents. In addition, unexploded units were discovered planted in seats at Radio City Music Hall and the Roxy Theater.

By now the press was well aware of the Mad Bomber, the *New York Times* describing him in stories as a "mysterious bomb terrorist." The New York City Police Department was growing frustrated in its efforts to apprehend the criminal, no doubt exacerbated by the letters it and the newspapers were receiving in which Metesky would alert authorities about impending attacks and challenge them to find hidden bombs, sometimes left months in advance. He would also occasionally call before an incident—additional warning— but there was nothing to indicate that he was about to stop anytime soon.

On February 21, 1956, a bomb that Metesky left in a toilet of a men's room in Penn Station exploded, seriously harming a seventy-four-year-old attendant, one of the most significant injuries inflicted by the Mad Bomber.

At this point, the police stepped up their pursuit of the Mad Bomber, forming a special unit solely tasked with his capture. They recognized that the culprit was most likely a former disgruntled Con Edison employee, but there were hundreds of people in that pool. They also had dozens of other leads and tips—in a city the size of New York, there was no shortage of possible suspects.

After having downplayed the Mad Bomber for years, the police finally went public. They alerted the entire metropolitan area for citizens to be on the lookout for a person who was a skilled mechanic, with access to a drill press and a stated hatred for Con Edison. Also circulated were samples of Metesky's distinctive writing style.

The increased police effort did not deter Metesky. In July, one of his units exploded in a phone booth on the main sales floor of Macy's. A month later, a security guard at the RCA Building in Rockefeller Center found a section of pipe in a phone booth and, thinking it might be useful for a home project—apparently, he hadn't seen the police warnings or noticed the sealed ends— brought it home, where it detonated in his kitchen the next the day. No one was hurt.

Unfortunately, that wasn't the case on December 2. In what turned out to be Metesky's most injurious attack—and the event that truly thrust the Mad Bomber into the limelight—six people were hurt, three seriously, when a unit went off during a Sunday evening show of *War and Peace* at the Paramount Theater in Brooklyn. The event generated a media storm, garnering headlines and forcing the police to up their defense of the city against the attack of an anonymous madman. The next day, New York City Police Commissioner Stephen P. Kennedy called together his top commanders, and after ranting a bit (and even promising a promotion to whoever was able to bring in the bomber), officially launched what he termed "the greatest manhunt in the history of the police department."

One of the biggest challenges was that although Metesky was a jerk, he was a cunning one, and—outside of his letters—he provided little with which the police could work. He left behind no fingerprints, and his explosive units were compact enough that he could transport them without bringing any attention to himself, thereby allowing less of an opportunity to be observed while hiding them. In an era before security cameras existed, there was also no record of his being at any of the crime scenes, all of which were public places, and he easily blended in with the crowd.

With no fresh leads or new evidence, Inspector Howard E. Finney of the New York City Police Department's crime lab and Captain John Cronin suggested that investigators try something that up to this point hadn't really been done in the history of law enforcement: They would have a psychiatrist study the case and then create a profile of the perpetrator that could be used to generate a lead. They turned to Dr. James A. Brussel.

Brussel was a distinguished psychiatrist who was the assistant commissioner of the New York State Commission for Mental Hygiene. In that role, Brussel had consulted with the police on multiple cases and had gained extensive insight into the criminal mind. He also had served during World War II and the Korean War, during which he had taken part in psychological counterintelligence for the Federal Bureau of Investigation and the US Army's Criminal Investigation Command.

Brussel was provided with the entire Mad Bomber case file, including information about the bombs and Metesky's letters to both the police and the newspapers. He pored over the evidence, employing his years of psychological expertise, and before long, was able to compile a detailed profile of the Mad Bomber. In retrospect, Brussel's accuracy was stunning, and ultimately, seminal in creating the field of criminal profiling.

In addition to the obvious—that the bomber was a former employee who had a grudge against Con Edison—Brussel first determined that the bomber was a middle-aged man and a textbook paranoid, which meant that he thought he was perfect and above mistakes. Brussel's reasoning was that bombers were historically male and the letters indicated that the bomber thought everyone was against him, a classic trait of paranoia, which usually peaks around the age of thirty-five. Adding the sixteen years since the first bomb in 1940 would make the bomber about fifty years old.

Metesky was fifty-three at the time, and certainly displayed enough "jerk" behavior to be considered "paranoid."

Brussel next deduced that bomber was neat, meticulous, and precise, all based on the letters and the construction of the units. He also would've been a model employee, setting high personal standards, as paranoids strenuously seek to attain perfection in order to avoid criticism.

Check on each count.

Based on the letters and the stilted writing, Brussel thought the bomber had received some education, maybe into high school. Based on the formal language used in the letters, Brussel also felt that the bomber was foreign or had spent extended time with immigrants—referring to Con Edison as "the Con Edison" was not something a native New Yorker would've done—and most likely was a Slav (a people who usually used bombs as weapons). That would've also made him a Roman Catholic, the prevalent religion of Slavic people.

The son of Lithuanian immigrants, Metesky regularly attended mass at St. Patrick's Cathedral in New York City.

By analyzing the handwriting in the letters, which was comprised of straight block letters except for the unusual breast-like Ws, and the phallic construction of the bombs, Brussel suggested that the bomber suffered from an oedipal complex, probably from having lost his mother when he was young. As such, the bomber would also be unmarried (possibly even a virgin) and sharing a residence with a female relative.

Metesky's mother had died when he was a child, and after serving in the Marines, he had moved in with his father and two unmarried sisters, Mae and Anna. His father had died but he was still living with his sisters in 1956.

Finally, Brussel surmised that the bomber was from Connecticut because many of the letters from "F. P." had been sent from Westchester County, which was conveniently halfway between Connecticut and New York City. Connecticut also had a high concentration of Slavic immigrants.

Metesky's home at 17 Fourth Street in Waterbury was square in the heart of Connecticut.

Bingo.

Inspector Finney was impressed with Brussel's work. (As well he should've been!) But Brussel wasn't quite done yet: He insisted that the police should publish the profile in newspapers immediately, which was far from standard operating procedure.

Although Finney initially resisted, Brussel explained that between the public revenge campaign and the indignation whenever one of his letters wasn't printed, the bomber desperately sought attention. Also based on what was fairly obvious—that the bomber was also an arrogant jerk—Brussel felt that if the madman saw the profile, he would be unable to help himself from pointing out any mistakes they had made in their evaluation, which could provide a much-needed lead.

Finney was concerned that if they went to the press with the profile, there might be all sorts of nut jobs coming out of the woodwork claiming to be the culprit. By the same token, he also trusted Brussel's expertise. If the psychiatrist was right, the real Mad Bomber would also come forward. He agreed to the plan.

Before the profile was published, Brussel made one final prediction: He told Finney that based on everything, that when they caught the man responsible, he would be wearing a double-breasted suit. *Buttoned.*

On Christmas Day 1956—the day after one of Metesky's undetonated units had been discovered in a phone booth at the New York Public Library—Dr. Brussel's profile of the Mad Bomber was printed in newspapers across the metropolitan area. In addition, a $26,000 reward was offered by the New York City Board of Estimate and the Patrolmen's Benevolent Association for the capture of the Mad Bomber. The game was on!

Years of acting like a dangerous jerk was finally bringing Metesky and his alleged cause the attention he craved, as Brussel had predicted. Also, as Finney feared, it brought tons of false bomb reports and confessions. Still, it had the desired effect.

When the profile was printed in the *New York Journal-American,* it was joined by an offer to print the Mad Bomber's grievances and a formal request from the New York City Police to turn himself in, after which he would receive a fair trial.

As Brussel had predicted, Metesky couldn't resist and responded immediately, refusing to give himself up but providing a full list of all the spots he had left bombs. He still wanted revenge on "THE CON EDISON" for their "DASTARDLY ACTS" and promised to continue to make the company miserable, even from his grave.

The newspaper printed Metesky's response on January 10, 1957, along with another open invitation from authorities to air his complaints.

Metesky again responded quickly, talking more about his frustration with how Con Edison had treated him after his accident, how he was disabled and had to pay for all his own medical expenses. He also provided details about how he constructed his units and even went so far as to suggest that he would refrain from planting any more bombs—a truce of sorts—until after March 1.

Still working with the police, the *Journal-American* printed Metesky's missive on January 15, and requested more information about his accident, suggesting that a new compensation hearing could be set up.

With the direct attention now stoking his ego, Metesky began to feel more confident, which would ultimately be his undoing.

Possibly it was the headiness caused by being the center of such intense scrutiny or the calm that comes with sensing that the end is near, but his Waterbury neighbors reported a change in Metesky around this time. As mentioned earlier, not much was known about the quiet, slightly eccentric but well-dressed man who lived with his sisters at 17 Fourth Street and worked in his garage at all hours. But as Mad Bomber mania was reaching its height in January 1957, the man who lived in "the crazy house" according to the local kids (they do see people more clearly than adults, right?) was now more outgoing and friendly.

The increased confidence also caused him to do things that were out of character for the calculating and elusive Mad Bomber. After the profile ran, Metesky allegedly called Brussel at his unlisted home phone and told him to "keep out" of the situation, which only confirmed what the psychiatrist had thought—the bomber would be unable to stop himself from reacting.

But it was in one final letter to the *Journal-American* in which he promised an end to the bombings that he made the kind of arrogant mistake that almost every comic book villain makes: He told police the exact date of his injurious accident.

Now armed with this key piece of information provided by Metsky himself, the investigation finally got the breakthrough it desperately needed.

Interestingly, after having been reluctant to cooperate with authorities and stating that they had no personnel files previous to 1940, Con Edison suddenly "discovered" the files of former employees and began sifting through them. (Maybe Metesky had been right about them, after all?) On January 18, a senior office assistant named Alice G. Kelly supposedly came across Metesky's file and recognized many similarities between his situation and the Mad Bomber's, including his having worked for the company around the same time, his having suffered an accident at a Con Edison plant, and his being disabled because of it. In the file, she also saw that Metesky had a penchant for corresponding with the company via the mail—angry letters in which he promised Con Edison would pay for its *"dastardly deeds."*

Metesky's file was immediately brought to the attention of the Mad Bomber task force. The Waterbury police were notified and asked to do a "discreet" check on Metesky, and three days later on January 21, 1957, four New York City Police detectives showed up at the door of 17 Fourth Street, late in the evening, arrest warrants in hand.

Metesky, dressed in a bathrobe, let them into the house and was completely courteous and cooperative. After a few minutes of small talk about an auto accident, he said, "I know why you're here. You think I'm the Mad Bomber." When the detectives replied that they did, he gave up all pretense and promptly confessed on the spot. He showed them his garage workshop, which was full of bomb-making equipment and pieces for new units, and pleasantly started answering questions, including why he called himself "F. P."

"Fair Play," he told them.

The detectives asked Metesky to get dressed so that they could take him back to New York City to be formally booked. Quietly, he put on his clothes: a double-breasted suit. *Buttoned.*

Metesky's arrest made newspaper headlines across the nation, and accompanying pictures show the formerly shy terrorist smiling and seeming to enjoy the attention, just as Brussel suggested he might. He also flashed some of his paranoid-induced jerkiness.

"'I'M GLAD I DID IT,' BOMBER STATES" was the headline splashed across the top of the *Springfield Union,* which was next to a picture of a beaming Metesky.

Psychiatric experts examined Metesky and believed him to be mentally ill. While awaiting trial, his tuberculosis also flared up, rendering him bedridden. Medical experts opined that he only had months to live. He was considered to be "a very sick man."

Despite that, Metesky was cooperative, ultimately admitting to planting thirty-two bombs in total. He was indicted on forty-seven separate charges, ranging from attempted murder to maliciously endangering life. After consulting with psychiatrists, medical experts, prosecutors, and police, however, Judge Samuel S. Leibowitz declared Metesky "hopeless and incurable" on April 18, 1957. The Mad Bomber was committed to the Matteawan Hospital for the Criminally Insane in Beacon, New York.

During his time at Matteawan, Metesky didn't really respond to treatment for his mental disorder, although he was a model inmate and caused no problems. Dr. Brussel, who gained acclaim and dramatically changed the way detective work would be done from his role in the Mad Bomber case, visited him from time to time, and while never accepting that anything was wrong with his mental makeup, Metesky would point out to the doctor that his bombs, although disruptive, had been designed not to be lethal.

Ironically, being captured did aid his physical health. Despite being ravaged by tuberculosis when arrested, he was given proper medical attention while at Matteawan and his condition improved. As a matter of fact, Metesky went on to live a long life.

In December 1973, at the age of seventy, after having been committed for almost seventeen years—two thirds of what would've been a maximum sentence of twenty-five years, had he gone to trial—and being deemed harmless, Metesky was released. He returned to his family home in Waterbury, where he took care of his ailing sister Mae (Anna had died a few years earlier) and lived in relative obscurity.

Metesky died in 1994 at the age of ninety. Like many jerks, the once-feared Mad Bomber went out quietly, rather than with a big bang.

CHAPTER 3

Lydia Sherman:
Connecticut's Own Black Widow

It can be argued that many times when someone is branded with a special nickname from the press, it's almost always for something notorious: "The Butcher of Bagdad," "Long Island Lolita," "The Mad Bomber of New York." Few do-gooders are recognized by the media in the same way because their acts aren't as sensational—"The Candy Man of Coventry" or "Mother Theresa of Thomaston" just wouldn't sell as many papers or get people buzzing.

Thus, if someone was trumpeted as "The Modern-Day Lucretia Borgia," "America's Queen Killer," "The Poison Fiend," or simply "The Derby Poisoner," you can bet that she was an extraordinary jerk. Such is the case of Lydia Sherman.

One of the most horrifying mass murderers of the nineteenth century, Sherman was the prototypical "black widow" serial killer, marrying and then murdering multiple husbands. What made Sherman's case extraordinarily shocking was that rather than be content with simply doing away with three spouses over less than a decade, she also extinguished the lives of eight children—six of them her own flesh and blood.

Now that's a level of jerkdom very few ever reach. Thankfully.

Before she would do mortal harm to her own children, Lydia herself was one, coming into the world as Lydia Danbury on Christmas Eve 1824. According to her published confession, *Lydia Sherman: Confession of the Arch Murderess of Connecticut*—a bestselling sensation in itself and something she apparently took great pleasure in providing, although its truthfulness and chronology is a bit questionable at times—she was born near Burlington, New Jersey, and less than a year later, her mother died. She was taken to live at her uncle's farm until she was sixteen, after

Portrait of Lydia Sherman c. 1824–c. 1878
ORIGINAL ART BY GREG SHEA

which she resided with one of her brothers in New Brunswick. She claimed to have worked for a reverend and his family for a few years, and then went on to become a tailor by the time she was nineteen years old.

The young Lydia was described as an attractive, slim woman with "rich chestnut hair, large blue eyes, and a milky complexion," and it appears that she would trade on her good looks throughout her life. She was also a devoted Methodist, and it was during a "love feast" (a communal religious dinner) in 1842 at her local church that she met Edward S. Struck, a carriage blacksmith and widower with six children.

Struck was apparently infatuated with the pious girl, and despite being nearly twenty years her senior, soon asked her to marry. She accepted, and they were wed a short time later. Over the course of the next eighteen years, the couple would welcome seven more children to the family: Lydia, John, George, Ann Eliza, Martha Ann, Edward Jr., Josephine, and William. Soon after the lady met the fellow, it didn't take more than a hunch to know that with so many kids, the group was significantly more than a bunch, so to speak. Struck transplanted his brood to New York City, where they kept moving to bigger residences as more children came along, finally settling in an apartment on 125th Street.

Realizing that he needed a better income than could be earned in the blacksmith shop, Edward Struck began to search for new employment and caught what he thought was a great break in January 1857, landing a job as an officer on the newly formed Metropolitan Police force. For the next six years he proudly walked a beat in the Manhattanville section of the city. During this time, things also got easier at home as all six children from his first marriage got older and moved out one by one. Everything seemed to be going well . . . until tragedy struck the Strucks. And that tragedy would turn out to be a double whammy, and very possibly self-inflicted.

Around 1863, two-year-old daughter Josephine suddenly was incapacitated by an attack of the measles that Lydia claimed eventually brought on a fierce cold. In a short time, the little girl was dead from her malady, a death that the attending physician simply chalked up to "inflammation of the bowels." At the time, no one had any reason to think that anything untoward had happened—sadly, young children dying of fairly innocuous diseases like measles was an accepted part of life in the mid-nineteenth century, even though the measles are not known to have the symptoms from which Lydia suggested the girl had suffered. Josephine was laid to rest with a fair number of tears and without an autopsy. In retrospect, however, her death may not have been as random as it seemed. It would be the first in a string of abrupt and unexpected fatalities in the family.

Meanwhile, the Strucks were about to endure another major event that would set the clan—and Lydia, in particular—down the road to ruin. Although what happened during the incident itself would be disputed, there was no question as to the horror that occurred in its wake.

One day during the fall of 1863 at Stratton's Hotel in Manhattan—part of Officer Edward Struck's beat—a knife-wielding man attacked the hotel's bartender and was shot by a detective who happened to be passing the scene, had heard the ruckus, and had investigated. At the inquest afterward, hotel employees at the scene alleged that when the clear cries for police assistance had gone up, Officer Struck, rather than intervene, had turned and fled the scene in fear that the assailant was brandishing a gun. Struck, on the other hand, claimed that when the assault went down, he had been blocks away from the crime, and by the time he arrived, the action had already ended.

The Metropolitan Police believed the multiple witnesses who had suggested that Struck had acted cowardly, and he was immediately dismissed. Struck, for his part, believed that he had been the victim of a setup, and insisted to his wife and anyone else who would listen that he had been targeted because he was the only honest cop in a corrupt force.

Suddenly unemployed and disgraced, and with a wife and seven young children to support, it appears that Struck spiraled downward into severe depression over the ensuing months. He eventually refused to leave his bed or home, and even threatened to kill himself. Lydia would later say that a few friends proposed that she have her husband committed to a lunatic asylum, but then another one made a more permanent suggestion: that Lydia "put him out of the way, as he would never be of any good" again.

It was an idea that only a truly diabolical jerk would consider.

Later, in her confession, the cold-blooded murderess would detail how she decided to put her beloved husband of eighteen years out of his misery—courtesy of a heaping dose of arsenic.

Back in the nineteenth century, arsenic was an incredibly easy poison to obtain. Unlike today, when only licensed professionals can get arsenic, Lydia Struck was able to walk into her local drug store and ask the pharmacist for a few ounces without raising any suspicion whatsoever, as it was commonly used to kill rats. She brought the poison home, mixed a "thimbleful" of it into a bowl of oatmeal gruel—only a few granules is enough to kill a man—and on the night of May 23, 1864, fed it to her spouse with the sole intent of murdering him.

Arsenic is an especially virulent toxin but a slow-acting one. Over the course of hours, Struck suffered from a burning throat, then uncontrollable vomiting and diarrhea, excruciating abdominal and intestinal pain, violent convulsions and, ultimately—mercifully—death. The fifty-nine-year-old Edward Struck was officially declared dead "of consumption" the next morning. (Although Lydia never admitted it, the circumstances of her young daughter Josephine's death were eerily similar to arsenic poisoning.)

Like many jerks, it doesn't appear as if Lydia Struck had fully considered the ramifications of her actions. With her husband now gone, no income, and six young children to care for, things were now very bleak. She claimed to be "much discouraged and downhearted." It probably would've made sense to get some psychological or financial help, but as evidenced by the murder of her husband, Lydia was more than capable of taking care of things in her own unique way.

Horrifyingly, she settled on the same method to "take care" of what remained of her own family.

Greatly upset by what had happened to her husband (as if someone else had caused his demise!), and after thinking "the matter over for several days," the widow Struck decided that her three youngest children—six-year-old Martha Ann, four-year-old Edward Jr., and nine-month-old William—"could do nothing for me or for themselves," and thus, would be better off if they were "out of the way." Except by "out of the way," she didn't mean to deposit her kids at an orphanage, but into premature graves.

In July 1864—less than six weeks after burying her husband—Struck gave arsenic to all three of her young children, and then sat back and let the poison do its gruesome work. In her confession, she described watching all three suffer terribly, casually remarking on how well they suffered the severe vomiting and gut-wrenching agony as their lives ebbed away. She described how son Edward, "a beautiful boy," "did not complain during his illness" and "was very patient."

All three children died within a single day.

As it had been with the sudden demises of little Josephine and husband Edward, no one suspected Lydia Struck of anything criminal. Again, it was an era when entire families were often felled by a single bout of sickness. The official record attributed the children's deaths to "remittent fever" and "bronchitis."

With the burden of the youngest members no longer weighing down the remaining Strucks, things did improve—for a while. John was working and George was able to find employment as a painter, while daughter Lydia was a clerk in a retail store, all of which provided income for the family. But soon George contracted lead poisoning, forcing the fourteen-year-old boy to quit his labors and take to his bed.

In a manner that was becoming all-too-familiar, Lydia had a "special" medicine for those who might be a drag on the family, and mixed it up in her son's tea. George was soon lying in a cold grave next to his father because his mother had once again become "discouraged."

"I know now that is not much of an excuse," she wrote in a gross understatement that only a heartless monster could fathom. "But I felt so much trouble that I did not think about that."

The Struck household was now down to Lydia and daughters Lydia, eighteen, and Ann Eliza, twelve; son John, now sixteen, had moved out and was supporting himself, which was probably the only thing that spared his life.

After the string of (seeming) tragedies that had befallen the poor widow—who still possessed her good looks and charm—one of the Struck family doctors took pity on her, and got Lydia work.

As a nurse.

That's right—the woman who had cruelly administered poison to her husband and four (maybe five) of her own children under the pretense of ending their (and her own) suffering, was now regularly tasked with attending to the sick on a daily basis.

Except Lydia Struck wasn't done attending to her own children yet. Worried that her daughter Ann Eliza, who had always been a sickly child, was not going to get any better, and thus, be relegated to a life of infirmity, Lydia sped up the natural process in her own unique way. By mid-March 1865, Ann Eliza—"the happiest child I ever saw," according to Lydia's confession—was gone after four days of suffering through arsenic poisoning. "Typhoid fever" was the cause listed on her death certificate.

At this point the two Lydias were left in the house, and that wouldn't last for long. In early May, young Lydia took ill and soon became bedridden—a condition that often became fatal in the Struck home. The girl struggled for nearly three weeks, but by May 19, she was dead, also of "typhoid fever." Although Struck admitted to poisoning her other children and husband, she claimed daughter Lydia's death had been by "natural causes." The symptoms, however, looked remarkably like arsenic poisoning.

By now, having "lost" seven immediate family members over the course of a few years to what appeared to be "mysterious" sicknesses, a few people were (finally) beginning to get suspicious. Lydia's stepson Cornelius—one of Edward Struck's adult children from his first marriage, and clearly not any sort of family physician seemingly content to sign off on death certificate after death certificate without batting an eyelash—went to the district attorney's office with his concerns. Although he got the promise that an investigation would be launched, nothing was done.

For the next year, Lydia continued to work as a nurse. In April 1866, the forty-one-year-old yet-to-be-discovered killer and her sole surviving son John—who, either an enabler in utter denial or truly oblivious to what had happened, and intent on financially helping his "unfortunate" mother—moved to Saylorsville (in Kidder township), Pennsylvania, to work for a family on a farm. They stayed throughout the summer, but Lydia realized that the hard manual labor was not really for her, and moved back to New York City. She landed a job selling sewing machines, and it was there that she met James Curtiss, one of the store's regular customers.

Impressed with the widow Struck's nursing reputation (and apparently not knowing anything about her true pain-ending skills), Curtiss offered her an opportunity to earn eight dollars a month—at the time, a substantial sum—plus room and board to take care of his elderly mother at his house in Stratford. With no family of her own requiring her support (her son John was on his own), and no doubt wanting to distance herself from the scene of her crimes, Lydia accepted. She relocated to Connecticut in 1867, moved in with Mrs. Curtiss, and hit it off with the old woman. All was well for the next eight months.

Lydia, however, was always looking to improve her situation. A golden opportunity soon came along.

One day while at the local grocery store, the still-attractive and personable Lydia got another caretaking offer, this time in the employ of Dennis Hurlburt, a wealthy older gentleman known around town as "Old Hurlburt." Recently widowed, Old Hurlburt was looking for "a good woman" to keep house on his successful farm in Huntington, in an area that is now near downtown Shelton. He and Lydia quickly came to an arrangement, so she packed her belongings at the Curtiss house and moved in with her new, affluent employer.

He may have been known as "Old" Hurlburt, but that doesn't mean he was "Dead" Hurlburt (not yet, anyway!). The rich widower was immediately taken with the comely Lydia . . . so much so that he asked her to be his wife only a few days after her arrival. Like a seasoned poker pro (or calculating murderer), Lydia considered the offer until Hurlburt sweetened the pot like a true sugar daddy, promising her "all that he was worth" if she agreed to the union.

They were married in Huntington on November 22, 1868, and true to his word, the grayed groom soon had his will rewritten to benefit his blushing bride. One can only imagine her self-satisfied smile as the lawyer signed the papers.

For the next fourteen months, life was good for the forty-four-year-old Lydia and the substantially older Old Hurlburt. One Sunday morning while helping him shave for church, Lydia noticed the elderly man's hands were shaking, and a short time later he said he felt dizzy. He tried to work it off by splitting some wood, but it was obvious that the grizzled farmer was suffering from some possibly age-related malady.

Unfortunately for Old Hurlburt, he would soon discover that his young wife "hated" to see someone "suffering."

The next day, Lydia was back to her old tricks. Ostensibly to make her husband feel better, she served him a steaming bowl of freshly made clam chowder—laced with arsenic. Old Hurlburt immediately took ill, calling for a glass of Hostetter's Stomach Bitters, a nineteenth-century cure-all that was more alcohol (ninety-four proof) than pharmaceutical. To help offset that ratio and speed up things, Lydia added some of her "special" medicine, just as she had done for her prior husband and a number of her own children.

By 6 p.m. on Thursday of that week, after three excruciating days of extended vomiting and wretched pain, Old Hurlburt was officially Dead Hurlburt.

Lydia Hurlburt was also now officially Rich Widow Hurlburt, coming into a tidy little fortune by late nineteenth-century standards: $20,000 in real estate and $10,000 in cash (worth roughly $500,000 today). In short, with a large bank account, no one suspicious of her crimes, and no one to tie her down, Lydia Danbury-Struck-Hurlburt was set for the rest of her life . . . if she hadn't been a complete jerk.

In the spring of 1870, only eight weeks or so after poor Old Hurlburt had been hastened to his premature grave, his forty-six-year-old widow was already on the make for her next husband/victim. Again recommended by someone who was duped by her charm and looks, Lydia came into contact with Horatio N. Sherman, a factory mechanic who lived across the Housatonic River in what was then the Birmingham section of Derby (now downtown). Another widower who had lost his wife just a few months earlier, Sherman was looking for someone to take care of his four children, his nuisance of an elderly mother-in-law, and his house.

Lydia obviously didn't need the money, which was good because Sherman had none, and in fact, had accrued debts that Lydia would generously pay off for him. In an effort to secure her and her services, he quickly proposed marriage. Cruelly toying with her prey, Lydia took her time considering his offer, putting off her suitor for a few months and forcing him to court her in proper fashion. In the meantime, she cozied up to Sherman's children: seventeen-year-old Nelson, four-year-old Nathaniel, and Frankie, a sickly infant, as well as fourteen-year-old Ada, the apple of Horatio's eye. She particularly bonded with Ada, who seemed to be looking for a female role model in the wake of her mother's death. Little did the vulnerable teenager know what a poor choice she had made.

Unable to keep the persistent and personable Sherman at bay any longer, Lydia finally relented. She took her third spouse on September 2, 1870, becoming Lydia Sherman in a small ceremony at Sherman's sister's home in Bridgewater, Massachusetts. Things were rocky from the start—Horatio Sherman was a heavy drinker, had been more in debt than he let on, and seemed incapable of keeping a job. In a moment of obvious alcohol-fueled frustration, he remarked to Lydia that he wished the fragile Frankie "would die" so as to be free of his misery, which would also free them from Horatio's former mother-in-law, who was still living with the family.

He didn't have to tell someone like Lydia Sherman twice.

"America's Queen Killer" "was full of trouble and, not knowing what to do" decided to give the child something "to get him out of the way" so "he would be better off." She quickly found arsenic that had been used to exterminate rats around the house and on November 15, 1870, put it in the baby's milk. Little Frankie succumbed before midnight.

Not surprisingly, this didn't help the situation as Lydia had thought it might. The mother-in-law didn't leave immediately, eventually requiring a substantial cash pay off before she would depart. Horatio Sherman hit the bottle even harder, maintaining such a constant state of drunkenness that he couldn't work. This only caused resentment from Lydia, who was forced to support the family with the fortune she had inherited from her previous victim—er, husband.

As bad as things were, they were only going to get worse.

A few weeks later, while helping get the local church ready for Christmas, Ada was stricken ill with what seemed to be the flu. Horatio Sherman, deeply concerned about his beloved daughter, called multiple doctors and then got so drunk that he couldn't stand upright. The doctors had no success curing the sweet Ada, so Lydia stepped in as she had done numerous times before to "end the suffering." She gave the girl two cups of her "specially brewed" tea—laced with arsenic—and Ada was dead by New Year's Eve 1870.

Absolutely devastated by his daughter's abrupt passing, Horatio Sherman went on a bender "working, drinking, and spending his money" without restraint. Concerned that her husband's protracted binge would eventually start draining her hard-earned wealth, Lydia tried to get him to join a temperance society to stop drinking. The situation temporarily improved before taking a final downward turn.

In late April, Horatio Sherman took $300 out of his bank account and went off to New Haven with a group of his friends for an extended drinking spree. They weren't heard from for a week, and only came back after Lydia sent Sherman's son Nelson to retrieve his wayward father. When Sherman returned home, he showed no sign of remorse and continued to drink for the next few days.

Lydia had reached her breaking point. If her spouse wanted to destroy himself, she certainly could oblige!

She spiked a pint of his favorite brandy with arsenic, and as she knew he would, he soon drank it down. Like all her prior victims, Horatio was soon felled with severe digestive and intestinal pains, as well as all the other nastiness associated with arsenic poisoning. The symptoms quickly became more and more intense, severely weakening the formerly robust man. The family physician, Dr. J. C. Beardsley of Derby, was quickly called in and, although perplexed by Sherman's condition—which didn't resemble the aftereffects of any of the prolific drinker's previous hangovers—prescribed medication that he thought would right his patient. He instructed Lydia to give her husband the medicine and nothing else.

Of course, Lydia "accidentally" left the poisoned bottle of brandy by the bedside, which was conveniently emptied before she could stop her spouse from drinking it. When Beardsley returned a day later, Sherman's condition had taken a grave turn. According to his court testimony, the doctor asked Lydia, "Pray what has he been taking? These symptoms cannot be the effects of a debauch, nor do they seem to be those of any ordinary diseases; what have you been giving him?" She said that she had only given him the prescribed medicine and nothing else.

"I did not mean to kill him," Lydia later claimed in her confession, evidently forgetting the lethal properties of arsenic despite murdering nearly a dozen people with it. "I only wanted to make him sick of liquor."

On May 12, 1871, after experiencing gut-wrenching agony for days—just like Lydia's other victims—Horatio Sherman died.

Except this time, it was different. Beardsley, knowing something was terribly wrong, had asked the man just before he had expired what else he had been ingesting. Sherman's response:

"Nothing but what you have ordered, and my wife has been particular to do as you have told her."

The competent Beardsley wasn't buying it. Unlike the other physicians who, maybe swayed by Lydia's charms, had never really questioned the woman's connection to so many heinous demises, he followed his suspicions and requested that he be allowed to conduct a post-mortem examination. Lydia, possibly wanting to get caught (as many serial killers do), agreed.

Beardsley and two other doctors removed the stomach and other internal organs from Horatio Sherman's corpse and sent them to Yale University to be analyzed by the accomplished professor of physiological chemistry and toxicology, George Frederick Barker. Two weeks later, Barker's results came back: Horatio Sherman had been killed by a substantial amount of arsenic.

After discovering that Lydia had done in her spouse with poison, authorities immediately exhumed the bodies of Ada and Frankie Sherman, as well as of Old Dennis Hurlburt, autopsied them all and sent the organs to Yale for examination. Barker discovered the three had also been killed with significant doses of arsenic.

The jig was up, but Lydia had taken off, returning to her family in New Brunswick shortly after Horatio Sherman's death. She hadn't tried to run too far, however, and on June 7, 1871, made no protest when she was arrested by police and brought back to New Haven to stand trial for murder.

The sensational case was called "The Horror of the Century," and consumed headlines across the nation. Lydia's trial finally opened on April 16, 1872, and from all accounts, she was in a good mood, smiling and pleasant throughout the trial. She was only tried for the murder of Horatio Sherman—for which she steadfastly maintained her innocence—but with such overwhelming evidence, it only took the prosecution eight days to convince the jury to find her guilty of murder in the second degree.

While awaiting her sentencing, she decided to do what many jerks do when they know they are in dire straits and "gave herself up to Christ." "Years ago I was a professor of religion and always thought I had religion, but I know now that I was never a Christian," the murderer of a dozen innocent people said in what could only be described as another dramatic understatement. "I always used to think I was, but I know I was not, or would not have done as I did."

After no longer being burdened spiritually, she then decided to abandon her innocent defense and provide a full confession of all her murderous acts. Interestingly, at the end of the document, she seemingly congratulated herself on her own cleverness—like a true jerk—stating, "It seemed strange to me that the doctors who were considered very talented, and were allowed to give me burial permits in New York, did not discover anything."

The forty-eight-year-old "Arch Murderess of Connecticut" was sentenced to life imprisonment at the state facility in Wethersfield. The judge who presided over the case regretted that "he could not send her to the scaffold instead." Many outside the court also called for her to be hanged, but then again, just as many bought her confession when it was published.

Lydia went peacefully to jail, and was not in the public eye again except for a week of freedom in May 1877 after she had taken advantage of a medical condition to walk out the front doors of the prison. Her escape went undetected long enough that she successfully traveled to Providence, Rhode Island, where she had somehow arranged a job as a housekeeper—to a wealthy widower!

Fourth time's a charm?

She was hauled back to the prison and died a year later on May 16, 1878, following a bout with cancer, at age fifty-four.

Like some of the murdering jerks of today, she was a true media sensation. And long after she was gone, her story lived on in verse:

> Lydia Sherman is plagued with rats
> Lydia has no faith in cats.
> So Lydia buys some arsenic,
> And then her husband gets sick;

And then her husband, he does die,
And Lydia's neighbors wonder why.

Lydia moves, but still has rats;
And still she puts no faith in cats;
So again she buys some arsenic,
This time her children, they get sick,
This time her children, they do die,
And Lydia's neighbors wonder why.

Lydia lies in Wethersfield jail,
And loudly does she moan and wail.
She blames her fate on a plague of rats;
She blames the laziness of cats.
But her neighbors' questions she can't deny—
So Lydia now in prison must lie.

To which, could be added one more verse:

Lydia mixed up the arsenic quick,
Gave it to her family and made them sick.
After they all found cold graves,
She tried to say that "Jesus saves."
But the poisoner had a nasty quirk—
Lydia Sherman, she was a jerk.

CHAPTER 4

Julius Schacknow:
Self-Made Prophet, Savior, and God

As in the story of Rev. Herbert Hayden (chapter 13), a jerk may sometimes employ a shallow veneer of deep faith to help mask deplorable behavior. Then there are some jerks who rather than hide behind a god, will just declare themselves God, and attempt to take advantage of all the glory and trappings that come with being a deity.

> *I'm your creator and I've come to punish the world for their sins, for their ungodliness, their crookedness, breaking my commandments . . . and threatening people who love me as Jesus with contempt . . .*
>
> *I am man sent from God. Julius. I am the son of God. This is no boast, no baloney. I am the real thing. I don't have to prove anything to you. You must prove yourselves to me.*

Those are the words of Julius Schacknow, a man who over the course of a few decades proclaimed himself a preacher, a prophet, the "sinful" reincarnation of Jesus, and ultimately, God. During that time, "Brother Julius," as Schacknow became known, would also inspire hundreds, make millions, and engage in behavior that many would hardly classify as "divine."

Unless they were talking about a divine jerk.

Still, there were some parallels between Brother Julius and other messiahs: Like Jesus, Julius Schacknow was born into a poor Jewish family, albeit 1,924 years later and on August 21; and rather than a manger in Bethlehem, it was a decidedly less sheep- and cow-filled home in Brooklyn, New York, that would receive the self-anointed savior. Also like Jesus, little is known about Schacknow's formative years other than he grew up during the tough days of the Great Depression. From there, the paths diverge quite a bit.

By the time Schacknow was eighteen, both his parents had died, so with World War II underway, he enlisted in the US Navy. He served during the war in the South Pacific as a radio man, and went AWOL a few times. While in Guam following the end of hostilities, he had his first experience with what he would later term as "God consciousness." He claimed that while in a "living vision" he was taken up to heaven where he had a private audience with the Lord. According to Schacknow, God told him to study the Bible for five years, that he was "a very special predestined chosen vessel" to rid the world of evil, and that he was "to be the light of the Gentiles and the hope of my people Israel."

Word of Schacknow's vision got to the base psychologist, and after a brief stint in the hospital there, he was honorably discharged from the navy. Soon afterward, he married Elsie Beville, with whom he had two children. In 1947, he applied to the Bible Institute of Los Angeles, and for the next few years, was devoted to studying Scripture. Apparently, he didn't dedicate himself quite so much to being a family man, and by 1950 Elsie filed for divorce, citing "religious incompatibility." In 1955, he met and married Mary Smith, with whom he had two more children; by 1960 Schacknow was divorced a second time, this time on grounds of marital infidelity.

Mary's charges had merit—Julius had been traveling around the country, taking odd jobs and pursuing his Bible studies, and it was while in Illinois during 1958 that he met a mysterious woman known as Joanne, who soon became the third Mrs. Schacknow. They were married in 1961, and with his four children, moved to New York.

The family soon resettled in New Jersey, and it was there that Schacknow landed a job as a buyer for International Telephone and Telegraph (IT&T) and started to build his following. From

The "Sinning Jesus," Brother Julius Schacknow
CONNECTICUT MAGAZINE

his time studying and preaching at various ministries across the nation, he had already developed a reputation as a devoted theologian and an impassioned speaker, demonstrating a charismatic and persuasive presence in the pulpit. During lunch breaks at IT&T, he would give sermons to rapt coworkers, who helped to spread the good word as Schacknow was telling it.

Before long, Schacknow was referencing the book of Revelation in his sermons, specifically calling attention to how St. John had promised that two "witnesses clad in sackcloth" would precede the Apocalypse. Schacknow eventually claimed to be one of those witnesses—his wife Joanne, who was known among the faithful as "the Holy Spirit," was the other. This declaration only further deepened the devotion of his followers.

In his role as a prophet, Schacknow continued to visit churches along the East Coast as a guest minister, yet as his reputation for his biblical knowledge was growing, so were the rumors that he was not a conventional holy man. For one thing, a crucial part of his ministry seemed to revolve around sex—in particular, that his female followers unquestioningly provide it to him.

Apparently, God had told Schacknow that he had placed him on this Earth to experience all the vices and evils of the world so he could better distinguish between right and wrong. God also allegedly informed Schacknow that he had a unique spirit, one that could indulge in debauchery and yet not be tainted by it. Such a spirit also lifted him above the judgment of others, which was handy when it came time to explain why he could enjoy alcohol and tobacco when the use of such items was forbidden among his flock.

According to former followers, the enthusiastic Schacknow was *very* devoted to not disappointing God, partaking especially heavily in the sins of the flesh. Some accusations also suggested that the younger the flesh, the better.

Conveniently, God also decided that it was at this point Schacknow needed to know the truth. During one vision, he said that God had proclaimed, "You are my son, the Lord . . . There's never been another." He added that God had made him flesh to complete the Messiah's mission—the end of the world was nigh, and he had been dispatched to save humanity.

As such, "Brother Julius" quit his regular job and took on the full-time mantle of "the sinning Jesus." With such an imperative calling at hand, his following graduated to official "cult" status and assumed a more formal structure with assigned roles: Schacknow appointed twelve apostles, assigning each a different sign of the zodiac and all the cult members who were born under that corresponding sign—it was the dawning of the Age of Aquarius, after all.

Speaking of free love, it was around this time that Brother Julius publicly swapped wives with one of his key followers, Paul Sweetman, a man whom Schackman had designated as his chief apostle. Joanne went to live with Sweetman, with whom she would stay for decades. Sweetman's wife Minnie moved in with Schacknow for a short time before she passed away. Although by this point, an earthly convention like marriage had no meaning for Brother Julius, who was regularly spreading his "divine seed" among the younger females of the group.

In 1970, during an outdoor revival in Trumbull, Brother Julius publicly revealed that God had shared with him the news that he was his one true son, thus severing ties with all other churches and religious organizations. Going forward, members were instructed to turn all their money and wealth over to the cult, and to renounce any further worldly possessions. Funds collected on behalf of the group were supposed to help spread the word of Brother Julius, although it seemed very little of the money went beyond serving the direct needs and wants of the cult's leadership.

Church followers were also told to leave their former lives, friends, and families behind, and to keep all their relationships— platonic and romantic—within the group.

Brother Julius played the physical part of messiah well: Although only about five foot seven, slightly overweight and balding, he kept his dark hair and beard long and flowing. He often dressed in a white robe, wore an earring, and used his deep, sonorous voice to shake the soul foundations of those around him. He also had eyes that were described as "piercing" and "mesmerizing," another tool he employed to convert followers, making them think that they were connecting with someone extraordinary.

Like many cult leaders, Schacknow excelled in identifying people who were lost emotionally or psychologically, or those looking for something more to their lives. He was as good at praying as he was at preying on the weak, often focusing on the drug or alcohol dependent, and other helpless folk who suffered from psychological issues. Much of his success came from giving a purpose to those who needed one, or from substituting his teachings as the pharmaceutical of choice for the addicted.

He also targeted vulnerable young adults who were still trying to "find themselves" and were quite impressionable. For a savvy salesman like Schacknow, it was easy to reel them in by telling them exactly what they needed to hear.

"I can release a little power and change you," he told one group of teenagers at a gathering in Meriden. "I can help you kick any habit, give you a life above sin and good grades in school. . . . If you really believe in me, I will give you the answers. You can be sitting in class and all you have to do is ask the Lord what the answer is and it'll flip on in your head like a television set."

To give Brother Julius his due, no doubt there were followers he approached at a time of crisis and for whom he was able to provide direction, possibly saving them from ending up in a worse place. Some claimed that he helped them kick their addictions, quell their demons, and find purpose in their lives. The problem was that for many other converts, the path Schacknow guided them to ultimately did more for Schacknow's own personal gratification (and bank account) than it did for their best interests.

After the Trumbull announcement declaring that he was the second coming of Jesus, Brother Julius and his church officially moved operations to Connecticut, choosing to set up headquarters in Meriden. In addition to proselytizing and separating his followers from their hard-earned money, Schacknow branched into other ventures, including music. The church founded The Anointed Music and Publishing Company (TAMPCO), an operation designed to support the organization's band, the Anointed, which was an obvious effort focused on drawing young people. Schacknow promised his followers that the funds they invested in producing the Anointed's albums—as well as publishing a seven-volume tome chronicling the life of Jesus as interpreted by Brother Julius—would provide a substantial windfall for the church.

The Anointed's 1972 debut release, *God is Alive,* was typical for the era—a folksy blend of '60s psychedelia, with lots of guitars, harmonies, and songs like the title track, "The Good Shepherd," "Yes We Have the Christ," and "Voice of the Seventh Angel." On the cover, the group asserted that they were introducing "a new sound" inspired by having discovered that the Messiah had "come again to the Earth in our twentieth century among the Gentiles." They also zealously attributed all their "talents and accomplishments" to their "God, the Messiah, Brother Julius."

Schacknow was a better cult leader than record producer, and due to a significant lack of interest on behalf of the record-buying public, the album tanked. The proposed biography of Jesus also met a similar fate after the first volume was published and was discovered to be such dreck that it essentially couldn't be given away. Evidently, the retail entertainment market wasn't quite ready to embrace the word from Brother Julius as eagerly as his devotees.

Despite the commercial failure, however, Schacknow was still a hit with the followers, and by 1974, they numbered almost five hundred. Brother Julius was on top of his game, attracting droves and promising answers and eternal glory to anyone who would believe that he was the Chosen One—and still sharing his personal divine touch with the younger, more nubile females of the group. Then again, making heavenly guarantees and delivering on them were two entirely different things, and to that point, no one had called him on it.

Still, the financial fiascos of the album and book caused a significant hit to the church's coffers, consequently shifting the cult over the next year from efforts that focused on creative endeavors to more stable (and lucrative) business enterprises. John Hill, TAMPCO's secretary and a key member of the church's leadership, had previous experience in real estate, and helped move the church in that direction. An entity dedicated to house sales and named J-Anne Inc. was formed, and it was soon affiliated with the reputable real estate company Century 21. Another group called County-Wide Home Improvement and Maintenance Company was organized; its focus was on home maintenance and construction.

Not so coincidentally, it was around this time that Brother Julius decided to reorganize the flock a bit, separating and elevating those who showed an ability that could be utilized by either J-Anne or County-Wide. Those who were still working on TAMPCO projects and others who didn't have anything to offer the new companies were soon ostracized and pushed out. Schack-now justified the shedding of the (useless to him) faithful by pro-claiming that 288—a multiple of 12—was a divine number, and that the group should operate with only that many members. He also began to arrange marriages but discouraged procreation in the ranks, ostensibly because the world was "an evil place." Subse-quently, a number of followers "voluntarily" had vasectomies: a cut below to please Him above, so to speak.

The change in philosophy to a more cash-flow-friendly opera-tion didn't go unnoticed by members, who began to question the cult's leadership. Reports of serious abuse by Schacknow, sexual and mental, were also starting to circulate, hinting of a much darker side to Brother Julius than previously suspected.

Beginning in 1975, TAMPCO was quietly phased out, and all the group's energies were refocused on J-Anne and County-Wide. It may have rankled some of the faithful, but as it turns out, Schacknow and his associates were as successful in building and selling physical homes as they were in collecting spiritual ones—for a little while, anyway.

The real estate and construction enterprises were soon bring-ing in significant income. By 1977, the Southington-based J-Anne Inc. was reportedly selling nearly $25 million worth of homes, and County-Wide was responsible for building dozens of houses in the region. The companies were doing so well that a separate entity, Jubilee Holding Co., was formed to tap into the commercial real estate market.

Staffing the businesses with church members also had another benefit for the bottom line. Believing that they were aiding Brother Julius in his mission, many members worked for well below stan-dard wages; one report claims that a church member repairing machinery for County-Wide was being paid a mere eighty dol-lars for his fifty-hour work week. Others told of being vigorously pressured by Schacknow and Joanne "Holy Spirit" Sweetman into "donating" the majority—if not all—of their wages back to the church. To help motivate employee-followers, they were informed on a regular basis that they had to meet lofty sales goals or face the wrath of God.

Oddly, just as his church was having great financial success, Brother Julius slowly started fading to the background. Once known for never having met a pulpit or microphone he didn't like, he started preaching less, as well as doing fewer and fewer interviews with media outlets. Still as fiery and passionate as ever— and never backing down from his claims of divinity or his habits as "the sinful messiah"—Schacknow seemed more interested in the Good Book rather than the company's financial books.

Some speculated that Schacknow's reticence had to do with what was perceived as a rift in the church's hierarchy. After John Hill, Paul and Joanne Sweetman, and the others who ran the real estate and construction divisions of the church had enjoyed such success without Brother Julius's direct input, it appears that some of the power and decision making swung over to their side. Given Schacknow's sexual predilections and the accusations that would come, however, he may have decided to keep a low profile for legal reasons.

Still, as the Connecticut real estate boom of the 1980s took off, so did J-Anne and County-Wide. At its peak, J-Anne controlled five Century 21 franchises and was annually scoring over $100 million in sales. Under the direction of the Sweetmans and Hill, the church reportedly had a net worth of better than $20 million.

As had often been the case from the beginning, no matter how much money was coming in, it didn't seem to be quite enough; members were still encouraged to live humbly and return the lion's share of their earnings to the church for discretionary use by Brother Julius and his inner circle. Although Schacknow apparently didn't have much use for material objects like expensive clothes or luxurious homes, his top advisers allegedly did. Still, there were no specific explanations to exactly how these monies were being spent.

One possible answer was on lawyers.

Karen Schacknow Goodwin, one of Schacknow's stepdaughters, filed a civil suit against her stepfather, alleging that he was sexually abusive. Karen claimed that Julius had physically exploited her for seven years, starting from when she was eleven years old. The case was settled out of court, resulting in no criminal charges for Julius, but there were other similar allegations from numerous church members during this time involving underage girls. No formal case was ever brought against Schacknow, primarily because most followers were too intimidated to stand up to their "God," and even more reluctant to report anything to the authorities.

"Sinning messiah" is one thing, but "sex-abusing pedophile" goes well beyond typical "jerk" territory.

Schacknow's need for a reliable attorney was far from over, however. As the real estate boom went bust in the late 1980s, so did the fortunes of J-Anne and County-Wide. The church's business enterprises were increasingly coming under legal attack, with several former members who had helped J-Anne and County-Wide to such great success suing Schacknow and his top apostles for back wages and damages. Many claims were settled out of court, usually involving tens of thousands of dollars.

The state of Connecticut also charged the Sweetmans with unemployment fraud, claiming they had bilked the system out of $40,000 and filed phony claims. Like Schacknow, the Sweetmans were able to negotiate a deal, one that involved paying $50,000 in restitution and serving accelerated probation instead of jail time. Century 21 eventually revoked J-Anne's franchise license, effectively snuffing out the company.

County-Wide had numerous issues of its own, including multiple lawsuits brought against it for failure to complete construction projects. An investigation from the Connecticut Labor Department uncovered that funds that were supposed to be used for employee pension plans had been diverted, and that Sweetman and others had taken millions of dollars in "personal" loans. After arranging payments to reimburse the pension funds and make other owed payments, County-Wide was forced to cease operations altogether.

The Lord giveth, the courts taketh away.

Out of quasi-legitimate business, Brother Julius's ministry turned back to its former expertise, recruiting and exploiting the young and vulnerable. By this point, Schacknow had all but withdrawn from the public eye, letting his apostles and younger followers do the initial recruiting. As opposed to the large, open gatherings of the 1970s where Brother Julius was the star attraction who would vigorously exhort his flock from the pulpit, the church instead tried to lure new converts by quietly advertising Bible study classes with a focus on the Apocalypse and other yet-to-be-fulfilled prophesies. After they had fully committed to the church and were properly indoctrinated, the converts would then get an audience with the living God.

Although Schacknow wasn't the visible front of the group any longer, it certainly didn't mean he wasn't active behind the scenes. He still led Bible-study groups and was involved with most of the church's spiritual practices. Unfortunately, it appears he was also undertaking the same liberties that he felt compelled to take to better "know sin."

By the early 1990s, Brother Julius's flock had dwindled to fewer than fifty stalwarts, and a number of those had seemingly lost faith. The years of abuses, lawsuits, and empty promises had taken their toll. Disillusioned, many of the long-time top apostles had departed, which further disrupted the church's harmony; others lower in the hierarchy followed suit. The days of cheery folk songs, free love, and open devotion were long gone.

Former members reported that in later years, when they tried to leave the cult, they were often "threatened" by Schacknow, who rather than specify a direct physical action that he might take, would instead insinuate that all sorts of ills might befall them due to divine providence. In other words: "Depart at your own peril, and expect a smiting (of sorts)."

They still left.

In a 1993 television interview—the first one he had done in over a decade—for a New England Cable News special called "Who is Brother Julius?," Schacknow boldly asserted to reporter

Alan Cohn that "I am the Lord God," and it was time for everyone on Earth to know him. He also said that the Apocalypse was at hand, and that after not being able not find a single "good" person, he was going to end the world in a fiery judgment.

During the same interview, Schacknow also suggested that he was the inspiration for Hollywood's selection of George Burns as the titular character in *Oh God!* based on Burns's physical likeness to Brother Julius (a divine joke?). The program also displayed Schacknow's personal letterhead, which was emblazoned "From the Desk of the Lord God" across the top of the page.

In the program, which turned out to be a full-out exposé, another of Schacknow's estranged daughters, LaRay, suggested that her father was worse than infamous Branch Davidian leader David Koresh, saying, "The damage that David Koresh did is minimal compared to the potential my father could do." She stated that he even wanted her to become one of his wives (in every sense), and that after her time with him, she felt "like I tangled with Satan himself."

Other former followers detailed a variety of physical and mental abuses perpetrated on church members in addition to Schacknow's well-reported sexual activities, including numerous accounts of child sexual abuse. When confronted by Cohn about the claims and lawsuits against him, Schacknow immediately became belligerent, declared the interview over, and stormed off. It would be the last television appearance he would make.

Brother Julius continued maintaining a low profile, partially due to his various legal issues, and also due to his deteriorating health. Now seventy-one, a life of vice and excess was catching up to the "sinning messiah," and he reportedly was suffering from a number of undisclosed ailments.

On July 28, 1996, Julius Schacknow died in his sleep while staying at the New Britain home of one of his seven wives, finally getting to meet his Maker. (Or was he just returning to his heavenly kingdom?) Fittingly, it was a Sunday morning.

Oh, and that's right: At the time of his death, Schacknow reportedly had seven unofficial "wives," different women around

Connecticut with whom he shared a bed. Evidently, he would be shuttled by one follower—God apparently wasn't in the habit of driving himself anywhere—between Cheshire, Berlin, Southington, and New Britain, spending a day or two in each town enjoying the company of one mate before moving on to the next. (He probably got out of cutting the lawn and other husbandly chores, too.)

Upon hearing of Schacknow's passing, many former followers expressed relief. Others were less charitable, angry that they had been taken advantage of emotionally, spiritually, physically, and financially over the course of years, even decades in some cases.

While alive, Schacknow didn't condone elaborate funeral rites, and church members were often buried quietly and without ceremony. Although what specifically happened to his remains isn't of public record, there was no indication of any sort of resurrection, even though some may still be waiting for one.

Schacknow has been dead for a number of years, yet some of his most loyal and ardent followers are still around, accepting the mantle of prophets and spreading the gospel according to Brother Julius. They occasionally will attend conventional services—churches in the Southeastern region and Fairfield County seem to be their most popular targets—interrupting services to tell those assembled that they are sinners in an evil world who are being led astray by "false shepherds." They will then try to help save others from eternal damnation by offering the true path as promised by their god, their one and only "Lord Julius Christ." Often, they end up being escorted from the churches and asked not to return.

In one of his last interviews, Schacknow said, "Very few people will believe that I'm the real Lord. But that won't offend me because there are true sheep who will hear my voice, and they will know."

Others don't need to hear his voice to know that Brother Julius Schacknow was a true jerk.

CHAPTER 5

Uncas:
Last (and Likely Worst)
of the Mohicans

Sometimes determining if someone is a jerk can truly be a question of perspective—depending on what side of an issue one falls can go a long way in deciding if someone else's behavior is "jerk-y" or not.

Such is the case of Uncas, chief of the Mohegan tribe and one of the most controversial Native Americans in state history. Some branded him a hero for befriending "the white man" and repeatedly siding with colonists during Indian conflicts, and for ultimately preserving his tribe and its legacy. Others were not as kind, despising him as a remorseless opportunist, a willing traitor, and a tyrannical sachem (leader), whose cruel ambition led him to slaughter members of his own race whenever necessary. Blurred by the passing of centuries and the myopic lens of recorded history, the truth was somewhere in between, although the evidence does seem to be stacked a bit higher on the latter side.

Not helping matters was that the real-life Uncas was also the inspiration for the fictional Uncas in James Fenimore Cooper's epic tale *The Last of the Mohicans,* written a century and a half after the powerful sachem died. The enduring popularity of the story—as demonstrated by its multiple cinematic adaptations— has dramatically shaped perceptions of Native Americans, and in particular, of Uncas, with romantic notions of noble savages and proud warriors. Again, history (and reality) was not as rosy as novelists and filmmakers would have audiences believe.

Also complicating the process of sharing Uncas's story is that he existed over four hundred years ago at a time when accurate— and objective—reporting of events involving Native Americans was a challenge. Uncas also primarily spoke Algonquian and little English, and there were no extensive written histories or detailed biographies compiled during his time. Most of what is known about the influential chief was recorded second- and thirdhand, and often decades later.

Still, it seems as though Uncas caused enough suffering and destruction among his fellow Native Americans to qualify as a jerk to pretty much everyone outside the Mohegan tribe.

As the Mohegan did not use the Julian calendar to mark time or keep written birth records, it's generally accepted that Uncas (also Unkas or Onkas, depending on whom you ask, and which means "the fox") was born at the tail end of the sixteenth century, approximately around 1598. He entered this world on the Mohegan tribal lands, which generally stretched west from the Thames River to the middle of the present-day state of Connecticut (or "Quinnehtukqut," Algonquian for "beside the long tidal river"), mostly in the area between what is now New London and Norwich—well beyond what is currently Uncasville, home to his best-known legacy, Mohegan Sun Casino and Resort. (That's another story for another day and book.) The Mohegan main village was Shantok, the location of which sits in the shadow of the casino and can also still be visited today.

Uncas was born to be a sachem, the result of careful and politically advantageous breeding, not unlike the tradition of royal families intermarrying to consolidate power. His paternal great-grandfather was Woipequuund, a principal sachem of the rival Pequot, who had married Mukunnup, the daughter of a leader of the Narragansett, who were farther to the east in Rhode Island. In addition, his father, Owaneco, already a Mohegan sachem, was also descended from the chief of another nearby Moheagan tribe on his mother's side.

With such a pedigree, Uncas was destined to rule his tribe, and would've been trained from an early age to do so. Unlike the kings European colonists were used to, sachems generally were not absolute monarchs whose word and whim were law, but more

*Uncas, chief of the Mohegan tribe, executes Miantonomi of the Narragan-
sett tribe after a battle in present-day Norwich, Connecticut, in 1643*
CASSELL'S *HISTORY OF THE UNITED STATES,* VOLUME I, 1874

benevolent caretakers who could not rule without the approval of their followers. They often consulted with the tribe's elders before making decisions, and usually would not set up laws or go to war without support of the majority of the tribe. Sachems also had to be skilled in working with other tribes in terms of trade and alliances.

Uncas also would've been instructed in the other ways of Native American life, including hunting, fishing, and fighting, as well as learning to harvest shellfish, trap beaver, dance, worship, and gamble—actual Native American life was very different than the way it's often portrayed in cinema or television. From one description, Uncas grew into a typical Mohegan, "a man of large frame and great physical strength."

Uncas was probably just entering his teenage years when European explorers started arriving on the shores of Connecticut in the early seventeenth century. The Dutch were first to visit, primarily in search of beaver pelts, which were plentiful in the region. Again, contrary to popular belief, most Native American tribes welcomed their European guests and were eager to trade with them, and that was certainly true of the Mohegan. However, the rival Pequot were a little quicker and more successful in forming a trading partnership with the Dutch, and were soon benefitting from the alliance, becoming one of the most powerful tribes in the region.

Seeing that an alliance with their prosperous neighbors would be beneficial for his people, Uncas's father Owaneco, the Mohegan sachem, approached Tatobem, the Pequot sachem, and suggested that Uncas's older brother marry one of Tatobem's daughters. Tatobem agreed to the union, but Uncas's brother unexpectedly died before the marriage could be consummated. Both sachems decided that the son next in line—Uncas—should take the place of his deceased brother, to which Uncas agreed. In about 1626, Uncas then took his first wife.

Unfortunately, Owaneco wouldn't live to see his people benefit from the union, as he died shortly after the marriage took place. With Owaneco gone, Uncas was forced to kowtow to his new father-in-law Tatobem, an indignity for which he apparently didn't care, although it didn't last long. In 1633 after a misunderstanding, Tatobem was captured and murdered by the Dutch, weakening the Pequot power base. His eldest son and immediate successor was also killed, which left the Pequot under the control of next-in-line Sassacus, who attempted to stabilize the deteriorating situation.

Making things difficult was that English colonists were now arriving in droves in the "New World," obtaining large swaths of tribal land through trade or purchase. Smallpox was also ravaging the Native American peoples of New England, an unintentional "gift" from the newcomers to their new neighbors, whose immune systems had never encountered the deadly disease.

Sensing that his brother-in-law Sassacus was vulnerable due to these factors, Uncas saw an opportunity to get the Mohegan—and himself—out from under Pequot control. With the support of the Narragansett (who also stood to benefit from any Pequot losses), Uncas attempted on five separate occasions to expand Mohegan territory at the expense of the Pequot hunting grounds. Each time, however, the Pequot were able to fend off the Mohegan, eventually defeating Uncas and sending him into exile among the Narragansett.

Being banished didn't particularly suit Uncas, so he soon returned to Connecticut to make amends with Sassacus. He ritually humiliated himself before the Pequot sachem, who, apparently unable to gather tribal support to execute his upstart brother-in-law, restored a portion of Uncas's lands and power, possibly in the hopes that Uncas would once again become an ally. It may have been a mistake.

Back in his home territory, it first appeared that the diminished Uncas and his lessened tribe were working with the Pequot, and were even reported to be secretly helping them to attack English settlements so as to maintain positive relations. Apparently however, Uncas was working both sides. While he may have been surreptitiously involved in killing English colonists in some areas, he was also forging an alliance with other English settlers, particularly Captain John Mason, who would be a trusted friend for life.

Uncas's full plan soon became evident: to use the English, their weapons, and manpower to strike back at the Pequot.

He suggested to his new allies that Sassacus had been personally involved in the high-profile murder of an English settler, and then warned of an impending raid on a British ship by a rogue band of Pequot. Uncas also helped to create general fear and distrust of the Pequot across the region by spreading rumors that the tribe was on the verge of attacking colonial settlements along the Thames River. By willingly casting such aspersions on his Native American brethren (who up to this point, had not really done anything substantially negative to the English), he was able to gain the trust of a number of well-placed English leaders—and a growing reputation as a jerk.

Tensions between the Pequot and the English—and by extension, the Mohegan—continued to escalate, and after a number of violent incidents, war was officially declared on May 1, 1637. Uncas immediately gathered his warriors to join Capt. Mason and the English forces, and within days was aiding in attacks on the Pequot. At first some of Mason's fellow Englishmen questioned whether Uncas was truly loyal to them, so the sachem had twenty of his braves raid a group of nearby Pequot; they brought back the heads of five Pequot and one live prisoner, whom Uncas then allegedly tortured over a fire before tearing his charred body to pieces. Legend has it that Uncas then feasted on the flesh of his victim, although there are no accounts from the English soldiers involved that any cannibalism occurred. As it turned out, just simple torture of a fellow Native American was enough to erase any doubts of fidelity in the minds of Uncas's new confederates.

The joined forces moved quickly to take the fight to the Pequot. Mason devised a plan that involved circling south around the Pequot lands via Long Island Sound, landing to the Pequot's east in Narragansett territory. After the journey, they gained the support of the Narragansett sachem Miantonomi, and then went to launch a surprise attack on the Pequot "from behind."

In late May, the English-Mohegan forces (with a handful of Narragansett in tow) struck one of the main Pequot strongholds along the Mystic River, a large fort that protected a thriving village. Despite catching the Pequot unaware and killing many warriors, Mason ordered the entire settlement to be set on fire—an unusually vicious tactic, as many of the estimated two thousand Pequot there were women and children. Sadly, those who weren't extinguished by the flames were slaughtered by the Mohegan and English when they tried to escape.

The attack sent shock waves through the Native American community. Although atrocities and cruelties were certainly part of war as they knew it, women and children were almost always spared. The fact that the English had committed such a massacre—and that Uncas had been a willing partner—delivered a message that the landscape had changed, and not for the better. It also altered the Native American view of Uncas, and again, not in a positive way.

Eager to completely eradicate his former rivals, Uncas played a significant role in helping to hunt down and exterminate any remaining Pequot. Those who somehow survived were eventually absorbed into the Mohegan tribe, which following Uncas's successes, had nearly doubled.

Jerk or not, Uncas was quite shrewd. To keep his lands and take control of the territory that had belonged to the Pequot, he negotiated with the English at every turn. He traveled to Boston in June 1638 and obtained an agreement with the leaders of the Massachusetts Bay Colony that gave him access to what had been Pequot land, although the claims were disputed by Miantonomi and the Narragansett.

To help consolidate his power and gain allies, Uncas took multiple wives, high-ranking daughters of other sachems, including one of the widows of his former father-in-law Tatobem. He also married into the Hammonasset tribe, and immediately sold much of their land along the central Connecticut coastline to colonists. By doing this, he further spread his influence among other tribes and better ingratiated himself with the English, building a great empire for himself in the process. Only Miantonomi posed a true threat to his authority, and the two sachems were constantly at odds.

Recognizing that in order to secure the safety of their colonies there needed to be peace between the Narragansett and Mohegan, the leaders of Connecticut and Rhode Island decided to meet in Hartford to try to secure a peace treaty between the two powerful sachems. Being a less-than-gracious host, Uncas instructed bands of Mohegan to hassle Miantonomi and Rhode Island governor Roger Williams during their journey to the meeting in the hopes that they would get discouraged and not attend. They nonetheless persevered and arrived in September 1638, and negotiations began.

From the outset it was clear that Uncas and Miantonomi hated and greatly distrusted each other, and had no interest in making any deal. The colonial leaders persisted and eventually were able to get both men to agree to a few terms, among them that if there were any conflicts between the two tribes, they would turn to a colonial commission for adjudication, especially in serious matters involving prisoners or murder. Both also agreed not to harbor any colonial fugitives or enemies of the English, to respect each other's lands and claims, and generally, to play nice. Both sachems reluctantly signed the treaty.

Like many peace accords throughout history, putting names on a piece of paper didn't magically put an end to conflict between the parties involved. While Miantonomi and the Narragansett struggled to coexist with the ever-growing colonist population, Uncas made move after move that seemed engineered to curry favor with his English allies, no matter how costly they were to his own people. For instance, in 1640, he gave a sizable chunk of Mohegan lands to the English without any compensation—a curious transaction that apparently wasn't any sort of benefit to the Mohegan other than providing Uncas with more personal clout among the Connecticut colony's leadership.

Uncas also continued to employ the English military might whenever possible, raiding and plundering small villages of Narragansett allies that he "suspected" of harboring Pequot. The Narragansett were leery of attacking the joint forces for fear of incurring the full wrath of the English, whom they recognized as having superior firepower. Like a kid having to stand by while the class weasel takes his lunch money with help of the neighborhood bully, Miantonomi watched idly as the Mohegan and English looted and burned the wigwams of his comrades.

Uncas also continued to slander Miantonomi at every turn, creating rumors that the Narragansett were constantly "plotting mischief" against the colonists in Connecticut and Massachusetts. It appears that the smear campaign was effective, frustrating Miantonomi to the point that he started trying to unite the other enemies of the English and Mohegan, including the Mohawk, who were particularly feared by colonists and many Connecticut tribes. Of course, Uncas shared every shred of information he heard about Miantonomi's war plans with colonial leaders.

In the late summer of 1643, after numerous incidents between the two tribes—including an alleged attempt on Uncas's life by an agent of Miantonomi—official war broke out after Uncas was attacked by an ally of Miantonomi and retaliated by raiding and burning the ally's village to the ground. After getting permission from the governor of the Massachusetts Bay colony to "take his own course" against the Mohegan, Miantonomi gathered a force of nearly one thousand braves and set out for Uncas's stronghold of Shantok. Being informed that the Narragansett were literally on the warpath, Uncas gathered four hundred of his own men and went out to meet them. Before attacking, however, he requested a powwow with Miantonomi.

According to later accounts, having concluded that he was vastly outnumbered, Uncas challenged his old rival Miantonomi to a one-on-one battle. One can only imagine Miantonomi momentarily considering the tantalizing offer to potentially rid himself of his bitter enemy—by burying his own cold knife deep in the heart of Uncas—before remembering that he was the one with the man-power advantage. Apparently this had been Uncas's plan all along.

Knowing that Miantonomi would never agree to such a fight, Uncas had instructed his men to wait for his signal. When the Narragansett leader refused the personal challenge, Uncas immediately dropped to the ground, at which point the Mohegan "let fly a shower of arrows upon the Narragansett." Catching the enemy completely by surprise—it was supposed to be a peaceful meeting to avoid a battle, after all—chaos erupted as many Narragansett were instantly killed. Others turned and fled, including Miantonomi.

The Narragansett leader didn't make it far before he was caught and brought to Uncas. When Miantonomi refused to speak to or acknowledge the Mohegan sachem, Uncas began to split open the skulls of Miantonomi's men right in front of him—an effective, if brutal, method to get someone's attention. Abiding by the agreement that both sachems had signed back in 1638, Uncas eventually brought Miantonomi to Hartford for judgment by Connecticut's colonial commission.

The years of kissing up to English and acceding to their wishes paid off. Knowing that they needed the influential Uncas's support to help control the Native Americans across the colony and that there would be no peace while both men lived, the commission decreed that for trying to have Uncas killed and attacking the Mohegan, Miantonomi should be put to death. Rather than have Miantonomi's blood directly on their hands, however, they stipulated that the execution should be carried out by a Mohegan leader on Mohegan land, and that any retaliation by the Narragansett would be met with English force.

Uncas immediately took his enemy to Mohegan territory and had his brother Wawequa carry out the sentence. With a fierce blow to the back of Miantonomi's skull, the Narragansett sachem was dispatched and Uncas's plan of eliminating his chief rival was complete. One unsubstantiated (and dubious) story says that after his foe was slain, Uncas cut out a piece of Miantonomi's flesh and feasted upon it, proclaiming it "the sweetest meat I ever ate."

Of course, the problem for Uncas was that although his main adversary was dead, there were plenty of others. The way he had gone about using the English to help dispose of Miantonomi didn't sit well with many Native American tribes in the region, and he was cursed and branded an amoral servant boy of the colonial leadership who would do anything—no matter how violent or reprehensible—to protect his own interests. (Which, the evidence suggests, he did.)

The surviving Narragansett led the pack of those who were interested in seeing Uncas meet a violent fate not unlike Miantonomi's, and were the most active against the Mohegan. Starting in June 1644, they launched raids against Uncas and his followers, striking smaller villages at the outskirts of their territory, and then steadily increasing the frequency and scope of their assaults. In due course, they laid siege to Shantok, posting themselves around the village to starve out the Mohegan and kill anyone who would dare to leave or get in to try to assist Uncas.

Uncas was still able to get word to his English allies that he was in dire circumstances. After many Mohegan men were lost and Uncas was on the verge of defeat, the siege was broken in July 1645 when colonists were able to sneak through the Narragansett lines to deliver arms and supplies. Sensing that they had the Mohegan on the ropes, however, the Narragansett continued their attacks.

The colonial leadership throughout the region, knowing that they still relied on Uncas to protect their interests, soon moved to take a more active role in quelling the situation. Calling on Uncas's old compatriot Capt. Mason and others, a military force of over three hundred was assembled, tasked with taking the fight to the Narragansett and their allies. Possibly recalling what had happened to the Pequot when they had stood up against colonial might, the Narragansett grudgingly backed down and signed a new peace treaty in 1645.

As had happened before, as soon as Uncas had taken care of one rival, another one popped up. This time it was a small group of

English under the leadership of John Winthrop Jr., son of the Massachusetts Bay Colony governor, who decided to settle at Nameag (just north of what is currently New London). The lands were formerly Pequot, and were under the control of Robin Cassacinamon, a regional Pequot leader whose tribe had not participated in the Pequot War.

During the summer of 1646, Winthrop's people were short of food, so he went to Cassacinamon to ask for help. In the spirit of good will, the Pequot sachem sent out a hunting party to oblige. Thinking they had permission from another regional sachem, the group inadvertently crossed the Thames River and into Mohegan lands.

Uncas didn't quite agree that the lower sachem had the authority to grant such hunting rights, and was upset by the intrusion. He gathered a force of three hundred and descended upon the unsuspecting Pequot hunting party. Making a big show of his superiority (like any bully), he attacked—but did not kill— the interlopers, instead chasing them all the way back to the colonial settlement at Nameag. Once there, he went on a rampage, ordering his men to sack homes and to rough up Cassacinamon's men. Amid the turmoil, he made verbal threats in English, supposedly proclaiming to everyone, "I am the victor!"

The raid produced no deaths, but it certainly upset the colonists and Pequot. It also served as a message to both the English and Native Americans that Uncas was no "little dog" of the colonial leadership, and that he was still someone to be feared and respected.

If he was trying to gain attention, it worked. He soon found himself explaining his actions before the colonial commissioners, to whom he claimed he had merely been acting in self defense. Despite the testimony of Winthrop and some Pequot describing the harm Uncas had caused, the Mohegan sachem got off with what constituted a verbal reprimand.

Not content with the ruling, Winthrop and Cassacinamon spent the next few years slowly chipping away at Uncas's authority. Winthrop constantly went to the colonial commission to complain about ongoing harassment of colonists by Uncas, while Cassacinamon, after claiming Uncas had "abused" and "defiled" numerous Pequot, formally petitioned to have the Pequot at Nameag be placed under the authority of the commission rather than the Mohegan. The quarrel raged back and forth for years, until the Pequot were finally granted their independence from Uncas in 1655.

Before then, however, there was more conflict with other tribes. The Narragansett, who had never really gotten over the execution of Miantonomi, tried repeatedly to usurp Uncas's power, while he continued to fabricate plots involving their supposed treachery against the English. In April 1649, Uncas was wounded when an assassin—allegedly hired by the Narragansett—made an attempt on his life; the case went before the colonial commission, and even though there was evidence that Uncas might have concocted the whole murder plot just to get official permission to deal with the would-be killer (and the Narragansett) as he saw fit, the assassin was found guilty and ultimately executed by the Mohegan.

By continually siding with the English against various Native American tribes, Uncas enjoyed favorable decisions from the colonial commission and armed protection. Still, by the mid 1650s, he was beginning to lose his control over the smaller tribes that made up his empire. More and more disenfranchised Pequot-Mohegans were moving away from places that Uncas controlled and joining other tribes, free of tyrannical rule.

As his power began to slip away, Uncas became more desperate to keep it. One story tells of how in 1656, after being discouraged by the colonial commission from making war on the neighboring Podunk for revenge over the murder of a kinsman, Uncas staged a raid that made it seem as though he had enlisted the feared Mohawk as allies. He burned a Podunk wigwam and planted Mohawk weapons at the scene, fooling the Podunk sachem, who surrendered those responsible for the murder. Uncas had them executed immediately.

Relying on his English protection, Uncas also continued to provoke the Narragansett and other tribes into various skirmishes.

By 1658, however, the colonial commission could no longer turn a blind eye to Uncas's dishonesty, rumor mongering, and use of English might for his personal vendettas. Deciding that he was now more of an annoyance than an ally, they started withdrawing support, leaving him to fend for himself among the Native American tribes whom he had antagonized for years.

Various tribes, including the Pocumtucks, Tunxis, and Narragansett, started weakening Uncas's power base, aggressively invading Mohegan territory. Uncas fought back, repeatedly defending Shantok from attacks. Even with constant calls from the English to live peaceably, he still sought strife on a regular basis, not hesitating to raid other Native American settlements when it suited his needs.

By the early 1660s and well into his middle age, Uncas seemed to have figured out how to manage his allies and enemies without much English involvement. Official records mention him less frequently, showing that either he had learned to live generally in peace, or that with the burgeoning colonial expansion, his activities were no longer as much a concern.

Now surrounded by European settlements on almost all sides and expecting further encroachment, he made an agreement with John Mason in 1665 that entrusted a large swath of Mohegan territory to his longstanding friend for sale to future settlers (the profit from which would be divided evenly between Mason and his heirs and Uncas and his heirs—not the tribe). The deal also stipulated that a significant tract of tribal acreage, including Shantok, would belong to the Mohegan in perpetuity—land on which the current reservation (and its Mohegan Sun casino) now sits. In 1670, the two men reworded the agreement to include two of Uncas's grown sons, Owaneco and Attawanhood, who were now sachems in their own right.

Although now in his seventies and somewhat more mellow, Uncas still had a bit of fight left in him. In June 1675, a conflict that would become known as King Philip's War broke out between colonists and a coalition of Native American tribes (including a large number of Narragansett) that had been banded together by a Wampanoag sachem named Philip. As on previous occasions, Uncas was quick to offer his loyalty and warriors to the English to help put down the insurrection, no doubt hoping to curry what remaining favor he could manage. An attack in August orchestrated by Uncas's son Owaneco inflicted significant losses on Philip's forces, and once again gained a strong measure of trust and appreciation from Connecticut colonists.

Uncas himself, even at his advanced age, led a few raids. After the initial campaign, however, he pulled the majority of his warriors back to protect Mohegan territory around Shantok, letting the English fend for themselves. He did respond to direct calls for aid, sending out war parties led by Owaneco to help the colonial forces when necessary, although he seemed to be more interested in using the war as an excuse to attack old enemies.

In May 1676, Uncas's son Attawanhood died, possibly as a result of a long illness, and it seemed to take a toll on the elderly sachem. The Mohegan essentially withdrew altogether from King Philip's War because they were "much saddened" by Attawanhood's passing, and it was reported that Uncas's grief was particularly pronounced. The fighting was mostly over by this point, and although the English would triumph—in great part because of the Mohegan—it didn't quite feel like a victory for Uncas.

Uncas had seen some of his fiercest rivals crushed, and although he was once again the most influential Native American in the region, it wasn't like when the Mohegan had thrived after the victory over the Pequot. They were no longer the most powerful group in Connecticut; the colonists were now atop the totem pole, so to speak, and they would never give up the top spot.

The once-mighty, respected, and feared sachem of the Mohegan died sometime between June 1683 and June 1684. The exact date of Uncas's passing was not recorded in the official Connecticut records—a sign of how dramatically his stature had diminished. Despite Uncas's influence in settling the lands "by the long tidal river," his demise was not commemorated by the colony until well after he had gone to join the spirits of his ancestors.

After decades of war and conflict, the English had become distrustful of all Native Americans. Even though Uncas had always stood by their side and was considered a friend, he had become more of an annoyance by the end. By the same token, many regional Native Americans tribes had grown to despise him after all his scheming, empire building, aggression and outright treachery. His death was not mourned by many outside of Shantok. In short, like a true jerk—or a great leader, in some cases—he had antagonized everyone except his own people.

At the end of *The Last of the Mohicans,* the elder Chingachgook says, "When Uncas follows in my footsteps, there will no longer be any of the blood of the sagamores, for my boy is the last of the Mohicans."

The real-life Uncas, however, was far from the last of the jerks.

CHAPTER 6

Rev. Samuel A. Peters:
Exiled Loyalist and
"Victim of Pseudomania"

To paraphrase William Congreve's famous quotation: "Hell hath no fury like a jerk scorned."

In the case of Rev. Samuel A. Peters, it wasn't exactly with fire and brimstone that the residents of Connecticut were smited, but rather with eternal damnation.

Okay, that might be a bit strong, but the not-so-good man of the cloth was responsible for hanging a bad reputation on the state that continues to linger centuries after his nefarious acts.

Peters was the author of *A General History of Connecticut,* a 1781 work that chronicled the state's development while "exposing" the misbegotten religious fanatics who lived within its borders. In addition, it introduced the rest of the world to the notorious Blue Laws, a harsh, puritanical code that allegedly restricted all facets of colonial Connecticut life and is still quoted today.

As it turns out, *A General History of Connecticut* was also a confection of lies, cooked up by an unrepentant liar and pompous egomaniac who used it to serve a heaping dish of cold revenge to those whom he believed were responsible for forcing him from the land of his birth. Peters's efforts also managed to mar their descendants as well as generations of innocent bystanders, Connecticut residents who would be unfairly prejudged for decades.

Granted, there were extenuating circumstances in the form of the American Revolution that prompted Peters's actions, but it still doesn't make his efforts seem any less jerk-like, nor does it absolve his legacy. Ezra Stiles, the president of Yale College during the American Revolution, later called Parson Peters an "infamous parricide," while nineteenth-century pastor Horace Bushnell branded him "one of the two greatest disasters that ever befell Connecticut"—the other being Benedict Arnold. Others were equally less charitable in their disregard for a jerk who seemed unable to contain himself from antagonizing others at every turn.

Samuel Andrew Peters was born on December 1, 1735, in the small town of Hebron. He was the third youngest in the twelve-child brood of Mary Marks and John Peters, a thriving farmer who was instrumental in establishing the town's first Episcopal church. As much of the region was comprised of Congregationalists—who had left England for America to enjoy freedom from the Anglican Church of England in the first place—this didn't exactly endear the Peters clan to the locals. Nevertheless, Samuel grew up in a fairly affluent household, and his parents were able to send him to study at Yale when he was seventeen years old.

Although the school was strict and rigorous, Peters graduated. He was ranked thirty-fifth in a class of forty, but that may have been more reflective of his social status and religious beliefs than his scholarly efforts. Or not.

In 1754, his father and an older brother died, leaving Samuel a sizable inheritance that included one thousand acres; in addition, he gained the burden of having to care for his siblings and widowed mother. He also found himself trying to fill the void left in the Hebron Episcopal Church by his father's death, and after his graduation from Yale in 1757, got himself elected rector. A year later, he formally requested the opportunity to become a fully ordained minister in the Church of England, which was met with approval by his fellow local Anglicans.

In 1758, Peters traveled to England to further his religious education. During his stay in London, the grandeur and pageantry of the clergy there made a strong impression on him, which only deepened what was already a fervent appreciation for things British. Despite a serious bout with smallpox—which left him physically scarred for life—he finished his studies and was ordained a priest in the Church of England on September 25, 1759.

Peters shortly thereafter returned to Hebron as a missionary and duly appointed representative of the church, and settled in as head of St. Peter's parish. An eager cleric, he traveled extensively preaching the Episcopalian word, and was also able to grow his congregation.

Like many good and affluent men of the Anglican cloth, Peters was also interested in finding a wife, and on Valentine's Day 1760 was married to twenty-year-old Hannah Owen. They were fruitful and multiplied quickly, having three daughters in five years. Sadly, two of the girls and Hannah had died by 1765, leaving the thirty-year-old clergyman to tend to his surviving daughter—also named Hannah—and his elderly mother.

The loss of his young wife and daughters didn't impact his ability to deliver a sermon, however, and his untiring devotion to his calling made Peters one of the most respected Anglican clergymen in the area. Unfortunately, with the growing unrest between the American colonies and the British crown courtesy of events like the Stamp and Sugar acts, this also occasionally made Episcopalians like Peters the targets of abuse.

Still, this didn't slow the enterprising Peters from continuing to build his personal wealth. He provided loans to area businessmen that upon repayment, helped make his cup runneth over. He also kept his stock rising in the eyes of local Episcopalian leaders, undertaking an extended missionary expedition up the Connecticut River to convert and baptize the uninitiated. After the trip, he would tell others that he personally gave the eventual state of "Verdmont" its name, a dubious claim at best.

His economic and professional successes, however, didn't extend to his personal life. In June of 1769, Peters married seventeen-year-old Abigail Gilbert; less than three weeks later, he was burying his teenage bride. A third time wouldn't be much of a charm for Peters, either, who took another young wife in Mary Birdseye in April 1773—she was twenty-three to his thirty-six. Fourteen months later, on June 5, 1774, she gave him a son, William, but then died less than two weeks afterward.

If being a widower yet again wasn't enough of a problem for Peters, the growing resentment of perceived English tyranny and the increasing possibility of an American revolution would become a true predicament for him, one that could have been avoided if he had possessed anything resembling humility, tact, or discretion.

From his halcyon years studying in London to his own successes developed through his embrace of the Church of England, it was no surprise that Peters had developed a strong affinity for and healthy respect of the Crown. A staunch and proud Tory—and a jerk who couldn't keep his mouth shut—he had always been predisposed to sharing his Loyalist views with his fellow Hebron residents, even if they didn't care to hear about them. But as the flames of independence continued to be fanned, Peters's words and actions would prove to be potent fuel for the fire.

Granted, today differing political views and intellectual debate are welcome, and often encouraged, in the United States. In 1774, however, the situation was markedly different as there was no such thing as the United States, let alone a right to free speech. The outspoken Peters would soon draw the ire of his neighbors and, in particular, the local chapter of the Sons of Liberty.

Following the Boston Tea Party in December 1773 and the closure of Boston Harbor, revolutionary spirits were running especially high. Connecticut Governor Jonathan Trumbull circulated a request to all towns of the colony to help support the distressed residents of Boston as well as the cause for liberty. The call was generally received well, except in Hebron, where the vociferous Peters led opposition to providing any support. He suggested that the India Tea Company be fully compensated for their losses at the hands of "patriot upstarts," and then sarcastically added if that happened and Boston Harbor was still not opened to business, then he would be more than happy to personally send "1,000 sheep and 10 fat oxen" to help make good.

Evidently, the Sons of Liberty didn't think that Peters's offer was as amusing as the parson himself did, and on the morning of

August 15, two hundred to three hundred of them showed up on his doorstep to tell him so.

The truth of what happened that day is probably somewhere between the two varying accounts. In Peters's version, he alleged that after he let in a few of the rowdy mob to search his home for materials "against the liberty and rights of America," which turned up nothing, they belligerently demanded that he read and sign thirteen "resolves" (public resolutions) that had been prepared for publication, and then forcefully extracted a sworn promise from Peters that he would no longer communicate to authorities anything about current events.

According to the Bolton Committee of Correspondence, the visitors were civil in asking about rumors that Peters was preparing a report to send to England regarding local activities and when they came upon the resolves—which they say Peters had already prepared prior to their arrival, and given their condescending tone, hardly seem to be something the patriots would've drafted—he gave them up without issue. Both versions agreed that Peters promised no further communication with the crown regarding revolutionary events. The controversial resolves eventually were published in the *Connecticut Gazette*.

Despite his oath, the published resolves, and strong suggestions that going forward Peters keep dissenting opinions to himself, a few weeks later, he was once again at the center of events involving the Sons of Liberty.

At the beginning of September 1774 came a false report that Boston was under siege by the British. In response, a group of local militia started out to Massachusetts to aid the rebel cause, over the public protests of Rev. Peters, who went so far as to state that those who participated should be hanged as traitors. Unfortunately for Peters, six hundred to nine hundred of those "traitors" discovered that there had been no clash before they had gotten too far. All fired up with no fight to be had, they instead turned up at the Peters house on the night of September 6.

This time, however, Peters was a little better prepared, with a small group of men on hand to protect him. Again, accounts of exactly what happened varied; Peters himself penned multiple conflicting versions of the event. In one of his accounts, he claimed that the Sons of Liberty supposedly threatened to hang him from a liberty pole and then were going to tar and feather him, a threat that despite sounding outlandish today was very real then. Another Peters's version says that the mob wasn't quite so vicious at first, but still in a foul mood, and before he could properly answer the accusations regarding his pro-Crown views, they rushed in, physically accosted him and his family, and then trashed his home, breaking windows, furniture, and other personal items.

Peters also insisted that he was taken from his home, dragged to the town green and forced to sign a retraction to his notorious resolves. Before he could be tarred and feathered, however, the defiant reverend was saved by friends or declared "insane" by the mob and spared—again, Peters's own accounts vary—and allowed to return to his broken home.

Sworn testimony from other witnesses on hand was a lot less dramatic than Peters's word. The group of concerned citizens that showed up had requested that he explain the intent behind his published resolves, and that he sign prepared statements of retraction. Only after the parson had repeatedly refused, had the patriots then taken matters into their own hands, removing him from the house and bringing him to the green, where he finally relented and signed the retraction. The crowd then allegedly gave three cheers and peacefully dispersed, inflicting no physical harm on Peters and his family, nor causing any real damage to his house.

Despite whatever really did happen that night, a public retraction and apology from Peters did appear in the *Connecticut Gazette* on September 16. Still, the possible continued threat of injury to Peters was genuine even after he was made to publicly agree "without equivocation or mental reservation" that he would wholeheartedly support the rebellious effort. He personally went to both Governor Trumbull and the Connecticut Superior Court seeking protection from physical reprisals, but his requests were met with general indifference. Trumbull did eventually send a cursory letter to authorities in Hebron suggesting that Peters be left alone, but it wasn't exactly any sort of binding action.

Hoping to find refuge among other Anglicans, Peters traveled to New Haven, which harbored a significant Episcopalian community, except his growing reputation as a Loyalist jerk preceded him. When he arrived, he was angrily greeted by the New Haven chapter of the Sons of Liberty, led by Benedict Arnold, who was still a bright-eyed patriot and years away from becoming known as one of the most notorious traitors in American history (see chapter 1). Rattled by Arnold's less-than-welcoming visit—nothing much happened beyond an exchange of threats—Peters quickly realized that New Haven would be no haven at all for him, and quietly returned to his home in Hebron.

Faced with the unmistakable intent of the Sons of Liberty and the ever-growing severity of the situation for Loyalists in general and for him in particular, Peters formulated a plan familiar to many jerks: He gave a final sermon to his Hebron congregation on Sunday, September 18, gathered a few of his personal belongings, said good-bye to his family, and then under the cover of night, ran like hell. (Or since he was a man of the cloth, ran like heck.) This time his destination was Boston, a Loyalist stronghold still firmly under British control.

Upon his arrival in Boston a few days later, Peters found some of the protection he was seeking, as well as a bit of appreciation from other Loyalists who hailed him for the difficulties he had endured. He was invited to a few Episcopalian churches to give guest sermons, and briefly enjoyed renewed stature in religious circles. He had even distanced himself from the Sons of Liberty and the angry mobs of Connecticut.

Unsurprisingly, Peters was unable to leave well enough alone.

Feeling secure in the sanctuary that Boston provided, and despite all his public pledges to the opposite, Peters started beating the Loyalist drums again. In addition to giving inflammatory public speeches, he started sending caustic letters to various Tory acquaintances, calling for extreme measures against patriots—even going so far as to suggest that British troops were getting ready to descend upon Connecticut to ferret out traitors and hang them.

A missive to his Anglican friend, the Reverend Dr. Auchmuty of New York, said: "The Sons of Liberty have destroyed my windows, rent my clothes, even my gown, etc., crying out down with the church, the rags of Popery, etc.; their rebellion is obvious—treason is common—and robbery is their daily diversion. The Lord deliver us from anarchy."

He also arrogantly called on Auchmuty and other Anglicans to send the word to England regarding the deteriorating situation in America and request that severe punishment be inflicted upon the enemies of the Crown.

Unfortunately, Peters used one of his brothers as a courier, who was intercepted by liberty-minded colonists. The letters were then published, which reignited the furor around Peters. Anglicans quickly disassociated themselves from him, a bounty was supposedly offered if he could be delivered into patriot hands, and the *Boston Evening Post* went so far as to call him "the most unnatural monster diabolical incendiary and detestable parricide to his country that ever appeared in America or disgraced humanity." In less than a month, the protection and good will that Boston had offered had evaporated.

Realizing that he possibly had gone too far this time, Peters appealed to Gen. Thomas Gage, the military royal governor of Massachusetts who was stationed in Boston, to take action against their common enemies. Gage, hands full with trying to keep the Sons of Liberty at bay and having no patience for the controversial Peters, instead proposed a clever solution to the reverend's plight.

Gage suggested that rather than stay and tangle with the revolutionaries, Peters should go to England to serve as a living example of the cruelties and indignities that were being inflicted upon those who remained loyal to the king. The British cause could be furthered, Peters would be safe, and he would gain acclaim for being a martyr of sorts. Oh, and not so coincidentally, there would be an ocean between Gage and the nuisance Peters.

A few weeks later, on October 27, 1774, Peters set sail for England. He would not return to his native land for thirty-one years.

When Peters arrived in London in late December of 1774, he received the kind of welcome of which he had probably only dared to dream. Being the first religious leader ostracized from America because of his British sympathies brought him acclaim both within the Church of England and from secular quarters. Peters even enjoyed a formal audience with His Majesty, King George III—one can only imagine the "poor, persecuted" parson reveling righteously in all the attention.

Once the novelty wore off, Peters settled in London, where he was able to procure a small stipend from Parliament as compensation for what he had lost as a result of his loyalty. His teenage daughter Hannah was able to join him in exile in 1776; son William stayed with his maternal grandparents in New York until well after the war. He occasionally was asked to deliver guest sermons, but in general, had to fill his days with tending to his daughter, talking politics with other Loyalist refugees, and venting his frustration at the failing British war effort through letters to old friends.

Thus, living in exile with no particular professional responsibilities, Peters had plenty of time to stew, and like anyone who felt as if they had been dramatically wronged, thought long and hard about taking revenge. Eventually, Peters came up with a plan that any jerk could appreciate: If he couldn't physically retaliate against his former countryman, then he would strike back in spirit.

He started with an article in the jingoistic *Political Magazine and Parliamentary, Naval, Military and Literary Journal* about his "old acquaintance" Benedict Arnold, who by this point had already turned on the American forces. He credited Arnold for being a talented field general, but not forgetting that night in New Haven when Arnold and the Sons of Liberty came a-callin', he questioned the turncoat's moral character, financial dealings, and religious tolerance. Later, when Arnold eventually arrived in England during his own exile, he made sure to not cross paths with his "old acquaintance."

Peters then went after his perceived nemesis Gov. Jonathan Trumbull. After casting dispersions on Trumbull's mother and the legitimacy of his birth, Peters insinuated that Trumbull was also corrupt and dishonest. "He will smile in the face of those he hates, and court their friendship, at the very moment he is endeavouring [*sic*] by every means in his power to affect their ruin," Peters wrote. "As to justice, he never had an idea of it; at least he never shewed [*sic*] any in practice." Not exactly a fond tribute.

As satisfying as these personal attacks may have been, Peters saved his best vitriol for his grand opus, a comprehensive work that chronicled the "history" of his homeland and "characterized" its peoples.

For the record, the official title of Peters's tome was *A General History of Connecticut, from its first settlement under George Fenwick, to its latest period of amity with Great Britain prior to the Revolution; including a description of the country, and many curious and interesting anecdotes. With an appendix, pointing out the causes of rebellion in America; together with the particular part taken by the people of Connecticut in its promotion. By a Gentleman of the Province.* Concise, he wasn't.

Although Peters was never known for his modesty, the book was published anonymously as he was concerned for the continued safety of both himself and his family. Considering the amount of spiteful exaggeration, willful misinformation, and flat-out lying, he might have been better not taking credit at all.

From the events regarding the founding of the colony (incorrectly attributed to Fenwick and the Rev. Thomas Peters, a supposed relative) to descriptions of the landscape (suggesting that the Connecticut River was over four miles wide at its mouth), Peters distorted every fact to his whim. He even concocted terrifying creatures such as the "bullfly," a giant insect that he claimed had horns!

In addition to the historical inaccuracies and other falsehoods, there were scathing gems like this: "From infancy their education as citizens points out no distinction between licentiousness and liberty; and their religion is so muffled with superstition, self-love, and provincial enmity, as not yet to have taught them that humanity and respect for others, which from others, they demand."

Of course, the most sensational sections of *A General History* revolve around the infamous "Blue Laws," the laughingly stringent rules that allegedly governed Connecticut going back to its roots in the colony of New Haven.

Although now to be "blue" means to be sad, and to work "blue" (as they sometimes say of comedians) means to incorporate profanity, the "blue" in the Blue Laws is derived from the concept of an old proverb, "true blue will never stain." Since it was believed that real blue dye would never fade or run, someone who was "true blue" would stick firmly to their beliefs, no matter how severe. Thus, the majority of Connecticut's colonists, with their puritanical heritage and faithful adherence to the strict laws of the church, were considered to be "blue."

One of the first mentions of the Blue Laws was in an anonymous satirical pamphlet published in 1762, referring to a set of purportedly austere governing rules created by early Connecticut Congregationalists. It's very likely that this provided inspiration for Peters, especially since the publication also extolled the virtues of the Church of England.

To forge his Blue Laws, Peters was able to embellish a few of the odd, archaic statutes that were floating around Connecticut and weave in a number of outright fibs. Some of the most outlandish include:

- Whoever says there is power and jurisdiction above and over this Dominion, shall suffer death and loss of property.
- No food or lodging shall be afforded to a Quaker, Adamite, or other Heretic.
- No Priest shall abide in this Dominion: he shall be banished, and suffer death on his return. Priests may be seized by any one without a warrant.

- No one is to cross a river, but with an authorized ferryman.
- No one shall run on the Sabbath day, or walk in his garden or elsewhere, except reverently to and from meeting.
- No woman shall kiss her child on the Sabbath or fasting day.
- Men-stealers shall suffer death.
- Whoever wears clothes trimmed with gold, silver, or bone lace, above two shillings by the yard, shall be presented by the grand jurors, and the selectman shall tax the offender at £300 estate.
- No one shall read Common-prayer, keep Christmas or saints-days, make minced pies, dance, play cards, or play on any instrument, except the drum, trumpet and Jews-harp.
- The selectman, on finding children ignorant, may take them away from their parents, and put them into better hands, at the expense of their parents.
- Fornication shall be punished by compelling the marriage, or as the Court may think proper.
- Adultery shall be punished by death.
- Married persons must live together, or be imprisoned.
- Every male shall have his hair cut round according to a cap.

To the last one, Peters added that, "When caps were not to be found, they substituted the hard shell of a pumpkin, which being put on the head every Saturday, the hair is cut, by the shell, all around the head."

Although Peters's Blue Laws seem clearly ludicrous—and many educated folks of the time immediately recognized them for the farce they were—others believed them because in 1781 the days of such harsh rules weren't all that far in the past. Capital punishment was still prevalent; most towns had (and actively used) whipping posts and pillories. Less than a century had passed since the last witch trials, and the tales of accused persons being hanged for consorting with the devil were easily recalled. Many smaller villages and parishes had official moral codes, and those who avoided church on the Sabbath sometimes did so at their own risk.

In short, Peters had a perfectly receptive audience for his erroneous history of Connecticut, including many readers who would not question the details or extremities because they didn't seem all that far from the norm.

Also consider that verifying or denying outlandish claims was a much trickier proposition in the late eighteenth century than it is today. Snopes.com was still over two hundred years away from busting urban legends, public research libraries were nonexistent, and investigative journalism simply didn't exist. Since the majority of the population wasn't literate, once a story got into the public consciousness, there were very few ways to purge it.

Upon its printing in 1781, *A General History of Connecticut* caused a bit of a stir; although many recognized that it was full of lies or simply considered it satire, tongues still went a-clucking on both sides of the Atlantic Ocean. It was a modest success as a second edition was printed a year later, and it was even translated into German a few years after that. Following American independence, it was carried in bookstores and sold throughout the United States, despite being predominantly acknowledged for the sham it was.

As for Peters, much of his time in exile post–American Revolution was spent in small trade dealings, attending to random church activities, and dabbling in politics—he continued to extol the Anglican cause and the supremacy of the British Crown. His sizeable Connecticut estate was seized, divided, and sold. His daughter Hannah was married in 1785 and left for Canada with her husband, a Connecticut Loyalist who served as a provincial secretary; son William finally came to England in 1788, and then went on to France for schooling before becoming an ensign in the British army.

Although assured that it was safe to come back to America, Peters stayed in England, trying to wrangle a return that included a prestigious post as a bishop. However, in the process, the ever-caustic Peters had made many enemies and the hierarchy in the Church of England had grown weary of his histrionics. Over decades, he failed in every attempt for restitution, and his pension was eventually revoked.

With no money, no professional prospects, and finally soured on England, he returned to America in the summer of 1805, in part to pursue a land grant in Minnesota that he claimed had been given to him. He stayed in New York City for the next dozen years, writing another tome—this one a fanciful history of supposed ancestor Rev. Hugh Peters, although there was much included about the unjustly persecuted Rev. Samuel Peters, too—that was a dismal failure. At the age of eighty-one, he undertook an arduous, year-long western journey in hopes of reaching the Minnesota land (that he was going to modestly name "Petersylvania"). He only went as far as Wisconsin, and was never able to gain official possession of his claim.

Peters returned to New York City, and over the next few years, watched the last of his health and influence dwindle away. In 1825, a nephew tried to get his ninety-year-old uncle to finally return to Hebron, but the bitter old parson allegedly proclaimed, "I won't go—I'll perish first."

And so he did, dying in New York on April 19, 1826.

As the years passed and A General History of Connecticut was increasingly viewed out of context, the book's reputation for untruths—and the infamy of the Blue Laws—gained credence.

In 1876, scholar and state librarian James Hammond Trumbull published The True-Blue Laws of Connecticut and New Haven, and the False Blue Laws Forged by Peters, an in-depth analysis of A General History of Connecticut that exposed the many falsehoods and inaccuracies that riddled the book.

Trumbull also unearthed an opinion about Peters documented in J. L. Kingsley's 1838 "Historical Discourse at New Haven" that is attributed to the historian, the Reverend Dr. Trumbull, who had known Peters from childhood and grown up with him. According to Kingsley: "Of all men with whom [Dr. Trumbull] had ever been acquainted, Dr. Peters, he had thought, from his first knowledge of him, the least to be depended upon as to any matter of fact; especially in storytelling. The best excuse that can be made for him is, that he was a victim of pseudomania; that his abhorrence of truth was in fact a disease, and that he was not morally responsible for its outbreaks."

Samuel Peters: A natural-born liar to some, and simply a jerk to others.

CHAPTER 7

Anastase A. Vonsiatsky:
Fascist Jerk in the Time of Hitler

One of the great principles upon which the United States was
founded is the inalienable right to freedom of speech, including being able to express a political opinion, no matter how radical.
In the case of Anastase A. Vonsiatsky, it's not that the self-styled
"count" was an ardent and vocal supporter of fascism (and by
extension, the Nazi party) that got him in trouble. Rather, it was
when (and how) he chose to express his admiration that earned
him the title of jerk: at the outset of World War II.

It's all about the timing, right?

Actually, it seems as though the generally well-liked Vonsiatsky was more of a misguided dreamer bent on eradicating communism and restoring the czars to power than a vindictive jerk,
but at a time when allegiances meant everything, the Russian-
born immigrant chose to associate himself with the enemies of his
adopted homeland, a decision that resulted in a prison sentence
and forged an unfortunate legacy. It also didn't help that he never
shied away from being the center of attention, paraded around the
quiet town of Thompson wearing a swastika-emblazoned uniform,
admitted to having perpetrated acts of torture and murder, regularly met with well-connected international Nazi collaborators,
and kept a fortified bunker, stocked and ready for war.

Possibly being a bigamist didn't help his reputation, either.

Like many jerks, the charismatic and virile Vonsiatsky apparently had an eye for the ladies, and seemed to have a bad habit
of using them as a means to an end. More than once he wooed a
woman and took advantage, bettering his situation and then moving on, occasionally before he had even legally ended the previous
relationship.

Photo of Anastase A. Vonsiatsky taken in 1938
CONNECTICUT MAGAZINE

But before the women, wayward plans of glory, and fascist friends, there was a more modest beginning half a world away. Anastase Andreivich Vonsiatsky was born on June 12, 1898, in the Citadel of Warsaw, which at the time was in part of what was considered to be White Russia. His father, Andrei Nikolayevich Vonsiatsky, was a colonel in the Russian Gendarmerie, and a loyal soldier of the czarist regime, as his forefathers had been. The

Vonsiatsky family had earned titles of nobility through the Holy Roman Empire, a connection that Anastase would later claim for his own.

Like his father, Anastase attended military preparatory schools from a young age, starting in 1908 at the age of ten. The discipline learned at the various institutions would serve the young man well as he was to endure a particularly unfortunate stretch of family tragedy. On June 16, 1910, Col. Andre Vonsiatsky was assassinated, and six years later, his wife and Anastase's mother, Nina, died of a heart attack in Moscow. Of the five Vonsiatsky siblings, one sister committed suicide in 1916 and older brother, Nikolai, died fighting the Bolsheviks in 1922. Another sister, Natasha, left for Shanghai and would later emigrate to the United States, where she was eventually reunited with her brother.

Despite all the familial turmoil, the teenage Vonsiatsky persevered in his studies, and in 1916, at the age of eighteen, enrolled in the Emperor Nicholas II Academy in St. Petersburg, which, at the time, was one of the most prestigious military schools in Russia. When the October Revolution broke out in November 1917, Vonsiatsky left school to join the fight against the communist revolutionaries who were spearheaded by Vladimir Lenin and the Bolshevik party. Vonsiatsky soon was a lieutenant with the White Army and saw extensive action—later, reports would surface that he was involved in various acts of kidnapping, torture, and murder while fighting in Crimea in the Ukraine. He never denied his role in the violence, stating that the murders were justified because "a civil war was raging and we were defending our country." Sometimes it's hard to distinguish between what happens during the heat of battle and proactively being a jerk.

During his service time, Vonsiatsky was repeatedly wounded, taking bullets in the arm, back, and stomach. In addition, he contracted typhoid fever and severe frostbite in 1919, which forced him from military action. In January 1920, he was in the Crimean city of Yalta recuperating when he met and married seventeen-year-old Liobouv Mouromsky, the daughter of a wealthy Jewish shop owner. The exact details of their relationship were a bit murky, other than it appears that Vonsiatsky discarded the young woman almost as quickly as he had met her.

By the time he was healthy enough to rejoin the cause in March, the White Russian forces were being decimated by the Bolsheviks and had scattered in retreat. Following the age-old wisdom of running away to fight another day, he made his way to France and began to search for a way to earn a living outside the military.

His civilian mission took him to London and then back to Paris, where he supposedly used his infamous charm to get close to a young French actress, who secured him a job as a scene shifter for ten francs a day. During his relationship with the actress, Vonsiatsky conveniently neglected to divulge that he was married, a fact that she would not know about until the money she had helped him procure had been used to bring his teenage wife and her parents to Paris. When the truth came to light, Vonsiatsky's brief career in theater came to an abrupt end.

Still, it didn't hinder Vonsiatsky, who soon found another, wealthier female benefactor. This time his target was Marion Buckingham Ream, heiress to what was then one of the largest fortunes in the United States. The daughter of Norman Bruce Ream, a capitalist who had made his wealth through speculation in livestock and grain, Marion Ream had joined the YMCA as a relief worker, and had been sent to France to help with the recovery from World War I. A demure, compassionate, graceful, and petite woman, she had met the strapping, gray-eyed Russian in the Folies-Bergère, a renowned French dance hall. At forty-four years old, she was literally twice his age, but that didn't seem to matter—she was soon thoroughly captivated by the young man whom she may have seen as a "bad boy" and an ideal way to break away from her strict, conservative family.

Like Vonsiatsky, Ream had been married previously—from 1903 to 1918 she had been Mrs. Marion Stephens, wife of Redmond Stephens, a Chicago attorney. Unlike Vonsiatsky, however, she had gone through the formal process of getting divorced before embarking upon another legally sanctioned union. She also probably would have insisted that Vonsiatsky do the same, but evidently he didn't think the subject of already being married was worth mentioning, especially when Ream had a substantial fortune and social connections that could be most beneficial to his long-term plans. With such a tremendous opportunity, why let trivial details—like his wife—get in the way?

In the summer of 1921, Vonsiatsky emigrated to the United States, although the exact details of how he was able to pay for the transatlantic journey aboard a luxurious French ocean liner were unclear; he claimed that he had made enough money moving scenery to afford the ticket, while others suggested that his rich new girlfriend had paid his way. Also convenient was that Vonsiatsky—who had been trained from his youth to serve in the military—was able to quickly find well-paying employment in New York City at a locomotive concern. One rumor even suggested that the former White Russian arrived daily in a limousine, another clue that he may have been financially supported by a more substantial, quasi-anonymous source.

Soon, there was no question where the money was coming from. On February 4, 1922, Anastase Vonsiatsky was married to Marion Ream at the Russian Orthodox Cathedral of St. Nicholas on the Upper East Side of Manhattan, a "Cinderfella"-like event that made social pages around the country. The couple was married for only two months and two days, however, when Liobouv Mouromsky appeared and filed a legal claim challenging the union. She stated that she was still married to Vonsiatsky, and that he was now a bigamist. She traveled to New York with a lawyer in the hopes of landing a large financial settlement.

The charge went to the ecclesiastical court. Vonsiatsky suggested that the only reason he had married the affluent young woman was to protect her from the chaos that had been unfolding around them in Yalta, and that the marriage had been nothing more than one of convenience. The judge apparently agreed, annulling the Vonsiatsky-Mouromsky marriage and upholding his union with Marion Ream—although given the Ream family's influence, any other outcome would've been a surprise.

The legality of their wedded status no longer in question, the couple purchased the 224-acre Quinnatisset Farm in rural Thompson, tucked away in the most northeastern part of the Quiet Corner of Connecticut, and moved in during June 1925. Vonsiatsky would rechristen the picturesque property "The Nineteenth Hole," a nod to the Quinnatisset County Club, built by Ream's father in 1905 and which was—and still is—across the road. Vonsiatsky would eventually transform the property into his own paramilitary playground, but first he assimilated to the role of Connecticut Yankee.

Anastase, now known to all as "Count Annie"—apparently he gave himself the title, created a regal Vonsiatsky crest and had it emblazoned on everything from silverware to dinner jackets—and his loyal wife Marion settled into the rosy life of a rich couple, existing quite easily on her vast fortune and engaging freely in all sorts of community activities. He golfed, organized, and performed in local theatrical productions (some of which he wrote himself), joined the local volunteer fire department, and was made a lieutenant in the US Army Reserve. Thanks to Marion's connections, he applied for and received US citizenship, becoming naturalized in September 1927. He also enrolled at Brown University, and although he dropped out after two years, he gained a deep appreciation for American football during his time there, regularly attending games for years afterward. He even reconnected with his sister Natasha, and set up her and her husband Lev Mamedov as the proprietors of the Russian Bear, a restaurant located on the Nineteenth Hole. The thirty-year-old immigrant was living the American Dream.

He was also living in the fast lane—literally, as he was repeatedly ticketed for speeding around the bucolic New England countryside in the many roadsters that Ream bought for him. He also threw wild parties in addition to being a heavy drinker and unabashed womanizer, allegedly partaking in numerous affairs.

At the other end of the spectrum, the low-key and gracious Marion Ream generously supported numerous local charities and causes, and seemed to patiently indulge her husband's vices and excesses. The house servants and residents of Thompson also tolerated the count's escapades and dalliances, mostly out of respect for Ream.

When Vonsiatsky wasn't busy carousing or playing at being a country squire, he devoted himself to a goal that sounds farfetched, but at the time, seemed obtainable (to Vonsiatsky, anyway): toppling Russia's communist regime and restoring the Romanov family to power. To do this, he saw fascism—the polar opposite of communism—as his best vehicle.

In his quixotic scheme for the reascension of the Romanovs, there would also be a plum, high-ranking position and great influence for the loyal Vonsiatsky. That was the plan, anyway—he even went so far as to print postage stamps bearing his likeness that were to be used in Russia once he assumed control of the nation.

To help bring those dreams to fruition, and relying heavily on his wife's riches and influence, the count started fashioning his own little piece of Russian restoration right in Thompson. He had a barracks constructed, where he openly trained and quartered recruits, and kept a printing press for the publication of his propaganda magazine, the *Fashist*. He also built a small granite fortress with sixteen-inch-thick walls, narrow windows, and an underground bunker, a Spartan structure that served as his headquarters. Stocked with guns, rifles, sabers, knives, grenades, and other military gear, it was designed by Vonsiatsky to survive an assault. Chances were strong that an unsuspecting assailant who rushed headlong into the building would tumble into the shaft that led to the bunker, and most likely fall to his death.

As part of the tower's defenses, Vonsiatsky kept a pack of German shepherds as watchdogs. He also had a nameplate bearing his name specially designed and installed—on the desk of his first lieutenant! A final bit of subterfuge that would decrease the risk of being assassinated as his father had been.

Vonsiatsky was very active in recruiting displaced Russians and furthering his cause, even hosting picnics at the Nineteenth Hole for fellow fascists. He never hesitated in talking to the local press about his machinations, no matter how much his actions were frowned upon—nowadays he might be called an attention whore in that he believed that any press was good press. He regularly granted interviews to national publications like *Life* and *Time* as well as local ones such as the *New York Times* and *Hartford Courant*. He would also visit local Elks clubs and American Legion halls to lecture about the glory of prerevolution Russia and the ills of communism. In addition to speaking Russian and English, Vonsiatsky was also fluent in German and French, so he could get his story across to almost any audience who would listen.

Vonsiatsky cast his net wide across the country. He joined the Brotherhood of Russian Truth in the late 1920s, which had worked to distribute anticommunist propaganda throughout Russia. After a falling out with the group's leadership in 1933, he founded his own anticommunist organization, the *Vserossiyskaya Fashistskaya Organizatsiya* or All-Russian Fascist Organization (or VRO for short). Of course, the count installed himself atop the party as the "vohzd," who would lead the way to reclaimed glory. The group adopted the swastika as its logo and used Hitler's familiar salute as a greeting.

The following year, Vonsiatsky merged the VRO with the Russian Fascist Party, which was based in Tokyo, Japan, to form the All Russian Fascist Party (RFP). This entity, however, only lasted a short time before Vonsiatsky broke away and formed yet another group, this one called the All Russian National Revolutionary Party (VNRP).

While mucking about in the alphabet soup of anticommunist factions, the count also managed to reach out beyond Russian groups, traveling the world to forge political relationships. He set up branches of the VNRP, which he called the "White Guard," in various locations around the United States, and claimed to have factions in Bulgaria, Brazil, Yugoslavia, and Egypt.

To help spread his influence, he undertook multiple international trips throughout the 1930s, visiting key cities such as Tokyo, Shanghai, Manila, Singapore, Hong Kong, Bombay, Budapest, Sofia, Paris and, most importantly (or unfortunately), Berlin. He also made sure that his propaganda manifesto the *Fashist* was in the hands of White Russians around the globe, printing and distributing hundreds of copies of each issue.

As Vonsiatsky became more consumed with trying to upend the communists in Russia, he also became less discerning in how he attained that goal. Watching the rise of the fascist Nazi party in Germany, Vonsiatsky saw Hitler not as an evil megalomaniac bent on global domination, but rather as a potential ally. "The enemy of my enemy is my friend," as the old proverb goes.

In the January 1937 issue of the *Fashist,* Vonsiatsky ran a picture of German soldiers with the title "The Army of the Holy Swastika," along with his own comments:

> *With the existence of Germany and Adolph Hitler, as a fortified base, and directing center for all anti-Communist movements, the beginning of a war by the U.S.S.R. with Germany can change with lightning-like rapidity into the end of international communism and the victory of the Russian National Revolution.*

That poor judgment is where the count crossed the line from harmless eccentric to potentially dangerous jerk—particularly in the eyes of the FBI, who in 1933 had started to track Vonsiatsky's movements and associations more closely, eventually compiling a nine thousand eight hundred-page file on him.

In the file, federal agents reported many interesting claims regarding Vonsiatsky's activities. One source asserted that he caught a bunch of turtles and painted swastikas on their shells; another suggested he wanted to purchase balloons to use to float his propaganda from Poland into Russia; yet another said that he purchased seven hundred battleship models, built and painted them to resemble ships in the old Imperial Russian Navy, and sailed them on a Nineteenth Hole pond.

Despite these shenanigans, there were more serious accusations. One report alleged that, during a trip to Berlin, Vonsiatsky had a brief audience with Hitler, and then dined with top Nazi *Reichsmarschall* Hermann Goering. When later confronted with these charges in court, Vonsiatsky would deny them; at other times he did admit to holding Hitler in high regard, and even having photographs of the German leader on the walls of his Thompson office.

Although he would make claims to the contrary regarding support of the entire Nazi agenda, it appears that Vonsiatsky wanted to have his cake and eat it, too. During the late 1930s, he reached out to and established an association with Fritz Kuhn, the notorious leader of the German American Bund, an organization of German-Americans dedicated to supporting the Nazi cause. Kuhn was an ardent and outspoken admirer of Adolph Hitler, and was able to generate significant sympathy for Germany's endeavors. He even met with *Der Fuhrer* during the 1936 Olympics, and although Hitler never acknowledged Kuhn or his group in an official capacity, he did not dismiss Kuhn's efforts, either.

By being on good terms with Kuhn, who referred to himself as the "American Fuhrer," Vonsiatsky thought that when the fascist German regime eventually turned its attention to Russia, he would be in prime position to take advantage if they were successful in defeating the communist regime.

Consequently, when Kuhn, one of the most visible Nazi adherents in the United States, made headlines in February 1939 after he brazenly addressed some twenty thousand followers at Madison Square Garden in New York City, disparaging President Franklin D. Roosevelt and nearly inciting a riot, Vonsiatsky was there. He also attended other Bund events, and allegedly provided funds for Kuhn to create and distribute pro-fascist (and pro-Nazi) propaganda. The *Fashist* even published photos of the two men together.

In July 1939, Kuhn was arrested for drunk and disorderly conduct in Webster, Massachusetts, just over the border from Thompson; Kuhn claimed he was visiting Vonsiatsky during the time, a charge that the count vigorously denied. Despite that, Vonsiatsky appeared in court with Kuhn, and also paid his bail when the time came.

Shortly thereafter, Kuhn encountered bigger legal problems and had to step down as head of the Bund after being sentenced to prison for tax evasion and embezzlement. He was replaced by Wilhelm Kunze, who would be instrumental in Vonsiatsky's ultimate downfall.

Meanwhile, Vonsiatsky continued his quest to liberate Russia, even though there were growing signs that publicly positioning himself alongside Hitler, his fascist government, and his Axis allies could be a dangerous prospect. In September 1939, Germany invaded Poland, officially igniting World War II in Europe, and although the United States would not join the fray for another two years, Hitler was not making many American friends.

Back at home in Thompson, the friendly count maintained good relations with the small community, regularly putting his small arsenal at the disposal of the state police, whom he let drink and eat on his tab at the Russian Bear.

With war on the horizon for the United States—and possibly sensing that he was under scrutiny, or maybe to just hedge his bets—Vonsiatsky began releasing statements separating himself from certain aspects of Hitler's Nazi party. In what he probably viewed as the ultimate patriotic American act, he published the following signed personal statement in the June–July 1940 issue of the *Fashist,* dated July 4, 1940:

> *The Russian National Revolutionary Party, of which I am the leader, does not support either Germany's or Japan's ambition for hegemony in Europe or the Far East.*
>
> *The Germans and the Japanese have never made clear their attitude toward a replacement of the present Stalinist rule by a Russian National Government.*

The sole aim of our organization is to return to Russia to free people with a government elected by the people, of the people and for the people.

Our intention is to form in Russia a truly democratic government.

Our party is not anti-Semitic.

Our party has no membership dues; it is financed solely by voluntary contributions from its members and sympathizers. It is not subsidized by any foreign power or foreign individuals.

Our organization is banned in Germany and Japan.

Only in the United States can we enjoy freedom of action and thought within the laws of the country.

I herewith state emphatically that the activities of our organization are against the present Soviet government alone and that in no way whatsoever does it act against the constitution of the United States or violate its laws, which we loyally support.

It may have been a little too late. By now, the FBI was intently following Vonsiatsky's movements and collecting evidence that would be used against him. In retrospect, it is fairly evident that the count had no specific agenda against the United States, yet his willful ignorance when it came to maintaining good relations with Hitler and the Axis in the hopes of being rewarded with Russia if it fell, was raising "red" flags.

In July 1941, a month after Hitler had invaded Russia, Vonsiatsky met with Wilhelm Kunze, the leader of the German American Bund. Hoping to further curry favor with the Nazi leadership, he allegedly gave Kunze $2,800, a cash "gift" that Kunze would use to pay for his own bail bond and subsequent departure from the United States. A few weeks later, Vonsiatsky was in Chicago, Illinois, where he rendezvoused with Dr. Otto Willumeit, the unit leader of the Chicago chapter of the Bund, and other Bund members. It was believed that Vonsiatsky was working with Willumeit to aid in Kunze's departure, and that the count was actively helping to finance the travel plans by providing funds for a fake passport and other necessary papers.

Unfortunately for Vonsiatsky, the meetings had been infiltrated by an undercover FBI agent, Alexius Pelypenko, who was reporting directly to the US State Department. Even though there was very little evidence that the German American Bund had any influence with Hitler, as far as American authorities were concerned, Vonsiatsky was actively aiding and abetting Nazi sympathizers—which, technically, he was.

A few months later, Japan attacked Pearl Harbor, formally drawing the United States into World War II. On the West Coast, thousands of innocent Japanese-Americans were rounded up and held in internment camps, and anyone else suspected of spying and conspiring to help the cause of the Axis, which included Adolf Hitler and Germany—officially enemies of the nation—were now under even more intense scrutiny. Over a decade of rubbing elbows with fellow fascist megalomaniacs was about to come back and bite Vonsiatsky in the Bund, so to speak.

On May 9, 1942, thirteen special agents of the FBI descended upon the Nineteenth Hole in Thompson and began searching the property, including all of the count's military offices. They seized boxes of damning documents, including correspondence between Vonsiatsky and his emissaries around the globe, as well as a full run of the *Fashist,* a significant cache of weapons, and multiple items emblazoned with swastikas. Although Vonsiatsky fully cooperated with the investigation, what was found was not exactly what any "good citizen" would be keeping in their home, unless they were enough of a jerk that they didn't think they could get in any trouble by overtly appearing to embrace the Nazi cause.

Published disclaimers and commie-busting intentions aside, on June 6, Anastase Vonsiatsky was formally indicted with Kunze, Willumeit, and two others as part of a conspiracy to violate the Espionage Act of 1917. He was arrested and taken to Hartford to be tried in federal court.

The count initially pleaded not guilty to the charges, and his wife's wealth meant that he could afford the best counsel. The prosecution countered with Thomas J. Dodd, an assistant to the US Attorney General, whose renowned political career would be launched by the case. The scene was set for a showdown, although it never materialized.

Vonsiatsky's legal team first tried to have him examined by mental health professionals in the hopes of having the count declared legally insane so that he wouldn't have to stand trial. When that didn't work, they quickly agreed to a deal. On June 22, 1942, Vonsiatsky officially changed his plea to guilty on charges of espionage and conspiracy.

Considering how cavalier he was in consorting with known Nazi sympathizers at a time when the United States was at war, it can be argued that he got off easy—he was sentenced to five years in the Medical Center for Federal Prisoners in Springfield, Missouri. He was released in February 1946 for good behavior, a few months after the end of World War II and seventeen months early. He was also allowed to keep his US citizenship.

The stint in prison appeared to have taken the jerk out of Vonsiatsky's sail, and shifted his priorities. After his release, and apparently contrite for the anguish he had brought Marion Ream, he moved to Florida so as not to cause her any additional embarrassment. With his sister Natasha and her husband in tow, he settled in St. Petersburg, which had a substantial population of Russian immigrants.

Although still married to Ream, Vonsiatsky soon met Edith Priscilla Royster, a waitress, and at age fifty-two he became a father for the first time when son Andre Anastase Vonsiatsky was born in July 1950. From all accounts, fatherhood agreed well with Vonsiatsky, who appeared to have been a caring parent. He still maintained a close friendship with Ream, and although they legally separated in 1952, there is no evidence that they ever divorced. Staying consistent with his earlier life, it was never clear if he married Royster, either—can't expect a jerk to change all his spots!

Ream was known as "Aunt Marion" to Andre, who would spend his childhood summers with her at the Nineteenth Hole in Thompson; she eventually even set up a small trust fund for him. Ream also continued to give the elder Vonsiatsky financial assistance, including $25,000 that he received upon her death in 1963.

Vonsiatsky kept busy during his years in Florida, watching football games and embracing his Russian roots. In addition to taking care of Andre, he wrote articles for several Russian immigrant newspapers and journals. In 1953, he opened the short-lived Tsar Nicholas II Museum in St. Petersburg, and even published a memoir he called *Rasplata* (Russian for "retribution"), in which he ranted against the communists, Franklin D. Roosevelt, and Thomas J. Dodd, among other political targets.

Speaking of politics and espionage, Vonsiatsky continued to stay in the loop. According to son Andre, during the communist scare of the 1950s, the FBI regularly visited the old count to seek his insight and opinion on potential enemies of the United States.

In his later years, Vonsiatsky certainly seemed more like an innocuous character than a true threat to national security. Some people, however, believed that he was still up to his old tricks and that he was involved in various plots to overthrow the communists in Russia, although there is scant (if any) evidence to prove it. One wild (and highly unlikely) Internet conspiracy theory even suggested that Vonsiatsky was somehow involved in the assassination of John F. Kennedy!

If he was up to anything untoward, the former White Russian managed to keep it to himself. On February 5, 1965, a few weeks after his sixty-sixth birthday, Anastase Andreivich Vonsiatsky died at his home from coronary thrombosis. He was interred at West Thompson Cemetery, a short distance from the Nineteenth Hole where he spent nearly two decades parading around in a swastika-emblazoned uniform, pursuing his fascist agenda, planning a triumphant return to Russia, and acting like a jerk.

CHAPTER 8

Amy Archer-Gilligan:
The True Story behind
Arsenic and Old Lace

It can be generally agreed that anyone who takes the life of another without provocation can be minimally classified as a jerk. But when they intentionally end multiple lives—including those of spouses, supposed friends, and others who trusted them to protect their well being—through a method that is extraordinarily painful and protracted, all the while hiding behind a moral righteousness that would put Job to shame, well, that's a special kind of jerk.

The name Amy Archer-Gilligan may not be immediately familiar, but the play (and subsequent movie) inspired by her life should be: *Arsenic and Old Lace* was a Broadway hit and the 1944 film adaptation, starring Cary Grant, is considered a cinematic classic. However, the darkly humorous tale of two charming spinsters who dispatch older gentlemen with poison and a laugh before burying them in their basement is a long cry from the disturbing actual events that unfolded in Windsor during the early part of the twentieth century.

Amy Archer-Gilligan's exact date of birth isn't known—some sources say 1873 or 1887, while others put it even earlier. Whenever it was, she was born in the Milton section of Litchfield, one of five children, to James and Mary Duggan. From most accounts, she had a decent upbringing, although there was evidence that the Duggan family was somewhat dysfunctional and plagued with mental illness: One brother was confined to an insane asylum in the 1890s, while a sister became an invalid after intentionally leaping from the roof of the family home. Amy was educated locally, and for a time worked as a bookkeeper.

Portrait of Amy Archer-Gilligan
M. WILLIAM PHELPS COLLECTION

According to Amy herself, she attended private school in New Milford and then went to Bellevue Hospital in Manhattan, New York, to train as a nurse, although neither of these claims were ever documented and seem to be suspect. She did, however, actually marry James Archer in 1897, and together they moved into one of the rented rooms in the Newington home of John D. Seymour, where they welcomed their only child, Mary, in 1899. Seymour died in 1904, but the Archers stayed on, continuing to care for the elderly boarders in the house. A few years later they left for Windsor to start their own nursing home as an economic enterprise.

The idea of a place for older folks to retire to finish out their days and receive medical attention (if necessary) was still a novel concept, so when the Archer Home for Elderly People and Chronic Invalids opened its doors in 1907 on Prospect Street in downtown Windsor, it was one of the first in the region. The business model was simple: Boarders would pay for a place to live, food to eat, and any medical attention. The rates varied—a resident could pay between $7 and $25 per week, or a flat fee of $1,000 to be taken care of for the remainder of their life. Amy also had residents agree to make her the beneficiary of their estates so she could "more easily" manage their finances once they passed. Occasionally, a boarder might sign a contract for a limited stay, but for most, once they signed on the dotted line with the Archers, they were part of the home until the day they died.

The problem was that apparently Amy often brought that day on a lot sooner than it needed to be.

"Sister Amy," as she became known in the small town of Windsor, was originally considered a pillar of the community. Often seen on the streets with a Bible in her hand, she was a staunch regular at Sunday services, and was also known as a generous financial supporter of the local Catholic church. Many neighbors thought highly of her because she undertook a task with which many of them didn't want to deal—providing care for the elderly and the infirm. Amy also made sure to stay in the good graces of the town's most influential families.

In retrospect, it was clear that she was working hard to project the image of a pious woman above reproach to mask her hideous crimes. Keep in mind that not only was this still a time in history when the concept of a serial murderer was novel, but also the idea of a *female* serial murderer was nearly inconceivable—Lydia Sherman aside, women were simply believed to be incapable of such horrors. This only aided Amy's deceptions, which worked so well and so long that she was able to run up a horrifying body count.

The first cracks in Amy's carefully crafted veneer, however, came in 1909 when charges started being made against the Archer Home in regard to the treatment of its residents (who were—ironically— called "inmates"). The family of one boarder even formally sued the Archers for $5,000, claiming that their relative had been subjected to unsanitary conditions inside the brick colonial, and had even been abused by Amy. Another resident complained about the uncomfortably close living quarters; shortly thereafter, Amy sent that resident to an insane asylum, which was a great way in the early twentieth century to make sure that someone wouldn't be heard from for a long, long time.

The Archer home's financial problems and resident-care issues were temporarily forgotten when Amy's husband James Archer unexpectedly died on February 10, 1910. According to the death certificate, Archer met his end as a result of Bright's disease, an acute kidney disorder. The only problem with this was that Bright's disease is a chronic ailment that often takes years before it claims a victim. James Archer had never been diagnosed with it, nor had he ever complained of any symptoms. He literally dropped dead at the age of fifty without any warning.

Of course, the signs were there if anyone had been looking for them. During the first four years of operation, more than twenty of the Archer home's residents died, a rate that was significantly higher than other similar residences. Even more telling, many were dying after very brief illnesses—particularly aggressive maladies that would come upon them in a matter of a few days or even hours.

Also suspicious (again, if neighbors and associates had been paying attention) was the speed and manner in which the bodies of deceased residents were removed from the house. Even if a passing occurred in the middle of the night, Amy would have the corpse removed immediately after death, so as not to "upset" the other residents. She also would make sure that the departed were embalmed and buried as soon as possible—obviously, the faster they were out of sight, the slimmer the chance that anyone could examine a body and discover the true cause of death.

During the majority of Amy's murderous spree, Dr. Howard King was the Windsor medical examiner. Conveniently, he was on Archer Home payroll as the house physician, and being compensated by Amy, would hastily sign off on deaths. From the high number of demises that he certified over such a short time, apparently the pay was good enough not to ask a lot of questions.

Oh, and there was one more obvious clue that something illicit might have been happening: the copious amounts of arsenic that Amy was purchasing for the home, often a few days before one of her residents would coincidentally die. Telling people that the poison was to get rid of rats and bedbugs, she was also buying nearly a pound at a time, which was enough to kill an army of any vermin a few times over, and certainly more than enough to exterminate a person.

As mentioned in the case of Lydia Sherman (chapter 3), arsenic is one of the most virulent poisons available. At first, it induces severe vomiting, diarrhea, and abdominal pain, and then it starts to cause extreme gastrointestinal bleeding. Victims then have trouble breathing, all the while also enduring dizziness, headaches, and labored breathing. Eventually they collapse, slipping—if they are lucky—into a coma before their systems shut down for good. It's very slow acting, sometimes taking days to be fatal. In short, to use it to kill someone is particularly cruel.

Even more disturbing—and to distance herself from her repugnant actions—Amy would often send the intended victim to nearby W. H. Mason's drugstore to make the arsenic purchase for her. Now that's a truly special kind of jerk!

After the unfortunate passing of a resident, Amy would play the sympathetic figure, always making a show of sending flowers to the funerals and families of her victims and expressing her deepest condolences, and even occasionally paying for final arrangements. She was bound to perform these tasks by the contracts she signed with her residents, but they weren't public documents, so no one knew she was just fulfilling her legal obligation.

Once James Archer died in 1910, to the unsuspecting residents of Windsor, Amy Archer was a poor widow with a child trying to make ends meet by running a respectable business that, from the outside, seemed to be doing well. The house was always at or near capacity, and from most accounts (other than from those who had been whisked away to insane asylums) life inside was pleasant enough, if a bit cozy. Sure, residents were dying at a higher-than-normal rate, but that was most likely an anomaly—it could simply be chalked up to a stretch of bad luck.

Speaking of speaking ill of the dead—after her beloved husband's death, Amy suggested that the reportedly poor treatment of some residents had come as a result of James's carelessness and occasional indifference. He wasn't around to argue.

Fortunately, the "tough times" at the Archer Home didn't go completely unnoticed, although they did go on much longer than they should have. Shortly after James Archer died, one of Amy's neighbors began to notice that residents seemed to be coming out dead from the Prospect Street residence almost faster than they were going in alive.

Carlan Goslee worked in the insurance industry by day, but in his spare time, was an active member of the Windsor Rogue Detecting Society, an amateur-like detective agency, and also wrote stories for the *Hartford Courant* and *Hartford Times*. Goslee's inquisitive instincts told him something wasn't quite right with what seemed to be happening on an all-too-regular basis, so he started to poke around, quietly talking to people around Windsor.

When Amy Archer heard that her neighbor was asking questions, she immediately went on the offensive. Like many jerks, when accused, she thumped her Bible more loudly and proclaimed that she was doing "God's work." Although she was almost always dressed in black, she portrayed (and no doubt saw) herself as a matronly angel, complete with long robes, feathered wings, and a shiny golden halo . . .

Amy was an angel, all right. An angel of death.

In May of 1911, after another *Courant* reporter, Robert Thayer, had also started looking into the unusually high death rate at the Archer Home (no stories accusing anyone of murder had been published yet), Amy sent a letter to the state's attorney indignantly suggesting that there was a conspiracy to smear her good name and to denigrate the Christian deeds she was undertaking. She claimed she was being unjustly persecuted, and rather than focusing on all the positive work she had done in caring for the unfortunate and infirm, her enemies were circulating wicked lies.

Two months later, she took her defense directly to her neighbors in Windsor, releasing a public statement in which she outright called any claims that she was poisoning her residents "absurd." Again, she played the Christian card and suggested that what was going on was all a misunderstanding, and that life in the Archer Home, despite the unusually high number of deaths, was good. The sick and elderly had a roof over their heads, hot meals, and medical attention, all without putting any burden on the community—for what more could they ask?

All Amy's protestations and her shrewd facade must've worked to an extent—almost five years and over fifty more "inmates" would pass before she was arrested and formally charged with murder.

In the meantime, the Archer Home was struggling financially. The flaw (literally, a fatal one) with Amy's business model was that after accepting a flat fee to care for a person for the rest of their life, once all the beds became full, there was no new income. With food, utilities, and the general upkeep of the house, plus all the money she was paying out to hide her lies (maintaining payments to Dr. King for his unquestioning cooperation, settling the lawsuit from the prior resident, donating to the local churches to protect her Christian reputation, taking care of the funeral arrangements of her victims, etc.), a cash infusion was needed.

Maybe not coincidentally, in 1912, the Archer Home saw fifteen of its residents die, more than a few of them rather abruptly.

In addition to freeing up beds by poisoning residents—and raising much-needed new income—Amy also began to quietly rework agreements, even asking for advances and borrowing money from her inmates. She took advantage of her station any way she could, preying on the pity of others to bail her out, and even turning to her womanly charms, such as they were, when things became dire.

A strapping divorcee of fifty-seven, Michael Gilligan moved into the Archer Home during the summer of 1913. A former farmhand and fireman, he was the picture of health, and by moving into Amy's place, he figured he would not be a burden to his five grown children and could live out the remainder of his days independently. A very social man—it was said that he never met a drink that he didn't like—Gilligan was generally well regarded about Windsor. Unlike Amy, he was welcome almost everywhere he went, and that certainly included the Archer Home.

Between the opportunity he provided to rehabilitate Amy's flagging reputation and the nice-sized nest egg he had accumulated over the years, it wasn't too long before Amy had snared Gilligan in her web. Despite the twenty-year difference in age, almost immediately after he moved in to the Prospect Street residence, he and Amy became romantically involved. By November, they were married.

Now Mrs. Archer-Gilligan, Amy had managed to temporarily stave off both the debt collectors and the gossip mongers. Marriage seemed to improve her disposition, and having a capable man around the house was certainly a benefit. General maintenance was being done and long-needed repairs were finally made to the overcrowded house.

All was going well, except for some, it's hard to stop being a jerk. Thirteen residents died in 1913, and it wasn't too long into

1914 before Amy was being overwhelmed by debt and becoming desperate again.

On February 19, 1914, she had her husband of only three months sign a new will that left his entire estate to Amy. Forty-eight hours later, Michael Gilligan was dead, abruptly felled by what was called an acute case of "indigestion."

Arsenic poisoning will do that to a man.

Even though witnesses had seen Gilligan in the days up to his end and took note of his hearty physical condition, Amy suggested that he had died of double pneumonia! Her paid physician, Dr. King, certified "valvular heart disease" as the cause of death, although he had never examined Gilligan before or after his death, nor had he done an autopsy. Later during her trial, one witness of Gilligan's death testified that Amy's husband had suffered from extreme nausea and a burning in the throat and stomach, which is consistent with arsenic poisoning.

Like the other residents who had met an untimely demise in the Archer Home, Gilligan was quickly embalmed and buried. The fact that he was dead only two days after signing a new will—giving everything to his new wife and leaving nothing for his five children—wasn't ignored, however. Reporter Carlan Goslee, who had been friendly with Michael Gilligan and was stunned by the man's sudden death, took the evidence he had of Amy's significant arsenic purchases and his suspicions, and went to Clifton Sherman, his editor at the *Hartford Courant*. Sherman, impressed by the evidence—circumstantial as it was—refrained from immediately publishing any stories blatantly accusing Amy. He instead went to the Connecticut state's attorney Hugh Alcorn, so that law enforcement could launch a proper investigation into the happenings at the Archer Home. A few of the relatives of Amy's other residents who had met unexpected deaths had also contacted Alcorn, who had begun to realize that something was sorely amiss in Windsor.

Unlike criminal investigations today, where investigators have numerous sophisticated tools and an abundance of technology at their disposal to quickly solve crimes, the wheels of justice turned much more slowly a century ago. After Michael Gilligan's passing, another eight residents of the Archer Home would die in 1914. Seven more would pass away in 1915, and another half dozen would expire by May of 1916 before authorities finally stepped in to end Amy's murderous spree.

But that's not to say that investigators sat back and did nothing during this time. In fact, near the end of 1914, Zola Bennett, an undercover private investigator for the Connecticut State Police, was sent to the Archer Home. Playing the part of a wealthy widow looking for a place to live, the older woman was quickly accepted by Amy and given a room. Once on the inside, Bennett began to gather evidence that would be used to arrest and eventually prosecute Amy.

It wasn't too long before she discovered that Amy had been swindling residents, draining their bank accounts, and bilking them of whatever other resources she could. Always maintaining her role as a poor pious widow down on her luck, Amy was able to get them to agree to give her substantial loans, or even property in some cases. Sadly, many of those who signed a new contract with Amy were literally making a deal with the devil. Only rather than harvesting their souls, she took their money and their lives.

Gathering and processing court-admissible evidence, especially in a case like this, was a much trickier process before the advent of forensic investigative teams and integrated law enforcement computer networks. Although a jerk, Amy was very crafty, never making an arsenic purchase herself, either sending Dr. King to do her dirty work or, as mentioned, one of her intended victims. Sure, there was an ever-growing body count and whispered accusations, but without a bloodied murder weapon, it was hard to say what exactly was killing the residents of the Archer Home at such a significant pace; remember, they were "infirm" and "aged." Death was no stranger to such a house even under normal circumstances.

Still, the authorities suspected that something unusual was happening, and eventually realized they needed to step up their investigation. It took almost a year to gather family permissions and court orders to start exhuming bodies, but by the spring of

1916, Amy's victims began coming out of the ground, and via the autopsy table, were finally able to provide the evidence needed to take down a murderous jerk.

Dead men (and women) do tell tales, it turns out.

The first body exhumed was that of Franklin Andrews, a sixty-one-year-old former factory worker who had been a resident of Amy's for twenty-one months before abruptly dying of "gastric ulcers." The coroner who examined his remains determined that there was enough arsenic in his system "to kill several men."

The second to be dug up was Alice Gowdy, who at sixty-nine had moved into the Archer home in June of 1914 with her husband Loren to live out her years. By November, she was dead of what was called "acute indigestion." Turns out her "upset stomach" was caused by arsenic, and lots of it.

Next to be examined was second husband Michael Gilligan. Instead of the "indigestion" that had felled him, it seems as though Amy had loaded him with enough arsenic to murder half a dozen husbands. (Not surprisingly, it would also come out that Amy's first, James Archer, hadn't been a victim of "kidney disease," as reported, but of arsenic poisoning.)

Fourth was widower Charles Smith. Over the course of two years, Amy had gotten the eighty-seven-year-old to withdraw his entire life savings (over $3,000) and give it to her before he suddenly—and conveniently—passed because of "a stroke," brought on by "old age." An autopsy determined that the end of the man's life had been brought on by arsenic.

Finally, the remains of Maude Lynch, a thirty-three-year-old woman who had been brought to Amy by her family, were scrutinized. Rather than having died from "epilepsy" and a form of "anemia," as was certified by Dr. King, it was revealed that she had been killed by a dose of strychnine, not arsenic. Still, she had been poisoned by Amy's hand.

Five dead bodies saturated with poison were more than a coincidence. Between the forensic evidence, the information that had been gathered by investigative journalists Carl Goslee and Robert

Thayer, and the reports gathered by Zola Bennett, the disturbing truth could no longer be disputed: Amy Archer-Gilligan was routinely murdering the inmates of the Archer Home, with money as her apparent sole motive.

Armed with what appeared to be ironclad evidence, authorities finally moved in and put a stop to the horror. On May 8, 1916, Amy was arrested at her residence on Prospect Avenue—also the crime scene. She didn't put up much of a protest, and went along peacefully with police, maintaining her composure throughout most of her processing. She was placed in jail, and in September was formally charged with five murders by a Hartford grand jury, with a trial set for June 1917.

While waiting for her case to come before a judge, however, Amy slipped back into jerk mode. As in the past when accused, she went on the offensive and began talking to the press, insisting that she had been framed for the murders—that the authorities had planted the arsenic in the bodies and had falsified the evidence about her scamming residents out of their life savings. Never mind that there was no practical (or sane) motive for anyone to do that to a God-fearing Christian widow like Amy purported to be; everyone was out to get her! She was innocent, and looking forward to getting her day in court, telling her version of events, and being cleared of all charges.

As the case came closer to trial, public interest in Amy's case grew exponentially. Thanks to the extensive coverage by the *Hartford Courant*—its reporters were allowed to break the story exclusively after they had cooperated with the authorities—the shocking tale of a woman who had poisoned her charges and husbands for money had gone national, being picked up and printed by newspapers across the country. Fearing that an unbiased jury could not be found, Amy's defense team asked for a change of venue, but it was denied.

Finally June came and the trial began. The prosecution, led by state's attorney Hugh Alcorn, initially focused on the murder of Franklin Andrews, and brought in multiple medical experts to testify that the poison that had been found in his remains was the cause of his death. Alcorn also made sure that the testimony of all his experts agreed that examination of Andrews's remains showed that the arsenic had been given to the victim while he was alive, and it hadn't somehow gotten into the body post mortem.

For three weeks, the prosecution made a clear case based on the evidence: Each of the victims had been residents of the Archer Home, each had been murdered by arsenic poisoning, Amy Archer-Gilligan had purchased massive amounts of arsenic, and Amy had benefited financially from every death.

Amy's defense team paraded their own team of experts to the stand, although their testimony primarily centered on other possible ways that the arsenic could've gotten into the remains of the victims. The defense's case only lasted two days, and at no point did Amy Archer-Gilligan, who had loudly thumped her Bible every time she'd been accused, ever testify in her own defense with a hand actually on a Bible.

After a mere four hours of deliberation, the jury reached a verdict. On July 13, 1917, Amy Archer-Gilligan was found guilty of murder in the first degree. She was immediately sentenced to be hanged.

Obviously, there was great emotion in the courtroom. The stoic Amy even broke down and sobbed uncontrollably at her fate. The families of the victims were relieved as they finally got retribution for the cold-blooded murder of their mothers and fathers, brothers and sisters, sons and daughters.

Or almost got retribution. Like many jerks, Amy caught a break as the governor of Connecticut stepped in and granted her a stay of execution until her case could be heard by the Supreme Court of Errors. As it turns out, the first trial was thrown out on a technicality, and she was given a second trial.

This time, however, the wily murderess came up with another plan. In the time before the second trial, it suspiciously came to light that Amy was a drug addict, and had been obtaining and allegedly taking significant amounts of morphine. It was the drug addiction that had caused her to lose control of her faculties, and had ultimately led her to do such terrible things. Also this time around, the mental illness that had supposedly plagued her family—her brother had been committed to an insane asylum, remember—had also conveniently manifested itself in poor old Amy.

The court proceedings began again in 1919, except this time the Archer-Gilligan defense team presented their case in a different way, painting their client as a drug-addled, mentally unstable woman. Having been spared a date with the hangman's noose, Amy deftly played her part during her incarceration leading up to the second trial, acting her best to be declared insane. She kept repeating the same phrase over and over again, "I want to go home," and would do other things that a "crazy" person might do.

When it came time to again prove her innocence, however, Amy and her defense team instead plead to second-degree murder by reason of insanity, which carried life imprisonment. The judge accepted it, and she was remanded to the state prison in Wethersfield for the rest of her days.

After a few years, the stress of being in prison plus pretending to be crazy may have been too much for the prolific killer, and in 1924 she was sent to live in the Connecticut Valley Hospital in Middletown, a state institution for the criminally insane.

Instead of caring for infirm "inmates," Amy was now the "inmate." She reportedly was "a quiet, cooperative patient" during her time in Middletown, spending most of her time with a Bible in hand and praying. In a twist that couldn't be made up, the woman who may have been responsible for poisoning as many as forty people was allowed to work in the cafeteria, serving food to other inmates. ("You want my special seasoning with your hash?")

She spent the rest of her life there, dying of age-related complications on April 23, 1962. Her obituary listed her as being eighty-nine, but with the uncertainty regarding her actual date of birth, no one was really sure.

One thing, however, was indisputable: Amy Archer-Gilligan was a jerk.

CHAPTER 9

P. T. Barnum:
Prince of the Humbugs

Some jerks have bad behavior hardwired in their system and can't help it; other jerks come by the label courtesy of particular actions or events; and yet others just fall grandly into it and are never able to escape the reputation that follows.

Then there are some who openly embrace less-than-decent behavior, boldly declare it to the world, profit greatly, and then are beloved by the masses for their sheer audacity. Such is the story of P. T. Barnum: braggart, egomaniac, con man, prince of humbugs, the greatest showman in American history, and unapologetic jerk.

Not that there's anything wrong with it in this case. As Barnum ably demonstrated, people were happy to line up for the opportunity to fall for his hyped deceptions as long as in the end they felt that they had been entertained by something, even if it wasn't exactly what was promised.

The quote "I don't care what they say about me, just make sure they spell my name right!" is often attributed to Barnum, and even if he wasn't the first to utter it, he most likely said it at some point and undoubtedly lived by the sentiment. Certainly much was written and said about him, both good and bad, both in his time and long beyond his death. If he wasn't making headlines, he was often busy manipulating them.

He was also believed to have said "Every crowd has a silver lining," and again, even if he never said it, he certainly made no apologies for his love of making money. He shared his "golden rules" in how to generate a fortune and referred to himself as a "profitable philanthropist" who believed that if "adding to the pleasure and prosperity of my neighbors, I can do so at a profit, the incentive to 'good works' will be twice as strong as if it were otherwise." Nothing like helping others while helping yourself!

Barnum was also a visionary, a reformer, a debunker, and a politician—in short, he was a complicated man who at turns was brilliant and belligerent, humanitarian and huckster. An admirable jerk for the ages.

Phineas Taylor Barnum was born on July 5, 1810, in Bethel, and given his unsurpassed skills for self-promotion and hyperbole, it's hard to believe that the headline of the *Connecticut Journal* that day wasn't "THE GREAT BARNUM IS BORN" in seventy-two-point type. Although "humble" is rarely used to describe the entertainment icon, it can definitely be applied to his beginnings. One of five children of Irena Taylor and Philo F. Barnum, young P. T. was, in his own words, "always ready to concoct fun, or lay plans for moneymaking, but hard work was decidedly not in my line." Early on, he showed a strong aptitude for math, especially when it came to dollars and cents, and used this skill in youthful ventures such as selling cherry-rum to soldiers and owning livestock.

Despite his stated preference for easier work, P. T. was only fifteen when his father died, forcing the young man to support his mother and siblings by working in the family's country store. Over the next few years, he took on several other enterprises, additionally working as a clerk and a lottery agent, where he learned a great deal about the power of marketing.

If life wasn't busy enough, in the summer of 1829 he met Charity Hallett, a "fair, rosy-cheeked, buxom-looking" seamstress from Fairfield, and was immediately smitten. By November 8 they were married, and within four years, they would welcome their first daughter, Caroline. Over the next thirteen years, they would have three more girls.

In 1831, Barnum started his own newspaper in Danbury, the *Herald of Freedom and Truth,* which he used to further his own agenda, including his strong belief in Universalism. He also used the paper to "speak the truth" as he saw it about other members in the community, including one Deacon Seth Seeley, who accused

Portrait of P. T. Barnum, circa 1875

Barnum of libel and won. Barnum was consequently fined $100 and sentenced to serve sixty days in jail.

Being incarcerated didn't deter Barnum from continuing to edit his newspaper or holding court from his cell, entertaining dozens of visitors. At his liberation from jail on December 5, 1832, Barnum modestly orchestrated a grand spectacle to celebrate the freedom of the press that, according to the *New York Times,* included a band, a choir, a committee of "prominent citizens," and many speeches and toasts. It was followed by an enormous procession that featured forty horsemen, sixty private carriages, and Barnum himself in a special coach drawn by six horses, which paraded the three miles from the courthouse in Danbury to Barnum's home in Bethel.

Obviously, the penal system had done its job in reforming him.

In retrospect, it's clear that the spirit of the great showman had been sparked, and it was only a short time before Barnum would find himself in the spotlight once again.

In 1834, Barnum sold the family store and moved to New York City, where a year later, he discovered Joice Heth, a disabled African-American woman who claimed to be one hundred sixty-one years old and the nurse to infant George Washington. Thinking that he may have discovered something unusual that others might pay to see, he "acquired" documents that verified her story and then purchased the "rights" to exhibit her for $1,000. He then put his marketing might to work and before long had the public—and its money—flocking to his door.

Unfortunately, Heth died about a year later, and when an examination was done, it was determined that she had only been about eighty years old—a fact that Barnum met with "shock" and "indignation." Despite that, he claimed that "the public appears disposed to be amused even when they are conscious of being deceived."

If he had been unsure before then, making over $10,000 by exhibiting Heth left no doubt that an income—and quite a lucrative one—could be derived from lying to people, or simply taking advantage of their willful ignorance; the jerk within wasn't going to quibble over which it was.

Barnum put together a circus-like troupe and for the next few years toured the South and West as "Barnum's Grand Scientific and Musical Theater." Not in any way a prosperous venture, it did allow him to hone his prodigious theatrical skills and get a better sense of what people wanted to see.

In tough financial straits by 1841, Barnum was back in New York City with a renewed ambition and a plan for success. Cobbling together good references, promises of collateral he didn't have, and his own limitless bravado, he was able to acquire the struggling Scudder's American Museum on Broadway, including its modest collection of curiosities. He upgraded and expanded, and then relaunched it—with all the appropriate fanfare—as "Barnum's American Museum."

It was the hit that would make Barnum's name synonymous with showmanship.

Over the next twenty-three years, Barnum's American Museum would become one of the most famous attractions in the world, making him a fortune. As he had discovered, the public would tolerate his outrageous claims, true or not, as long as they felt they had been entertained in the process. In fact, it seemed like the bigger and louder of a jerk that Barnum acted in selling them "humbug" (as he referred to hype), the more the public embraced it. And he was more than happy to oblige.

Despite not always delivering on exactly what he promised, Barnum did provide an experience that people would be talking about long after they passed through "the egress" (another word for "exit" that Barnum made sound like a special exhibit in itself for people to enjoy). The American Museum was a wonder in itself, four buildings joined together to form an entertainment adventure unlike anything the world had known to that point. Festooned with lights and flags, it had a three-thousand-seat theater, giant paintings of exotic animals, a rooftop garden (that featured hot-air balloon rides), an enormous lecture hall, collections of unusual animals (both living and taxidermied), an aquarium, and wax figures of notable persons as well as a seemingly endless and ever-changing array of acts.

On any given day, a visitor might be thrilled by giants and midgets, jugglers and magicians, albinos and bearded women, conjoined twins and all manner of human oddity. The museum also had dozens of exhibitors demonstrating everything from African water dances to glassblowing.

Despite offering a cavalcade of legitimate entertainment, Barnum couldn't resist his jerk urges and would occasionally "exaggerate" to help get more people in through the door: He boasted a "great" working model of Niagara Falls, yet it was only eighteen inches tall; his woolly horse of the frozen Rockies was simply from Indiana. Then there were times when he would flat-out lie, as when he concocted one of greatest hoaxes of all time: the Feejee mermaid.

Early in the summer of 1842, newspapers around New York started receiving letters from various correspondents mentioning the imminent arrival of a Dr. J. Griffin, a naturalist from the British Lyceum of Natural History, who had obtained a mermaid that had been caught near the Feejee (Fiji) Islands in the South Pacific. Griffin was reluctant to display the specimen, but as "luck" would have it, Barnum had heard about the mermaid and wanted it at his museum. With the help of the press, Barnum—who conveniently had plenty of seductive mermaid images to publish and even distributed pamphlets regarding the subject—vigorously courted Griffin. The public, whipped into a frenzy by Barnum's machinations, demanded that the mermaid be exhibited. Bowing to the pressure, Griffin caved, allowing it to be shown for a week at nearby Concert Hall. When the response was overwhelming, he agreed to let it stay longer—at Barnum's American Museum, of course. People came in droves, filling the museum and Barnum's pockets, too.

What they quickly discovered, however, was that they had been duped. "Dr. Griffin" was no scientist but really Levi Lyman, an accomplice of Barnum's. The British Lyceum also didn't exist, and the mermaid itself was also a complete (and ugly) fraud, fashioned from the upper body of a desiccated monkey and the lower half of a fish. It had been on display in Boston for years, and Barnum, knowing it was a phony, had merely rented it from Boston showman Moses Kimball. Barnum had also sent the first letters to the newspapers that had generated the buzz, and with the unwitting help of the press, had managed to turn an old artifact that had been gathering dust into a genuine, moneymaking sensation.

The Feejee Mermaid was hardly the only time that Barnum would rely on his ability to be a lovable jerk. As mentioned, he went to great lengths to find all sorts of human "freaks," and then brought them to his museum so he could better exploit them.

Probably the most famous person Barnum took advantage of because of his unusual physical appearance was Bridgeport native Charles Sherwood Stratton, who would become known to history as Tom Thumb. Barnum first met the boy during a trip home to Connecticut in 1842, and realized immediately that the four-year-old, who only stood twenty-five inches tall and weighed fifteen pounds, would be a box-office smash. He made arrangements to bring young Charles (and his mother) to New York for exhibition, paying three dollars per week, plus room and board.

Barnum wasted no time making over Stratton, telling everyone he was eleven years old and teaching him to sing, dance, and do impressions. Cranking up his publicity machine, Barnum dubbed the boy General Tom Thumb—just arrived from England (although in what military an eleven-year-old would be able to attain such a rank wasn't really clear)—and unleashed him on the public. Gen. Tom Thumb quickly became one of Barnum's biggest acts ever, drawing thousands of visitors to the museum. By 1846, over four hundred thousand visitors had come through the turnstiles to see the diminutive performer.

Naturally, Barnum expanded the act; by the age of seven, Stratton was drinking wine and smoking cigars as part of the routine. He was also earning twenty-five dollars per week, so although the great impresario was profiting on the boy's physical handicap, he did treat and compensate his star well. A European tour was eventually arranged, and Gen. Tom Thumb was soon entertaining heads-of-state, including Queen Victoria. Soon, he was an international celebrity.

To be fair, Stratton never complained about Barnum's handling, and he and Barnum enjoyed a long, close, working friendship, from which they both made immense fortunes. Barnum was there to orchestrate—and publicize, of course—Stratton's grand wedding to fellow little person Lavinia Warren, and then eventually to honor Stratton's passing some forty-two years after they met.

Not all Barnum's relationships with his "talent" were as positive. Although he didn't have a formal relationship with the famed Siamese twins Chang and Eng Bunker when they came to America, Barnum did try to associate himself with them though they thought him "cheap and crude." He displayed wax representations of the twins at the museum and also published pamphlets detailing their history, misrepresenting his role in their rise to fame (Barnum had no part whatsoever). Unlike few other sideshow performers, the Bunkers were able to parlay their deformity into significant wealth, which they used to buy a North Carolina plantation, where they lived with their wives for decades. Only when they needed the money to help support their twenty-one children did they finally turn to Barnum. In 1860, they played a limited engagement at the museum, followed by an extended European tour organized by Barnum, which was lucrative for all involved.

Barnum also had some legitimate successes in which he didn't have to exaggerate or lie about the talent he had discovered, as was the case with Jenny Lind, the "Swedish Nightingale." Barnum arranged and wildly promoted the European singing sensation's tour of the United States in 1850, turning her into even a bigger star. Lind's vocal talent truly matched Barnum's fanfare, and was one example of why the public was so willing to give him the benefit of the doubt despite his being a jerk.

With the American Museum doing well and his place in the entertainment world deeply entrenched, Barnum moved back to Bridgeport in November 1848, but not to any shabby old shack. Sparing no expense and needing a residence large enough to contain his ego, he had an opulent Moorish Revival mansion built, a grand three-story edifice that sat upon seventeen acres and was surrounded by conservatories, stables, and gardens. He named it Iranistan, and it marked the beginning of an era that saw him invest heavily in the Park City, with occasionally disastrous results.

Barnum had dreams of developing Bridgeport into an industrial metropolis, and to bring that to fruition, he backed the Jerome Manufacturing Company, taking on much of the clock-making enterprise's debt. Unfortunately, the company went bankrupt, and by 1855, almost all of Barnum's fortune was wiped out. On top of that, Iranistan burned to the ground two years later.

Humbled and bankrupt, Barnum was forced to sell his American Museum and other enterprises. He was also ridiculed by critics, who saw Barnum's demise as his comeuppance for the numerous lies and hoaxes he had perpetrated on the public.

Of course, Barnum's mighty entrepreneurial spirit wasn't snuffed out so easily. He penned an autobiography, modestly titled *The Life of P. T. Barnum, Written by Himself,* which became a best seller. He also wrote *Humbugs of the World* and then later, another very popular book called *The Art of Money Getting,* in which he shared the details of business strategies that he had employed— and that any ordinary person could also employ—to build great wealth.

Many of the ideas he focused on are still valid today, sound concepts like "whatever you do, do it with all your might," "let hope predominate, but be not too visionary," "advertise your business" and, most importantly, "avoid debt." But he also had the audacity to suggest (without a hint of irony) practices like "don't blab" and "preserve integrity." Coming from someone who launched his career on aggressively using all the hype he could muster to pass off an eighty-year-old crippled woman as a one hundred sixty-one-year-old former nurse to George Washington, and then later, a decrepit monkey sewn together with a fish as a mermaid—all just to trick people into paying admission for his museum—this advice seems a tad hypocritical.

Still, people ate it up. Barnum toured extensively, giving lectures about how to create a fortune, and as it turned out, it was a great way to remake his. By 1860, the fifty-year-old was a wealthy man once again, able to buy back most of his prior assets, including the American Museum.

Although things were looking up for Barnum, the nation was not in such great shape. The outbreak of the Civil War in 1861 put a crimp in the entertainment business, although people were always happy to have diversion from the fighting and bloodshed. An avowed abolitionist, Barnum found himself becoming more involved with the slavery cause, and ultimately in politics.

Not surprisingly, with his prevarication skills, Barnum realized what many jerks do—that perhaps a career in public office would be for him. Declaring politics as "distasteful," he nonetheless held his nose and ran for the Connecticut legislature as a Republican, winning the first of two consecutive terms in 1865. He tried to run for US Congress in 1867, but apparently the voting public didn't think Barnum was quite a big enough jerk for that stage, and he lost. A few years later, in 1875, he would win a single, twelve-month term as mayor of Bridgeport. Despite his grandstanding tendencies, most of his time in office was productive and uneventful.

Before he would occupy the mayor's seat, however, Barnum would have a few more ups and downs. In 1865, his beloved American Museum was destroyed by fire, and although he rebuilt nearby, it burned again in 1868, almost forcing him out of the museum business altogether. He kept one smaller museum open, which was at the center of one of the greatest shams in archaeological history.

Barnum is credited for saying, "There's a sucker born every minute" (a jerk-like proclamation if there ever was one), but as it turns out, the great showman may never have said it—although it may have been said *about* him and his unmatched ability to separate people from their money. In this particular instance, Barnum was actually hoaxing a bunch of hoaxers, and in turn, hoaxing everyone else.

In 1869, a remarkable discovery was made at the farm of William "Stub" Newell in upstate New York, near the small town of Cardiff. While having a well dug on his property, the farmer claimed that workers had unearthed the petrified remains of a human being who measured over ten feet in height! Dubbing the find the "Cardiff Giant," Newell set up a tent and charged twenty-five cents a head to see the amazing sight. Thousands showed up, and before long, he was able to sell a portion of the rights for $30,000 to a group of investors led by David Hannum, who moved it to Syracuse so even more could witness the wonder.

As soon as Barnum heard about the fantastic artifact, he sent an agent to investigate. The agent reported the details—including the size of the crowds lining up to see it—to Barnum, who then immediately made an offer of $50,000 to Hannum for the rights to display it in his New York City museum. The offer was rejected.

Being a jerk—and recognizing a scam when he saw one—Barnum knew exactly what to do. He had his own ancient behemoth carved and put it on exhibition in his museum. He then told people that he had acquired the real Cardiff Giant, and that the other one up in Syracuse was a fake.

With the full fury of Barnum's media might behind it, his Cardiff Giant was soon outdrawing the original one, which didn't sit well with Hannum. Knowing that Barnum's was phony, he allegedly made the enduring "sucker" comment about those going to see it.

Ironically, Hannum sued Barnum for libel for suggesting that his Syracuse Cardiff Giant was a fraud. When the case went before a judge, however, Stub Newell, the farmer who originally discovered it, was forced to admit under oath that he and a partner had created the figure, and then had planted it to be found by the unsuspecting farm hands. It had been a hoax from the start, so the charges against Barnum were dismissed since he had been accurate in calling the other giant a fake.

As he was nearing his sixtieth birthday, the showman formally retired from entertainment, but he was still P. T. Barnum. He wouldn't stay out of the limelight for long—in fact, it was only about a year. In 1870 he started laying the groundwork for his return to center stage. Or actually, the center ring.

The idea of a circus was hardly a new concept, but with Barnum's involvement, it would reach new levels of popularity and profitability, and ultimately be his legacy. Although Barnum was initially invited to collaborate with a few partners from the Midwest, it wasn't long before Barnum himself, with his name and fame, was at the forefront. On April 10, 1871, "P. T. Barnum's Grand Traveling Museum, Menagerie, Caravan and Hippodrome" opened with much acclaim in Brooklyn, New York.

Featuring many of his old performers and contributors from the American Museum, plus, as he put it, "the largest group of wonders ever known," Barnum then billed it as only one of the biggest egomaniacs known to history could: "The Greatest Show on Earth."

It was a smash hit. Within a few years, he needed a bigger space for the circus for when it was home in New York, which led to the construction of the New York Hippodrome, at the time the largest public amusement venue ever, with seating for over ten thousand. Built at a cost of $150,000—equal to about $3 million today—it was a lavish showplace and hosted the circus for many years before expanding to other events, eventually becoming known as Madison Square Garden.

Barnum, ever the innovator, moved his circus around the country via railroad, which allowed the operation to travel easier and faster, meaning it could reach more places and play more shows, and thus generate more revenue.

Although he was enjoying great success with the circus, Barnum did endure some personal tragedy, as his wife of forty-two years, Charity, passed away in 1872. Maybe it was the era or his personal resiliency, but within a year, he was remarried, this time to Nancy Fish, an English woman who was forty years his junior. Was it a case of a trophy wife or a gold digger? Later gaining a significant inheritance after Barnum's death, Nancy would marry into money and privilege twice more, eventually ending up as a French baroness.

But the circus was opening up new vistas, leading to world tours and bringing in considerable income. As always, Barnum was constantly trying to outdo himself, acquiring new attractions and creating sensations, never shying from controversy.

In 1881, a year after joining forces with James Bailey's "Great London Show," Barnum purchased Jumbo, the largest-known elephant in captivity. At the time, Jumbo had been the most beloved attraction at the London Zoo and adored across England, so his sale to the brash American showman was a bitter pill for the reserved British to swallow. For Barnum, the scorn of a nation made the deal all that much sweeter.

England's loss was America's gain, and the nearly twelve-foot-tall Jumbo was another incredibly popular—and lucrative—attraction for Barnum. Sadly, Jumbo was accidentally killed by a train while on tour in Canada during September 1885. Ever able to capitalize, Barnum had the mighty beast stuffed and mounted, and continued to exhibit it.

Jumbo's demise couldn't slow down the momentum of Barnum's circus endeavors, but time did begin its inevitable drag on the dynamic showman. Nearing his eightieth birthday, the decades in the spotlight and on stage as well as on the road touring—not to mention the energies he expended on politics, writing, lecturing, and proselytizing about Universalism (still his religion of choice)—started catching up to Barnum. Although his mind remained as keen and ebullient as ever, his physical health began to suffer, forcing him to pass more control of his circus endeavors over to Bailey.

Even when the end was very near, the eighty-one-year-old Barnum, ever the egomaniac, still couldn't resist the urge to make headlines—literally. After having told reporters that no one was ever praised until after they were dead, the *New York Sun* ran his obituary on March 24, 1891, across the top of the front page (where else?) of the evening edition under the banner "Great And Only Barnum—He Wanted To Read His Obituary—Here It Is."

Two weeks later, on April 7, Barnum asked about the receipts from the box office the previous evening at Madison Square Garden; a few hours later, the consummate showman bowed out silently in his sleep.

Although a younger Barnum had once admitted that "my prime objective has been to put money in my purse," when he died, Barnum had overcome the years of openly being a jerk to the public—who realized that it had been part of the act—to become one of the most beloved characters of his era. Part of his redemption also came from his generosity; although a "profitable philanthropist," he was a philanthropist nonetheless, and that included giving tens of thousands to Universalist causes, to Tufts College to establish a museum of natural history (the grateful university's mascot is still called Jumbo), and to various local charities.

Taken as a whole, Barnum's life is one of the most amazing in American history. He put entertainment on the grandest of stages, and in the process, brought to light some of the most sensational, curious, and wonderful items and people ever to exist. His legacy can still be witnessed in every loud commercial or entertainment spectacular, while his presence is still felt across the state at the numerous places named in his honor.

As you head to the egress of this chapter, one final story.

Even from his grave, however, the Prince of Humbugs still had one last hoax left. In his Bridgeport office was a wooden crate imprinted with the words, "Not to Be Opened Until the Death of P. T. Barnum." After the mighty impresario had been laid to rest, the members of his staff eagerly opened the box, hoping that it might be full of cash or some other significant financial reward for their years of service.

When the lid was removed, they found that Barnum's last act of generosity was a copy of his autobiography for each staff member—a final parting gift that only a jerk would think was a treasure.

CHAPTER 10

Philip Musica:
Multiple Identities, One Jerk

What's in a name? That which we call a rose
By any other name would smell as sweet . . .

William Shakespeare never met Philip Musica or F. Donald Coster, but clearly the Bard understood that no matter what name a jerk goes by, he is still a jerk.

In the case of Musica/Coster, creating multiple identities gave one man a unique opportunity to perpetrate numerous criminal acts, including tax fraud and bootlegging, as well as masterminding one of the largest financial scandals of the twentieth century. At different times he was a grocer, an importer, a chemist, a physician, a law enforcement agent, a spy, a corporate executive, a socialite, and even a potential presidential candidate. Before he was through, Musica would fool thousands and pocket millions.

Sure, when it comes to duplicitous dealings and ripping off investors, the name Bernie Madoff may now come immediately to mind, but in 1938, the headlines in Connecticut—and across the United States—were touting the sensational scandal at the multimillion dollar corporation McKesson & Robbins, Ltd., and in particular, the downfall of its CEO, F. Donald Coster. Unlike Madoff, however, Coster wouldn't be brought to justice or serve time in prison for his dishonest acts, choosing instead to end his felonious work as a jerk—and his own crime-riddled double life—with a revolver.

Long before he would become a "respectable" resident of Connecticut's Gold Coast and be known as the aspiring Wall Street tycoon F. Donald Coster, Philip Mariano Fausto Musica was born in 1877 in Naples, Italy, to Antonio and Assunta Musica. The Musicas would have a total of four sons and four daughters, making for a feisty clan that would become a "crime family" in the

*Philip Musica (seated, left) with his attorney Sam Reich,
taken at his home during his arrest in 1938*
CONNECTICUT MAGAZINE

truest sense, eventually all becoming involved with Philip's illegal ventures.

The Musicas immigrated to the United States in 1880, coming through Ellis Island and settling in the Little Italy district of lower Manhattan. Although their Five Points neighborhood was a slum that could be tough and where crime was rampant, Antonio Musica seemed to be a legitimate businessman, starting out with a barber shop, and then with the profit from that, opening A. Musica and Son, a small grocery store. Using his connections back in Italy, he was able to directly import specialty products from Italy—cheese, olive oil, pasta, spices, etc.—and by cutting out wholesalers, sold his items for lower prices than other shops.

Philip quit school at fourteen to get into the family business, helping out in the retail part of the shop at first, but eventually getting involved in the importing aspect. Within a few years, he demonstrated a knack for successful business and jerk-like behavior (maybe they go hand in hand?), deciding that the honest profits from simply undercutting the competition weren't enough; he soon took advantage of New York City's notoriously corrupt waterfront and began to bribe dock officials to alter bills of landing to state that Musica's shipments weighed much less than they actually did. Lower rates meant lower tariffs, which in turn meant decreased operating costs and larger profits.

The scam was enormously successful—with the money they were saving through bribery, Philip Musica was able to expand the operation. Soon the Musicas were one of the largest importers in the city, making over $500,000 annually, and providing enough income that the clan was able to move to a much better home and community in the Bay Ridge section of Brooklyn. Supremely charming and manipulative, Philip Musica was also able to parlay his manufactured prosperity to advantages beyond financial, making key political and personal connections that would aid him later on.

All was going well, but the good times were to be short-lived. In 1909, during a public crackdown on waterfront crime, Musica's phony weight scheme was discovered. Philip and his father Antonio were arrested for tax evasion, fraud, and bribery.

But the young Musica was crafty. Feigning sincerity, he was able to convince the authorities that he had been an unwilling victim of a corrupt system that had necessitated bribery. Then, expertly playing the role of the good son, he agreed to plead guilty in exchange for having the charges against his father Antonio dropped. On October 29, Philip was fined $5,000 and sentenced to a year in the Elmira Reformatory in upstate New York.

Musica was serving his time in jail without incident when on April 12, 1910, he was mysteriously pardoned by US president William Howard Taft. The hefty fine was also remitted—apparently, the contacts Musica had made earlier paid off sooner than he anticipated.

Following his release in 1910, Musica eschewed the import business and went back to a different area of family expertise: hair. Rather than cutting it this time, however, Musica decided to form the United States Hair Company, an enterprise that provided high-quality human hair for stylish hairpieces and extensions, which were popular at the time. Setting up on Front Street on the edge of the Financial District, he made himself president of the company, and by using his old import business contacts, was able to arrange to have hair—which was selling for as much as eighty dollars per pound at the time—brought to North America from hard-to-track sources throughout Europe.

Or so it appeared.

Being a jerk, Musica couldn't run the business the honest way. Using the connections that Antonio had established during his time as a barber, Philip was able to have the worthless cuttings from barber shop floors collected and packed in crates, to which a top layer of good hair was added. To keep authorities from discovering his scheme, he had the crates—consisting of "the cheapest of hair and the finest of tissue paper," according to the *New York Times*—shipped back and forth across the Atlantic, which increased the paper value of the actually worthless cargo.

Still, using his keen interpersonal skills and charisma, as well as a fair amount of chicanery, he was able to convince investors that United States Hair was a $2 million company with numerous assets abroad, most of which were phony branch offices in England and France set up by Musica. By doing this, he was able to borrow nearly $1 million from twenty-two different banks, from which he was able to divert nearly $600,000 to his own accounts by falsifying invoices and pocketing the payments.

Musica also cashed in when the company went public—he offered shares in the business on the New York Curb Exchange (which would later become the American Stock Exchange). As the primary stockholder, he instantly became a millionaire when shares shot up to ten dollars each.

With the ill-gotten resources, the entire Musica family once again was living the high life, none higher than Philip. He bought his parents and siblings a bigger house in Bay Ridge while he took up residence at the ritzy Knickerbocker Hotel, right in the heart of Manhattan. He wore expensive suits from the finest Fifth Avenue tailors, with matching shoes and spats, and indulged heavily in New York's nightlife scene. He also ran in the top social circles and with Wall Street executives, counting luminaries such as famed opera singer Enrico Caruso among his friends.

It's now easy to see that United States Hair was a house of cards, and it was only a matter of time before creditors and stockholders would figure out that they were being swindled by Musica. The end came in the spring of 1913 when Musica and his father went to borrow another $370,000 against a new shipment. By then they were already heavily in arrears to a few lenders, making the banks suspicious enough to send investigators to check on United States Hair's "merchandise" down at the docks. When all the crates were opened and it was discovered that there was only about $250 worth of actual hair, the jig was up. The banks, suddenly realizing that they were out thousands of dollars, immediately filed criminal charges.

Police descended upon Musica's apartment and the family home in Bay Ridge, but all they found were more piles of worthless hair and a book on extradition laws, opened to a chapter about Honduras. With the aid of private detectives, authorities were able to track the Musicas to New Orleans, where they were preparing to sail to freedom. Dramatically storming the decks of the S.S. *Heridia* just as it was preparing to cast off, the police quickly apprehended the entire family holed up in a stateroom under the name Martin.

In what would be an eerie foreshadowing, it was reported by the *Times* that when confronted by police, Philip Musica pulled out a revolver and tried to kill himself; other sources suggest it was his father Antonio who attempted suicide. Whoever it was, both father and son were taken back to New York to be arraigned.

Similar to when he had been caught in the previous swindle, Philip Musica took full blame for all the illegal activity to protect his seventy-two-year-old father, even though the elder Musica's signature had been on many of the phony invoices. He again cut a deal with prosecutors, pleading to grand larceny and exchanging his freedom for that of the rest of his family.

This time Musica was sentenced to "The Tombs," the Manhattan Detention Complex, which allowed him to stay in close contact with the district attorney's office. The cozy relationship with the authorities was important because Musica would spend his jail time giving the district attorney significant information about his illegal hair business activities. It appears that he was also a jailhouse snitch, reporting on the illicit activities and other crimes of fellow inmates at the Tombs.

Thanks to Musica's cooperation, his sentence was commuted to less than three years and he was released in 1916. With political tensions ramping up and World War I soon to begin, Musica was able to engage his contacts and employ his skills as a tattletale, becoming part of an effort to find German spies in the United States. When the war formally started, he got involved in trying to track down draft dodgers.

It was also during this time that Musica took his first alias, working for the district attorney under the name William Johnson. Musica apparently used the false identity as a means to settle some old scores, trying to get indictments against a few former business associates, including an attempt to send one to the gallows. His efforts eventually failed, and with them, so did the brief crime-fighting career of William Johnson.

It was 1920, and both Johnson and Musica had now vanished, but the man who had lived in both of their skins was far from gone. He created his third persona, Frank D. Costa, who would make a foray into a new line of business: bootlegging.

Prohibition had just officially come into existence, making the manufacturing, sale, and transportation of alcohol in the United States an illegal act. Therefore, to get alcohol to the millions who still wanted it, thousands of illicit ventures were launched, from unauthorized production and importation to fraudulent bottling and private speakeasy clubs. Musica/Costa found his own clever niche in the "industry," forming the Adelphi Pharmaceutical Manufacturing Company, which specialized in creating "medicinal" products such as hair tonic and cosmetics that were high in alcohol content—*really* high [*wink wink*] in alcohol content.

The scam was that other bootleggers would purchase large quantities of Adelphi's overly alcohol-saturated—yet still legally manufactured—products, and then distill the alcohol out of them for use in making liquor. In essence, Costa's company was supplying other criminals, and as with his prior ventures, it became immensely profitable in a brief amount of time. Also like his other schemes, it would be short-lived; by 1923, Adelphi was no more, due in part to a squabble with a business partner.

Speaking of partners, it was around this time that Musica took on one in his personal life. Given he was a cheat (and jerk), it's no surprise that he would wreck someone else's marriage to get the woman he wanted. The target of his affection was Carol Jenkins Hubbard, the wife of former business partner and soon-to-be victim of Musica's conniving efforts, Edward Hubbard.

Musica systematically went about destroying Hubbard's credibility, first with his other business partners (by forging documents to imply Hubbard was embezzling), next at his church (sending an anonymous letter suggesting that Hubbard was having an affair with a young girl), and finally with authorities (manufacturing evidence that resulted in Hubbard's arrest). By the time Musica was done, Hubbard was disgraced and Carol divorced him. She immediately married Musica in 1921.

Although Adelphi—and Frank D. Costa—were now defunct, Musica was far from leaving the financial community or done reinventing himself. In fact, what would turn out to be his most successful incarnation was ready to do business. It was now time for F. Donald Coster to step upon the stage.

Musica would eventually provide an impressive biography of F. Donald Coster for *Who's Who,* with intriguing details that painted a picture of a true Renaissance man. Allegedly born in Washington, D.C., in 1884—at 125 A Street NE, the site of the US Supreme Court, no less—it was claimed that Coster had studied abroad at the prestigious University of Heidelberg in Germany, earning a PhD in 1909 and an MD in 1911. An expert in chemistry, he then eventually returned to the United States and had supposedly practiced medicine in New York from 1912 to 1914 before deciding to try his hand in the world of commerce.

Although Musica had a shiny new alias, he was still in the same old business of bootlegging. To avoid being recognized, he initially set up operations in the quiet upstate New York town of Mount Vernon. He called his latest venture Girard & Co., and it prospered, manufacturing alleged pharmaceutical items that had (conveniently) higher-than-necessary amounts of alcohol. Girard sold a portion of its products to drug stores to maintain legitimacy, but the major share of its inventory was purchased by bootleggers.

As with his other enterprises, Musica/Coster brought his family on board, also under pseudonyms. His brothers George and Robert changed their surnames to Dietrich and were given high-ranking positions within the company. His other brother, Arthur, was now known as George Venard, and was installed as president of W. W. Smith & Co., a separate phony company set up by Philip that would become Girard & Co.'s biggest customer—on paper.

Although bootleggers were purchasing large quantities of illegal alcohol through Girard & Co., the creation of the fictional business gave the Musicas the ability to "cook the books." With the brothers all in key positions, they were able to create the illusion that orders were being placed through W. W. Smith, products were being shipped from Girard & Co., and that revenue was coming in. Nothing was actually being purchased—they were just shifting funds around in a manner that simulated sales. In reality, the Musicas were skimming money and pocketing profits.

Not satisfied with the scope of the scheme, Musica/Coster decided it was time to expand Girard & Co. He brought in Julian F. Thompson, a legitimate financial expert who was working for Bond & Goodwin, Inc., a major Wall Street investment house, to examine the company's books. At the time, it wasn't customary for accountants to check anything other than balance sheets, so without ever seeing the company's inventory, Thompson was impressed enough by Girard & Co.'s bottom line to recommend that they be extended a substantial line of credit.

With the new infusion of capital, Musica/Coster was able to move Girard & Co. to Fairfield, where he opened a new and larger plant in 1925. A year later, he again took advantage of Thompson's unwitting aid and influence, using him to procure $1 million from a number of Connecticut investors in order to set up his largest and most lucrative swindle of all.

Having learned (somewhat) from his past failures, Musica/Coster realized one of the keys of sustaining a fraud was the necessity of mixing in legitimate concerns to keep suspicion at bay. To that extent, he purchased controlling interest of McKesson & Robbins, a one-hundred-and-five-year-old corporation renowned for being one of the biggest pharmaceutical distributors in the nation. When Coster came along in 1926, McKesson & Robbins had fallen on hard times, relegated to one broken-down factory in Brooklyn that was turning out tooth powder and a few other odd products.

All that was left was the company's venerable name and reputation, which was what Coster was really after.

For his efforts, the earnest Julian Thompson was made treasurer of McKesson & Robbins, a decision by Musica/Coster that would ultimately lead to his own downfall. To start out, however, Thompson would be a significant part of the effort to get McKesson & Robbins back on its financial feet.

Despite being a complete fraud, Coster—"the business genius" as hailed by Thompson—did have some legitimate financial acumen. He immediately shut down the Brooklyn facility and moved what working equipment there was to the new Girard & Co. plant in Fairfield. He then went about gaining McKesson & Robbins some honest profits by putting out a new line of pharmaceutical products. Of course, generously mixed in with these new items were high-alcohol bootlegger-friendly ones, which quickly became best sellers.

Wanting to be closer to his factory—and farther away from anyone in New York who could possibly identify him—Coster moved with his wife to Fairfield in 1926. They bought a stately eighteen-room mansion on Mill Plain Road that was modeled after an Italian villa with stucco walls and a terracotta tile roof. They decorated it in "a heavy, bourgeois manner," according to the *New Yorker,* including one room made to resemble "a sultan's bedchamber." It was nestled on a well-manicured seven-acre parcel and was also home to two dozen chows, a Saint Bernard, a sheep, and a parrot named Ricky.

Coster also spent lavishly on recreational activities, such as $125,000 (well over $1.5 million today) on a grand 133-foot yacht, which he named *Carolita* after his wife and used primarily to entertain close friends and exclusive business acquaintances. He was also a member of the New York and Black Rock yacht clubs, and he bought a number of racehorses and expensive cars.

Although Coster endeavored to physically stay out of the public eye, he kept busy in local circles, serving on the board of directors of the Bridgeport City Trust Co., founding a cardiac clinic for the poor in Bridgeport, and donating to various charitable causes around town. He regularly attended the Methodist church, and became involved with politics, supporting local Republican candidates. To many, he seemed like a respectable entrepreneur.

Musica/Coster kept a small set of executive offices in midtown Manhattan, which he would visit only when necessary. At the time no one thought it was all that unusual that the reticent tycoon kept such a low profile—he hardly ever visited the Business District in Manhattan, rarely stayed overnight, and then always hurried to Grand Central Station to catch the first train back to Fairfield. If anyone had suspected the secret life he was keeping, they might've paid more attention.

Possibly hoping to somehow erase his earlier days as a scammer, Coster worked tirelessly behind the scenes—with treasurer Thompson as the public face of his efforts—to grow McKesson & Robbins substantially, establishing and selling stock for subsidiaries in Canada, Maryland, and London, among other places. In 1927, Coster was able to broker a megadeal with the backing of Wall Street investment houses that brought sixty-six family-owned regional wholesale drug companies under McKesson & Robbins's control; the individual owners benefitted by exchanging their private, family-owned stock for McKesson & Robbins's securities, therefore avoiding substantial inheritance taxes and other issues.

These efforts were immensely lucrative for the company, and in turn, its largest shareholder, Coster. The stock market crash in October 1929 put a bit of a damper on McKesson & Robbins's growth, with Coster allegedly losing an estimated $1 million of his own money. But the company was seemingly able to right itself quickly under Coster's strong leadership.

Interestingly, despite his perceived ability to successfully guide the company in economic matters, "The Duke," as McKesson & Robbins employees unflatteringly referred to Coster when he wasn't around, wasn't exactly beloved. He kept to himself, didn't socialize with anyone outside the top tier of management, abhorred anyone who asked too many questions, and was often brusque with low-level employees, to whom he referred as "the maggots."

Over the course of the twelve years Coster was based in Connecticut, he made McKesson & Robbins an economic force in the state and beyond, employing hundreds in thirty-five states and seemingly withstanding the clutches of the Great Depression. By 1937, McKesson & Robbins was the third-largest drug company in the world, claiming annual sales of $174 million, profits of $4 million, and assets of $87 million.

Such success attracted national attention for Coster. In December of 1937, leaders of the Republican Party courted Coster to make a run for the presidency against Franklin Delano Roosevelt. The "publicity-shy" CEO, however, politely declined.

It seemed that F. Donald Coster was on top of the world. For Philip Musica, however, it was all about to come crashing down yet again.

While the legitimate retail sales segment of McKesson & Robbins had been going strong over the years, Coster/Musica had surreptitiously kept his focus on another aspect of the corporation. Citing his "background" in chemistry, the grade school dropout had devoted much of his energy to the division involved with the supposed buying and selling of international crude drugs. Primarily working through the Canadian subsidiary of McKesson & Robbins, Ltd., this area was handled exclusively by Coster and the "Dietrich" brothers (aka Robert and George Musica), who dealt extensively with W. W. Smith Co. and its president "George Venard," better known as their brother Arthur Musica.

In a complicated ruse that involved fraudulent billing, phony sales receipts, and phantom inventory (methods they had used in their previous scams), the Musicas were using this operation as a means to bilk McKesson & Robbins out of millions. Rather than actually going into company bank accounts, sales income went directly into their pockets!

Yeah, despite what appeared to be overwhelming honest success, Musica/Coster had been up to his old jerk ways all along.

Musica/Coster's losses during the Wall Street collapse had been a lot more extensive than what was reported, and he had spent the next eight years trying to recoup them by siphoning off funds through the crude drug division of McKesson & Robbins.

The Musicas might have gotten away with it if it weren't for McKesson & Robbins's honest treasurer Julian Thompson, who noticed some discrepancies in the books in 1936. He questioned why the crude drug department, which had shown substantial profits on paper, had always reinvested in more inventory rather than diverting funds to other struggling parts of the company. Coster had quieted him with the excuse that he didn't want to tamper with a division that had been going so well, but the issue had stuck in the back of Thompson's mind. The following year, when funds were needed to shore up other divisions and Coster suggested that the company take a $3 million loan—despite showing a healthy bottom line because of the crude drug department—rather than simply transfer money around, Thompson got suspicious.

Later saying that he owed it to the stockholders, Thompson started secretly investigating the crude drug division as well as McKesson & Robbins's international subsidiaries. Over the next few months, he discovered that it was all almost nonexistent, and that W. W. Smith and Co. was also a sham. After realizing that something was terribly amiss and that an enormous number of assets was missing, he finally confronted Coster at the end of November 1938, in the hope that Coster would tell him that the money was hidden somewhere within the company.

Coster stalled Thompson, who continued to press for answers and concrete evidence of what had happened. Eventually, Coster finally snapped, shaking a finger in Thompson's face and threatening, "If you do anything to wreck the credit of McKesson & Robbins, you are going to regret it!"

While Thompson was trying to decide what to do, Coster, remarkably, moved to have the corporation put into a temporary equity receivership, meaning McKesson & Robbins was stopped from doing business and its books were impounded. On December 6, the Securities Exchange Commission announced it was launching a formal investigation of McKesson & Robbins. The company's stock plummeted and the story made headlines, complete with pictures of the company's CEO, F. Donald Coster.

Henry Unterweiser, a veteran investigator for the New York Attorney General's office, saw the story of McKesson & Robbins's plight in the *Daily News* and thought that the disgraced Coster looked remarkably like the former convict Philip Musica, with whom he had worked when Musica was in the Tombs. He alerted investigators in the McKesson & Robbins case.

Given the sensational way that Musica's schemes previous to the McKesson & Robbins scandal had been so publicly exposed, it seems as though someone should've noticed the resemblance between Musica and Coster a lot sooner than 1938. Then again, when Musica was first making headlines in the early decades of the twentieth century, there were no television or nightly news programs on which his face would've been plastered. Newspapers weren't really nationwide enterprises, and even if they were, photography wasn't what it is today. It took a trained observer with a good memory to make the connection.

On December 13, 1938, Coster—along with George Dietrich and George Venard—were arrested for fraud and conspiracy. Coster, who claimed he was too sick to leave Fairfield, was processed at his home, where he immediately posted bail. After resisting officers for twenty minutes, he begrudgingly let himself be fingerprinted. Following up on Unterweiser's tip, Coster's prints were run against Musica's. They were, naturally, a match.

By the afternoon of December 15, newspapers and radio stations across the country were trumpeting the remarkable story of how the president of one of the most successful corporations in the nation was, in fact, a two-time felon who had swindled millions.

On December 16, the US Department of Justice got involved in the investigation, and a marshal was sent to the mansion on Mill Plain Road to arraign Coster on additional charges.

At the Coster home, things were quiet. According to Coster's brother-in-law, Leonard Jenkins, the former tycoon was drinking heavily and talking to no one other than Ricky the parrot.

Everyone in the house had heard the report of a federal marshal on the way, but Coster hadn't commented on it. Instead, he went upstairs—with a .38-caliber police revolver he had hidden on himself—and locked himself in the bathroom.

When the authorities arrived, Jenkins went to check on Coster, knocking on the bathroom door. A very tired-sounding Philip Musica said, "Yes, I'll be right out."

A moment later, a single gunshot rang out.

The door was broken down. Musica's body—rendered lifeless by the bullet through his right ear—was in the tub, his wire-rimmed glasses were in the sink, and the smoking revolver was on the floor.

In addition to a stunning scandal that would take years to unravel and where it was later determined that some $3.2 million was missing from McKesson & Robbins coffers, Musica left a grieving widow, three brothers to do penance for his schemes, and a four-page suicide note.

In the hand-written note, "Coster" proclaimed that he was one of the only "virtuous" individuals at McKesson & Robbins, and railed against all the bankers, lawyers, auditors, and other incompetents involved with the company, suggesting they were plotting against him. In the ultimate act of denial, he then wrote: "As God is my judge, I am the victim of Wall Street plunder and blackmail in a struggle for honest existence . . . Oh merciful God, bring the truth to light . . ."

When investigators were going through the house, they discovered that Musica had taken from his bedside table a plaque with a quote from Harriet Beecher Stowe inscribed on it, and had placed it by his sleeping wife before going upstairs to kill himself. The quote was: "When you get into a tight place and everything goes against you till it seems as if you just couldn't hold on a minute longer—never give up then, for that is just the place and time when the tide will turn."

Alas, the tide never turned for Philip Musica. He was a jerk right to the end.

CHAPTER 11

Samuel Colt:
The Jerk Who Won the West

If I can't be first, I won't be second in anything.

—SAMUEL COLT, 1844

If you ain't first, you're last.

—RICKY BOBBY, *TALLADEGA NIGHTS:*
THE BALLAD OF RICKY BOBBY, 2006

Chances are most people will recognize the second quote from the fictional race car driver portrayed by Will Ferrell before they even recognize the name Samuel Colt, let alone how Colt actually impacted the course of human events. Still, it's the unadulterated ambition of both—and the inherent jerkiness that comes with such unbridled ambition—that drives both stories.

For the purpose of this book, however, let's focus on Colt, who was one of the most influential inventors and industrialists in American history. His lasting contributions to munitions manufacturing—in particular, the popularization of the revolver—were only outsized by his ego and his ability to never let a little thing like morals or conscience get in the way of making a dollar. In short, if by making yourself incredibly wealthy and famous by creating better and more efficient weapons with which to kill people can be considered the work of a jerk, then Colt was a fantastic jerk.

Unlike some others, however, Colt warmly embraced his jerkiness, as illustrated by this comment from a letter to his brother: "It is better to be at the head of a louse than at the tail of a lion."

Samuel Colt was born on a farm near Hartford on July 19, 1814, one of eight children, to Christopher and Sarah Caldwell Colt. When Sam was only seven, his mother Sarah died, but like many men with large families, Christopher was soon remarried. His second wife, Olivia Sargent, was not exactly the motherly type, although she did her best with the large brood. When the Colts struggled financially, she placed her stepchildren with other family and friends, mostly in situations where they had to work for their keep. Sam was put with a farmer, and enjoyed a modest upbringing, tending to chores around the property. Similar to many children, the future inventor didn't care much for formal schooling despite possessing a keenly curious mind, practical intelligence, and natural mechanical ability.

In July of 1829, while working at a textile mill in Ware, Massachusetts, where his father was an agent, then fifteen-year-old Sam was able to fashion an underwater mine that he was able to detonate from shore with an electric cable and crude battery, an experiment he would repeat later on a much larger scale and with a more critical audience. At that point, however, the stunt—to which he was able to draw a crowd to witness by passing around handbills announcing the event—proved a testament to his budding ingenuity in terms of mechanical and self-promotional skills, talents that would eventually be key in creating his empire. The explosion was more massive than he planned, drenching many of the onlookers and not exactly endearing the enterprising young man to them.

Thirteen months later, Colt, eager for adventure, found himself headed to sea aboard the brig *Corvo* for the next year of his life, a critical period during which he not only was able to broaden his cultural horizons but also conceived one of his most important notions. According to Colt, it was while watching the ship's wheel turn during his long journey that he came up with the basic design of a rotating cylinder that would become the revolver, a weapon that could be fired faster and more efficiently.

While at sea, he carved some prototypes from wood, and when he returned to America in 1831, convinced his father to finance the production of actual guns. While he endeavored to get them manufactured, Colt constantly worked on various designs of the revolver as well as the concept of making it with interchangeable machined parts via an assembly line, a groundbreaking idea

COLONEL COLT.

Sketch of Samuel Colt
LIBRARY OF CONGRESS

in arms manufacturing that he believed would be the key to his eventual success. Soon, he devised a unique plan that not only helped him raise the funds he'd need but also provided him with an opportunity to further hone his promotional skills.

Having discovered the intoxicating properties of the recently formulated nitrous oxide, aka "laughing gas," Colt set himself up as "the celebrated Dr. Coult, of New York, London, and Calcutta," and began touring North America, putting on carnival-like demonstrations. He charged twenty-five cents admission and would entertain audiences by letting various patrons take hits of the gas and then perform outlandish feats under its influence. It's easy to imagine the bold and brash Colt embracing the role of the evening's ringmaster, leading the crowd in raucous shenanigans, filling their lungs with his laughing gas and his pockets with their money.

Meanwhile, his prototype revolvers, which had taken years to produce, were finally ready. Unfortunately, when the time came to test the weapons, one would not fire at all. The second one exploded, and up in smoke with it went any significant financial support he could expect from his father.

Over the next three years he focused on building up his bank account—and his showmanship—on the back of "Dr. Coult" while he worked out the design kinks of his revolvers. The money, however, went quickly; in 1834, he hired gunsmith John Pearson to refine his revolver prototypes, and Colt constantly struggled to stay ahead of expenses. Despite the fiscal crunch, he was soon able to obtain patents in England, France, and the United States for the first practical revolver.

Having a patent and realizing that he could not self-finance for much longer, the go-getting Colt turned to family and friends. Staked again by his wary father, conservative cousin Dudley Selden, and a few venture capitalists, he was able to raise enough funds to found the Patent Arms Manufacturing Company in Paterson, New Jersey, in April 1836. Only twenty-one years old, he was on the verge of making his mark as a death merchant.

Like many young men, the flamboyant Colt excelled at spending other people's money. He used much of the funds he had borrowed in the process of trying to drum up sales by wining and dining potential customers as well as throwing lavish parties for influential politicians he thought might be helpful for business. He often neglected to pay his gunsmith and creditors in addition to others in his employ—not a particularly successful business practice.

Although many appreciated Colt's generous attention and the quality of his weapons, it wasn't quite enough to get the volume of orders needed to make his company economically viable. A war with the Seminoles in Florida provided a significant order for Colt weapons—a small burst of success—but by 1842, the Patent Arms Manufacturing Company was forced to fold.

Colt, ever the ambitious entrepreneur, had other irons—and inventions—in the fire. At this point, he had returned to his experiments with underwater mines that could be controlled from shore, concentrating on improving the quality and potency of the blasts. In one rather public exhibition for the US Navy and a host of congressmen that echoed his earlier stunt, in April 1843 he successfully obliterated a sixty-ton schooner in the Potomac River with one of his mines, an imposing feat in a string of demonstrations that he figured would have the government clamoring for his manufacturing services.

Unfortunately, although the thousands who had gathered enjoyed the spectacle of Colt blowing up a ship, and the decision-making military and political folk in attendance were impressed with the scale of damage and potential for death, Colt was not able to reap any direct orders for his explosive underwater device.

The experiment wasn't a total failure, however. The US Army was interested in the charges he had created, and ordered a small amount of them. More importantly, however, to detonate the mine, Colt had fashioned—with the help of Samuel F. B. Morse, a recent acquaintance—a waterproof cable capable of carrying an electrical current. Realizing another use for the cable in that it could easily carry a telegraph signal under water, Colt was contracted to manufacture forty miles of the cable that would be laid from Washington to Baltimore.

Despite the promise of being on the ground floor of long-distance communication, Colt's waterproof cable company failed pretty quickly, due in no small part to Colt's management. He was still interested in making guns, and had continued tinkering with his revolver designs. Unbeknownst to Colt, fate was about to take a turn in his favor.

As Colt had been struggling financially in the four years since his Patent Arms gun factory had ceased operations, the weapons that had been manufactured in New Jersey and had been used in the war against the Seminoles had continued to perform well beyond the fighting in Florida. Colt revolvers had become the preferred weapon of the Western frontier, their reputation primarily made by then-notorious Texas Rangers who employed them to effectively dispatch Native Americans, Mexicans, and the occasional criminal. To those who were trying to "tame the savages," the name Colt had become synonymous with killing efficiency.

In 1846, war with Mexico broke out, and sensing another opportunity, Colt was able to win an endorsement from Capt. Samuel H. Walker, a battle-tested Texas Ranger, who praised the weapons and said (via a letter to Colt) that "without your pistols, we would not have had the confidence to have undertaken such daring adventures. . . . The people throughout Texas are anxious to procure your pistols & I doubt not you would find sale for a large number at this time."

Walker was right. Soon, Colt was able to win an order for one thousand guns and a $25,000 contract from the US Army. Captain Walker made a few suggestions that he thought would improve the weapon's effectiveness, including making it larger in both caliber (.44) and number of shots (six). Colt incorporated these changes into the new model, which became known as the Walker Colt, and then in January 1847 starting producing them at Eli Whitney Jr.'s armory in New Haven. One of the most powerful handguns ever produced, it proved to be quite a capable weapon.

This fortuitous turn of events also provided the success that Colt needed to permanently reenter the munitions manufacturing business, and once he began production, he never looked back. Following the Walker Colt, he was able to win another large army contract, and with it, the much-needed major financial backing that would allow him to start a new armory. This time, however, the prodigal son returned to open up shop in his hometown of Hartford.

In August 1847, Colt leased a factory on Pearl Street, hired a sizable work force and got to making guns. In the time from when he had first envisioned producing guns on an assembly line, precision machine manufacturing had made great strides, and Colt was able to incorporate these changes into his process. Before long, quality Colt revolvers were being produced quickly in Hartford, and Colt's reputation—and business—really began to take off.

Within two years, Colt had paid off his creditors and was finally turning a profit from manufacturing weapons that were becoming increasingly popular, including the 1849 Pocket Revolver, which also packed surprising power for a handgun. One of the best-selling Colt firearms ever, some 325,000 pocket revolvers came off assembly lines and found their way to the front lines of America's westward expansion, helping blaze the way for the Gold Rush of 1849. With every Native American cut down or dispute settled by a pocket revolver, the Colt legend grew.

Of course, the former "Dr. Coult" was actively involved in shaping his own legend, employing the showmanship gained from those years traveling the country putting on nitrous oxide demonstrations. Long before the term "product placement" was conceived, Colt was focused heavily on marketing, doing everything he could to make sure that his weapon was in the hands of decision makers. In addition to the aforementioned penchant for plying prospective customers with alcohol and fine food (and the occasional bribe), Colt would constantly make gifts of his guns to military personnel and politicians; some sources suggest that he gave away over two thousand five hundred weapons to "help business."

He was also fond of keeping good relations with journalists. If a newspaper ran a story about a Colt being used successfully on a grizzly bear, Indian, or Mexican, he would request one hundred copies of the publication and send the editor a pistol as a gift.

Colt also frequently traveled abroad, bringing his celebrity and weapons to Europe—a place where war was also big business. "The good people of this world are very far from being satisfied with each other and my arms are the best peacemakers," he said, and with Italy, Austria, France, and Russia, among other countries, all regularly embroiled in conflict during this period, Colt played no favorites, eagerly selling weapons to any side in a dispute. Or both sides.

Actually, it was this habit of unabashedly providing weapons to all paying parties involved in a fight (including Native Americans—so much for the romantic notion of Colt's "Peacemaker" being instrumental in the settling of the Old West) that would raise some questions regarding Colt's ethics—or more precisely, would erase all doubt that he might just be a money-grubbing jerk.

Regardless of to whom he was selling—and he sold to everyone—before long his brand had became so well known that the name "Colt" essentially replaced the word "pistol" in common vernacular. Between the deadly efficiency of his weapons and his uncanny ability for self-promotion, Colt's fortune grew rapidly, making him a millionaire well before his fortieth birthday. He was even able to buy himself a military commission: Colonel Samuel Colt. Soon, the quote "The Lord made man, but Sam Colt made them equal," was familiar to all.

Colt unabashedly indulged in the extravagant lifestyle that comes with great fame and wealth, hobnobbing within the upper circles of society. It was around this period, in 1852, that he first met Elizabeth Hart Jarvis, the daughter of well-to-do Episcopalian minister William Jarvis. Twelve years his junior, the generous, gracious, and goodhearted Elizabeth caught the eye of the flamboyant Colt, and before long, his heart. Coming from "money," as they say, she would ultimately turn out to be a perfect partner for Colt. After he died years later, she not only successfully ran the Colt empire for decades and preserved the family legacy for generations, but was also one of the greatest philanthropists in state history.

In the meantime, Colt didn't hesitate to fully enjoy his successes, nor was he shy about reinvesting some of his new-found fortune back into his own company. He hired the best machinists and designers available, which helped him to improve the quality of both his manufacturing processes and handguns. Before long, Colt decided that in order to keep up with demand, he would require more space.

Being Colt, his grand design involved more than simply building a new factory, however. He decided he wanted to create an idyllic work community that could serve as a shining example to future generations of industrialists. Starting with a state-of-the-art manufacturing facility, he wanted housing for his workers, plus a school, church, general store, library, gardens, and social halls. His plan also called for roads and a rail depot, as well as sewers, gas works, and even a dock along the river. Essentially, he wanted to create a mini city, dedicated solely to making Colt guns.

Over the course of a few years, through buying, bullying, and bribing, Colt was able to acquire two hundred fifty acres of the South Meadows section of Hartford, land that was primarily in the flood plain of the Connecticut River. Reportedly, one local resident didn't want to sell, so Colt liberally "encouraged" a local newspaper to write negative stories to damage the man's reputation. When that didn't work, Colt allegedly set up a brothel across the street to shame the hold-out out of the neighborhood.

Although he was greatly appreciated (by most) for almost single-handedly reviving the Hartford economic base—despite repeatedly threatening to move his operations elsewhere whenever he came into conflict with the community—there were more than a few who still questioned his judgment. Building a massive, self-contained commercial complex in a lowland riverside area that could flood at any moment, and spending his own cash to do so, without insuring it (in Hartford, of all places!) was almost incomprehensible. The project was even deemed "Colt's Folly" by some.

Nevertheless, Colt had more than enough self-confidence to survive the derisive comments and naysayers. Even when a massive flood *did* happen in 1854 and wiped out the early stages of construction, Colt pressed on with his vision. Rather than move to a better-situated location, he had a two-mile-long, forty-foot-wide embankment erected along the river to protect the land.

The factory, the homes for the laborers, and all the ancillary pieces were soon rising out of the former wetlands. As completion was nearing, Colt had an ornate, onion-shaped blue dome constructed to cap his masterpiece—definitely a piece of architecture that didn't fit in with the white church steeples and flat mill roofs of New England. If that wasn't ostentatious enough, Colt commissioned a shining bronze statue of a rampant colt (what else?), rearing back on its hind legs with a spear in its teeth, a fitting, fiery symbol of the industrialist's own boldness. It was placed atop the blue dome, making for one of the most distinctive icons in Connecticut history.

Naturally, the ever-modest Colt named his ideal manufacturing development after his ideal manufacturer: Coltsville.

By August 1855, the stunning new armory and most of Coltsville was completed. Upon opening, the armory was the largest private weapons maker in the world, capable of churning out one hundred fifty guns a day. As was his habit, Colt paid his male workers well, but in return, demanded their best, which he often got.

When it came to his female employees, however, Colt was hardly a shining knight. He paid women less, which was standard at the time, but he was in the practice of hiring single, immigrant women to fill ammunition cartridges with gunpowder, a job that was much more dangerous than working on the assembly line—so dangerous, in fact, that the munitions facility was set far from the armory itself. So much for the "fairer" sex!

With an abundance of labor in the state due to an influx of immigrants, if a worker didn't put forth an effort that was in line with Colt's expectations—which included a ten-hour work day amid the hazardous, noisy machinery in the armory—they would quickly find themselves unemployed.

Colt may never have actually said, "My way or the highway," but it was certainly the message.

Although he could be a demanding jerk to his workers, that didn't carry over to his personal life. Ten months after the armory opened, on June 5, 1856, the forty-one-year-old Colonel Samuel Colt and twenty-nine-year-old Elizabeth Jarvis were married in her hometown of Middletown. They honeymooned in Europe for six months—as the privileged were wont to do—and upon their return, Sam built a "bold and unusual" dream mansion for them on a small hilltop in Coltsville.

Primarily constructed from stone, the manor, which Colt would christen Armsmear, was as original and eclectic as its lord—part Italianate villa, it featured Turkish domes and towers, rounded arches and windows, iron balconies and glass-domed conservatories. It was full of specially commissioned paintings and art, and peacocks and deer roamed the grounds freely. It also featured an enormous greenhouse, in which were grown grapes, peaches, figs, and exotic plants. Like everything else Colt did, Armsmear was ostentatious and larger than life.

Although Sam and Elizabeth now had a palatial home, they were not destined to fill it with a big, happy family. Over the next few years, they would suffer the loss of four children, three dying in infancy and one at three years old. Even more sadly, their one son who lived to adulthood, Caldwell, and who would've been the sole heir of the Colt fortune, died from tonsillitis in 1894 at only thirty-five years old. In addition, Colt also buried two brothers, one of whom, John, killed himself just before he was going to hang for murder.

Despite his personal tragedies, Colt's professional life continued to reach new heights, in large part because of his unbridled—and arguably, amoral—ambition. If there was some question as to whether Colt was a jerk or just a product of his era, his actions in the ramp up to the Civil War pretty much answered it.

As the issue of slavery began to come to a head and thus, more actively divide the nation, it was clear that an armed conflict was inevitable. A great war was brewing, one that would pit brother against brother. With each side irrevocably dug in, there would be no compromise and no doubt that the fighting would be fierce. Before one side could emerge victorious, a lot of American blood would need to be spilled.

And what better to spill a lot of blood, even if it was all American, than guns? Lots and lots of guns, and preferably Colt revolvers.

With forces on both sides massing millions of troops, a sales opportunity like never before was there for the taking. Just like he had done earlier in conflicts in the West and in Europe, Colt did business with both sides, enthusiastically selling arms to both the North and the South.

Ever savvy, old Colonel Colt made sure to keep his rhetoric somewhat down the middle. He publicly came out against abolitionists, yet also made sure to say that he wasn't in favor of slavery (because it was a flawed business practice). He staunchly voted Democratic—then, the party of big business and industry—and against Abraham Lincoln because he was concerned that Lincoln's election might ultimately be bad for business (which it turns out wasn't exactly the case). Although he even went so far as to fire over fifty employees who voted Republican, he claimed it was for work-related performance issues.

As the Civil War drew closer, Colt ran the armory around the clock and seven days a week (at a time when working on Sunday was still considered scandalous), employing over one thousand four hundred workers and cranking out sixty thousand guns a year, enough so that anyone who wanted a Colt firearm in the hands—regardless of their feelings on slavery—would have one. Annual earnings shot up through the onion-shaped roof, nearly quadrupling to over $1 million.

Although Colt himself referred to the flurry in sales as "my latest work on 'Moral Reform,'" others were less generous in their assessment of his actions. Some suspected him of being a Southern sympathizer, while newspapers like the *New York Times* flat out accused him of treason.

In fact, after fighting broke out on April 12, 1861, with the Confederate attack on Fort Sumter in South Carolina, and the Union formally declaring war three days later, Colt stopped selling arms to the South, but he had cut it close. Evidence was discovered that he had shipped weapons to Virginia for use by the Confederacy as late as April 15, a potentially traitorous act against the Union for which he was accused in Congress a few months later.

The ever-clever Colt carefully responded publicly that he never took an order from the South once the war started. Artfully timing his shipment as well as playing semantics only as a jerk could, he insisted that "taking an order" and "fulfilling an order" were two different things, and as a good businessman, he was obligated to complete an order for a paying customer as it had been placed *before* hostilities had officially started.

As Colt had completely halted commerce with the Confederacy, the accusations were dropped.

The Civil War brought Colt booming business and nearly unimaginable wealth, but with such prosperity can come a heavy burden. In addition to the stress of keeping it all going, Colt, an avid cigar smoker, also suffered from a number of chronic maladies—gout and rheumatism, among them. When combined with his penchant for being a workaholic and the go-go world-traveler lifestyle in which he immersed himself, it all took a dramatic physical toll on him. He had constantly pushed himself past the point of exhaustion, and after losing four children (the death of three-year-old daughter Elizabeth was especially tough), he was also emotionally drained. Ambitious jerks only have one gear—high—and Colt was no exception. Even when ill, he commanded his vast munitions corporation from his bed. Like the rock star of the age he was, he was destined to burn out rather than fade away.

After taking ill shortly after Christmas 1861 with what might have been pneumonia but could've been any combination of ailments, Col. Samuel Colt died on Friday, January 10, 1862, at the age of forty-seven, with his loving wife Elizabeth at his side. He was buried on the grounds of Armsmear following a lavish funeral that saw workers, business rivals, military leaders, political acquaintances, friends, and family all pay their respects. He left behind a young widow, a young son, and an estate of $15 million, which would be worth almost $320 million today. His death also created an enormous personality and energy void atop the Colt Patent Fire Arms Manufacturing empire, as well as in the ranks of American industry.

As a brash man who invited controversy, lived audaciously, and made nearly as many enemies as friends through his arguably amoral dealings, Colt also left behind a considerable amount of rumor and speculation. For instance, one popular legend is that he actually died from complications of chronic syphilis, a consequence of indulgences from his wild, younger days. Colt was also charged with regularly stealing design ideas and manufacturing processes without crediting—or paying—his sources, and then making them his own.

Another long-whispered assertion that seems to have more than a bit of veracity to it was that his favored nephew, Samuel Caldwell Colt, was not the offspring of his brother John (who had killed himself before having to hang for murder) but in fact, Colt's own bastard son, Samuel Colt Jr. The story goes that Colt had enjoyed an intimate relationship with a German woman he met abroad named Caroline Henshaw, and after she came to the United States, they secretly lived together as a couple (possibly married) for five years. Rather than go public with the union after so much time, he conveniently married her to his brother John just hours before his execution so that Sam could provide legally for the boy without raising eyebrows. The boy had, in fact, been born well before Caroline and John's sham union, and in his will, Samuel Colt also left his "nephew" close to $2 million, an exorbitant amount compared to what he left his other relatives.

If true—and the evidence certainly lends itself to it—then it demonstrates that Colt's jerkiness almost knew no bounds.

Even with his foibles and flaws, Samuel Colt is a hero to many, an undaunted and ambitious visionary who is rightly credited with making an everlasting impact on world warfare and manufacturing, in addition to helping Connecticut achieve great prosperity. His widow Elizabeth is one of the greatest benefactors in Hartford history, a grand dame whose unbridled generosity can still be felt today, over a century after she died. Her successful stewardship of Colt Fire Arms and shaping of her husband's legacy has helped to shift the primary focus to his positive contributions as opposed to his flaws.

Still, gun to your head, you'd have to admit that Sam Colt was a jerk.

CHAPTER 12

Hannah Hovey:
The Wicked Witch of Monroe

When thinking of witches in the historical context, many people immediately think of Salem, Massachusetts, and the infamous witch trials—and executions—that took place there. Connecticut, however, has a much darker history when it comes to witchcraft, executing at least nine (and possibly eleven—records aren't exactly clear) for "familiarity with the devil" by 1663, which was almost thirty years before the Salem trials even got underway.

The first person in Connecticut to be put to death for being a witch was Alse Young, who was hanged in Windsor in the spring of 1647. A year later, Mary Johnson was physically coerced (read: tortured) into "confessing" her satanic acts in Wethersfield and executed. In 1692, during her trial for witchcraft, Mercy Desborough was accused of making words disappear from the Bible, causing streams to rise and fall at will, and changing into numerous animals—she was eventually given the "water test," where she floated rather than sank, which brought a guilty verdict and a death sentence, although she was granted a reprieve when cooler heads prevailed.

In all, records show that thirty-five people were put on trial for witchcraft in the seventeenth century, with twenty-nine being convicted—those who were not executed either fled the colony or were somehow pardoned. No doubt many others were accused of trafficking in the black arts during these years. The last person to be officially tried for the crime was in 1768, when a woman named Alice Norton was accused of "riding through the air on a broomstick to attend a witches meeting in Albany."

Safe to say, it can be argued that in terms of jerks, there was no shortage of them during this period—accusing and executing innocent people because of one's own fears and ignorance certainly qualifies. At the time, however, most of them thought they were the ones doing away with the jerks. We now know otherwise.

Still, all this just illustrates that the specter of witchcraft was very real in Connecticut in 1783, the year that Hannah Hovey—who would go on to be known as "Hannah Cranna, the Wicked Witch of Monroe"—was born.

Unlike the majority of the other jerks here, there is very little historical record as to the actual life of Hannah Hovey, although she was definitely a real person and spent the bulk of her life, if not all of it, in the Stepney area of what is now known as Monroe. The years of her birth and death are known (sort of), as are a smattering of events in between, all of which are not enough to merit their inclusion here. Rather it's the numerous secondhand stories of her alleged deeds from those around her that cemented her nefarious reputation. In short, she didn't earn the immortal title of "witch" without having been a bit of jerk during her living years.

As mentioned, Hannah was born in 1783 (or thereabouts), near the end of the American Revolution, and there's evidence that her eventual husband, Captain Joseph Hovey, had served during the war. If so, it would've made him significantly older whenever the couple eventually met and got married. They set up house near the summit of Cragley Hill, which is in the vicinity of the Cutler's Farm Road and Elm Street in present-day Monroe. She would allegedly look out over her property from a large rock that was marked with a cut that looked like a cloven footprint—a sure sign that she was favored by Satan.

Again, not much is known about the Hoveys' life together other than they never had any children. The notion that Captain Hovey was a good deal older than his bride fits Hannah's story as it appears he died well before she did. Actually, the first suggestion from neighbors that Hannah may have possessed supernatural powers revolved around Captain Hovey's untimely demise.

The story goes that one evening Captain Hovey went out for a walk and, although he was in an area that he knew quite well, he somehow became disoriented and eventually toppled over a cliff and to his tragic end. Not believing that the good captain could have been the victim of such an unfortunate and unusual accident, the neighbors began to whisper that he had been bewitched by Hannah, and once dazed by her powers, became confused and inadvertently fell.

It's quite possible that it was after Captain Hovey's "suspicious" death that his widow picked up the nickname Hannah Cranna. It's also not quite clear why she was called "Cranna" aside from the rhyming aspect, although the surname "Cranna" is Scottish and means "rocky or lofty place"—maybe a nod to the Satan-stamped rock on her property? No matter how she got the moniker, it stuck fast and forever.

After the loss of her husband, the shrewish Hannah never remarried, choosing to live alone on her property in her ramshackle home with no other company aside from her chickens. As was the tradition, she always dressed in widow's black, including a long skirt and a large shawl that would flap wildly in the breeze. Without a husband to bring in an income, she also was very poor and forced to survive on her wits as well as the bounty of her own land, regularly foraging in the woods and streams on her property for food.

It doesn't take much imagination to picture how an eccentric, solitary woman with a bit of a mean streak, who lived in a meager house in the forest and was always clad in billowy black clothes—which hid her feet, so no one could be sure she wasn't floating above the ground—could easily be "transformed" by local loose tongues into a witch.

From various accounts, it seems as though Hannah was a fiercely independent and shrewd woman, who was very aware of the rumors regarding her supernatural powers. She got along well with some of her neighbors but was not above using her otherworldly reputation to intimidate the others in providing firewood and food when necessary, even going so far as to put "curses" or "hexes" on those who would not cooperate. The more she traded on her witchy—and jerky—behavior, the larger her legend grew.

Grave marker for Hannah Hovey
RAY BENDICI PHOTO

Again, nowadays very few people would capitulate to such almost-comical behavior, but in early nineteenth-century Connecticut, with a dearth of education and a healthy respect for the notion of evil dealings—there are over thirty places across the state named in "honor" of the Dark Lord, from Satan's Kingdom to Devil's Den—Hannah's conduct proved to be convincing.

As Hannah took on the mantle of witch, her land was changed into a realm of nefarious wonders. Her house was supposedly guarded by an army of snakes, and the birds on her property were protected by an enchantment that Hannah wove that caused hunters to always miss when trying to shoot them without her blessing. Her witch's "familiar" (a supernatural creature assistant, often a black cat) was a rooster named Old Boreas that, like any proper minion of evil, only crowed exactly at midnight. It was said that any timepiece set by the big rooster's crowing would keep perfect time thereafter.

Numerous fanciful tales sprung up about the extent of Hannah's "powers," most likely based on mundane events that may have resulted from jerk-like behavior but were exaggerated for storytelling effect. One such story centered on a stream that ran through her modest property that teemed with brook trout. Many wanted to test their angling skills in Hannah's stocked waterway, but she forbade all from taking "her" fish. One day a young man sneaked onto her land to test his luck, and sure enough, quickly landed a prize trout. Before he could get his hook back in the water, however, Hannah appeared, crooked walking staff in hand, and angered by the unapproved poaching in her stream, cried, "Curses upon you and your fishing!" Now, in real life, the cranky old woman most likely just chased the trespasser off her land with a cuss or two and that was that. In the lore of Hannah Cranna, however, after encountering the wicked witch of Monroe, the young man was jinxed forever and supposedly never caught a fish again, no matter how many times he tried.

Another anecdote in which it's not too hard to discern how a simple incident got blown out of proportion involved one of Hannah's neighbors, who was renowned for her pie-making skills. One afternoon, after the woman had finished baking a number of pumpkin pies and had set them out to cool, Hannah happened to be walking past. After complimenting the woman on her succulent pies, the widow Hovey asked (or most likely, begged) to have one. The baker graciously gave her a small one, but apparently Hannah asked for one of the larger confections. The woman, obviously perturbed that her generosity wasn't quite enough, told the old witch that the small one was all she could spare. Hannah, angered by the defiance, summoned her powers and hexed the woman's baking ability so that from that day forward, her pies were never again anywhere as good as they had been.

Again, the reality of the situation was most likely that the impoverished Hannah either had tried to get "some more" (like a Dickensian waif), and was irked at being rebuffed, or that she had attempted her "I'm a witch and you better give me a pie or I will curse you" routine. Either way, her jerky reaction to being refused only bolstered her standing as a dark sorceress.

A third story that has often been told about Hannah involves some bullies who unwisely decided to test her witchery. On this occasion, the old crone was minding her own business tending to her garden when two men driving an oxcart full of hay passed by her decrepit little home. Seeing the aged woman alone out in the yard, they stopped the cart and began to taunt her, challenging the mighty witch to provide a display of her supposed influence.

"Before you pass yonder tree, your wish shall be granted," she simply said.

The men laughed, but when they went to leave, their oxen would not move no matter the amount of coaxing. They began to push, but before they knew it, the wheels had literally come off their hay wagon. The oxen then ran off, leaving the two men to lament their own foolishness in having dared Hannah.

Chances are that this story, like so many others, has a kernel of truth. No doubt many people mocked Hannah behind her back and to her face, and all it would take is one case of "misfortune" to befall someone a short time after having derided her for such a story like this to grow. Cursed by the witch!

As much as they feared Hannah, sometimes the locals appreciated her "magical" abilities, especially if they benefitted from them. Another yarn that "testified" to her powers revolved around a particularly nasty drought. Crops had wilted, wells were filled with dust, and the town was drier than kindling. Not knowing what to do, one of the farmers gathered up his nerve and went to visit Hannah, and asked if she could somehow employ her malevolent talents on their behalf. "If you have faith in Hannah," the old woman allegedly said, "by sundown on the morrow your wish shall be granted." The man pledged his and the town's allegiance, and sure enough, the next day the citizens of Monroe were awakened by thunder and heavy rains.

Hanna Cranna, the wicked witch of Monroe, had conjured the heavens to open and saved the town!

What really happened—if the incident occurred at all—is probably dramatically less miraculous. It's certainly thinkable that, desperate to try anything to break the long dry spell, the townspeople decided to give the "old witch" a chance, and after making a bold promise, Hannah lucked out. Like Jeanne Dixon or many other self-proclaimed psychics—or more aptly, a television weather forecaster—it's possible that Hannah's numerous failed prognostications were quickly forgotten in lieu of the one big prediction she got right.

Unfortunately, it appears that despite "saving" the town from certain doom via drought, Hannah was soon again on the undesirable list as she couldn't help being a jerk. Feeling even more entitled following the rain incident, she tested the limits of what she thought she could get away with, constantly asking for food and other privileges while holding the threat of magical retribution over the heads of the residents of Monroe.

At first, the grateful neighbors complied, but after a while, a few of them grew tired of Hannah's harassment and hocus pocus. Deciding to stand up to her—ostensibly out of fear but more likely to let her know that they were sick of her jerky behavior and if she was going to behave like a witch, they would damned well treat her like a witch—a group of residents banded together to formally accuse Hannah of practicing witchcraft.

Hannah was supposedly arraigned on charges of consorting with the devil, although the case never went to trial. As previously mentioned, it had been decades since the last witch trial in the state, and more enlightened heads were judging over the populace. Chances are that once each side called the other's bluff, both backed off—the locals probably didn't harass her as much and she didn't reach into her bag of tricks to cry "witch" quite so much. She was allowed to go back to her home and live quietly.

From that point on, Hannah seemed to avoid any witch-like incidents. She primarily kept to herself, tending to her meager garden and home, and occasionally interacting with the neighbors. The years passed and there were no noteworthy incidents until late 1859, when Old Boreas died.

Hannah was reportedly inconsolable at the passing of her beloved pet rooster, grieving mightily for the old bird. She allegedly buried him at night in the center of her garden, performing some unusual rites in the process. Some believed that the end of Old Boreas, her faithful familiar, was a signal from her spiritual masters to the old witch that her own demise was near. Others more skeptical might say that when an elderly woman lost her only true (feathered) friend, it could have a devastating emotional impact, but why let that ruin the end of a good story?

After the death of Old Boreas, the full brunt of a Connecticut winter set upon Monroe. As the snows came down, the frail, nearly eighty-year-old Hannah hunkered down in her tiny shack, trying to ride it out.

One day after a particularly heavy January snow, a neighbor was passing by when he heard a loud moan coming from Hannah's house. When he waded through the snow to the door and into the house, he found the old woman looking sick and haggard. "The spirits have called and it won't be but a short time before I will be in the great beyond," Hannah said to him, according to popular accounts. "I have a wish to make that must be carried out," she continued, "I am not to be buried until after sundown and there must be ample bearers to carry my coffin from the house to the grave." Nothing is noted as to what the neighbor's response was, although she made it clear that she expected her final request to be followed.

"Obey my wishes if you would avoid trouble and vexation," are her supposed last words, a parting curse from a woman who had never been afraid to play the jerk to get her way.

The next day, Hannah Cranna, the Wicked Witch of Monroe, was dead.

With the deep snow all around—remember, snowplows hadn't been invented yet—the locals thought it would be too difficult to honor the old woman's dying wish to carry her coffin from the house all the way to the cemetery. A sleigh was summoned, her modest coffin was loaded upon it, and the funeral party started off for the graveyard.

After a very short distance, however, something quite unusual happened. The coffin, which had been secured, came loose and fell off the sled. Not only that, it started sliding down the hill and back toward Hannah's house.

Spooked, Hannah's neighbors put the coffin back on the sled, chained it down even more securely, and, to make sure that it stayed in place, a few brave souls sat atop it. They again set out for the cemetery but had only gone a little ways before the sleigh and coffin began to inexplicably shake, throwing everyone off.

That was enough. Rather than incur the full wrath of the witch from beyond the grave, those present decided to obey her request. They picked up the coffin, hoisted it up on their shoulders, and carried it all the way to the cemetery. By the time they got there, the sun had set, so they lowered the casket into the grave and quickly buried her.

Relieved that they had finally gotten the accursed Hannah Cranna into the ground where she could no longer get at them, the locals returned to her tiny domicile to go through her things only to find that the structure was engulfed in flames—a last salvo from the mighty witch. No doubt there were a few who heard the cackling of her laugher in the crackling of the embers as the house burned to the ground, leaving no trace of Hannah other than a pile of ashes, yet burning her memory into the minds of all forever.

Obviously, this all makes for a great finale to a fun story, although it seems highly unlikely. So what really happened at the end of the life of Hannah Hovey?

It doesn't take much to assume that the bitter cold of a Connecticut winter could easily cause the death of an elderly woman living alone in a hovel of a home that was probably neither insulated nor properly heated. Her headstone—a replica of which still stands in Gregory's Four Corners Burial Ground in Trumbull, right on the border with Monroe—lists 1859-60 as the "date" of her death, giving credence to the idea that Hannah probably died by herself sometime over the long winter and her body was not discovered until well afterward. That, of course, would somewhat discredit her remarks in regard to her final wishes.

As for the story of the coffin falling off the sleigh during transport, again, it's not hard to picture that an actual funeral procession mishap involving a person with such a bad reputation might become overblown as the years passed. Considering her lowly stature in town and her miserable life, it'd be surprising if anyone other than the gravedigger and a minister were present at her funeral.

Finally, if Hannah's abandoned, probably poorly constructed shack of a home accidentally caught fire, well, they used to burn witches, right? The perfect fiery exclamation mark at the end of the story.

However, there are some who believe the story of Hannah Hovey isn't exactly over yet. As the decades have passed, various spooky stories have popped up about the Wicked Witch of Monroe. The most popular one is that on certain misty nights, the specter of a mysterious old woman will suddenly appear in the middle of the road that runs alongside the cemetery, causing an unfortunate driver to swerve, lose control of his car—and eventually his life— as he crashes into the gravestone of Hannah Cranna.

If you drive along Spring Hill Road, you can see that Hannah's white gravestone is up on the hill overlooking the road and would require a spectacular aerial crash that would put Evel Knievel to shame, but again, why let truth ruin the legend? There's no doubt that the old woman who was happy to embrace the idea of being a witch and all the evils that came with it would be pleased to see that long after she was gone, she was still being blamed for being a jerk.

A portrait of Rev. Herbert H. Hayden from his autobiography

THE REV. HERBERT H. HAYDEN, AN AUTOBIOGRAPHY, HERBERT H. HAYDEN

CHAPTER 13

Rev. Herbert H. Hayden:
Minister Turned Murderer

Man cheats on wife: Jerk.

Man cheats on pregnant wife and allegedly impregnates other woman: Bigger jerk.

Man cheats on pregnant wife, allegedly impregnates other woman, kills other woman to solve problem, then gets betrayed wife to lie in court on his behalf to help clear his name: Legendary jerk.

Although there have been many gruesome and cruel murders in Connecticut's history, very few of them feature the astonishing levels of hypocrisy and injustice that occurred in the brutal 1878 demise of Mary Stannard. In what was a sensational trial that hinged on the then-groundbreaking introduction of forensic evidence, Stannard's accused murderer, the Rev. Herbert H. Hayden, was able to avoid a trip to the gallows even though witness testimony and physical proof overwhelmingly demonstrated his guilt.

Then again, it shouldn't come as a surprise that over a century ago a charismatic jerk like Hayden could get away with premeditated murder. There's at least one semi-recent, infamous murder case that also involved a vicious stabbing, an incompetent judge, a star witness who was willing to lie under oath, a brilliant defense team that was able to discredit expert testimony, unsubstantiated claims of planted evidence by authorities, and a jury who came to a decision based on personal sentiment rather than the facts. In 1878, however, there were no white Ford Broncos or suggestions that, if a certain hand garment fit, the jury must acquit.

Also coincidentally, the accused penned his take on events, giving it the certainly-not-suspicious title *Rev. Herbert H. Hayden; An Autobiography: The Mary Stannard Murder—Tried on Circumstantial Evidence.* After a brief recounting of his life, the majority of the book is the direct court transcription of his and his wife's testimony as well as his attorney's arguments. It ends with his release, and although it doesn't specifically say, "If I did it, here's how it happened," Hayden spent considerable time outlining the circumstances that put him in such a compromising situation—in addition to listing his sterling personal qualities.

You know, other than being a murdering, philandering jerk.

As to Hayden's story, according to the man himself, it was "In the year 1850, in Taunton, Mass., while the nation was celebrating the anniversary of its first President," that Herbert Hiram Hayden "first saw the light." (So humble a beginning!) He was one of three children, and his parents—lovingly referred to as "Mr." and "Mrs." Hayden—were of working, blue-collar stock. His father was the owner of a general store and young Herbert was often forced to work there, butchering animals in addition to other menial tasks while pursuing his education.

Speaking of school, Hayden recounts his first day there at age four, during which he fell and "shredded" his face, an event that he suggests could have been a portent of the doom that was to befall him throughout his life. He also tells of an incident from a church service when he was ten years old: During a sermon about Calvinistic decrees, he was (in his opinion) severely reprimanded for turning the pages of a Sunday school primer too loudly. The harsh rebuke would eventually push him down the path to Methodism.

In addition to such "hardships," Hayden was apprenticed to a carpenter for two years (like that well-known woodworker from Galilee). He had progressed to where he received a journeyman's wages when he experienced an undisclosed event in which "the finger of destiny pointed to another field of duty." Despite modestly describing himself as "a light-hearted, easy-going youth, apparently beloved by all," he suggests that he was forced to a higher calling by powers much larger than himself, although he prayed and fought mightily against it because he knew of his own unworthiness.

To avoid his destiny, Hayden tried to run off to Mansfield, Massachusetts. But fate would have it otherwise, and he stated that it was there that a mysterious stranger was sent to him to finally "lift his burden" and set him on the proper course to the pulpit. In the fall of 1869, Hayden enrolled in the Providence Conference Seminary in East Greenwich, Rhode Island, learning the skills he'd need for his chosen profession. He also worked on a farm, plied his trade as a carpenter, and sold books.

It was also during this period that Hayden met Rosa C. Shaw, a teacher from Carver, Massachusetts. They were married on Aug. 8, 1871, and a year later welcomed their first child, daughter Emma. After finishing his studies at the seminary, the twenty-three-year-old Hayden moved his family to Middletown, where in 1873 he started at Wesleyan University in hopes of getting the college degree needed to become a fully ordained Methodist minister.

The challenge of attaining a diploma while working and supporting a growing family—son Herbert was born in 1874—proved to be more than Hayden could handle. Whether it was the lingering effects of the typhoid fever he had contracted the summer before his studies, as he claimed, or his general inability as a student, as one of his professors would later suggest, he was done at Wesleyan by the spring of 1875.

Hayden managed to secure a spot preaching on Sundays at a West Rocky Hill church, but after leaving Wesleyan, he took a position serving at a church in Rockland, a lightly settled area between Durham and North Madison. He soon moved his family there, but there had been some sort of miscommunication regarding the minister prior to Hayden, who evidently wasn't quite ready to give up the pulpit. Hayden was an aspiring preacher without a congregation.

Despite Hayden's inability to become a fully ordained Methodist minister, his wife Rosa was still teaching and bringing in meager wages, which was the family's primary source of income. It was enough to put food on the table, but the Haydens' other long-term financial obligations were being neglected, and they found themselves sliding deeper and deeper into debt.

Hayden returned to farming in 1877, a process that recharged his spirit and made him "a new man." He also managed to land a temporary preaching position, filling in for a minister in Madison who had taken ill. A teaching opportunity also came along with this new position, and money being tight, Hayden was soon preaching, teaching, and farming. The distance from his home in Rockland to Madison made it more practical for him to spend the majority of the week in Madison, which only increased the stress on the family and added a few more bricks to Hayden's mental load. His growing frustration in his inability to become fully ordained wasn't helping his general disposition, either.

Things then got tougher for the Haydens when Rosa got ill and had to stop working for a while. With two young children in the house and Herbert away during the week, the family decided to bring in help. They turned to Mary Stannard, a comely twenty-one-year-old who lived on the property next to the Haydens' farm, less than a half mile away.

Stannard was a simple, hardworking, and cheerful young woman, known for her integrity, reliability, and honesty, and her willingness to care for others. Her family was very poor, so the able-bodied girl had been working from an early age to help out, which meant she didn't have much time for a formal education. She was a bit naive but always eager to please, which may have made her vulnerable to the whims of men.

In fact, Stannard had entered into a tryst with a married man from a previous family who had employed her, which had resulted in the birth of her son Willie in 1875. In spite of the stigma and scorn that came with having a child out of wedlock, she refused to divulge the father's name, and through her diligence and generally affable nature, the small Rockland community soon forgave her for what seemed to be a one-time lapse in judgment.

Stannard was a welcome—if costly—addition to the Hayden home, serving as a nanny to the children, a companion to Rosa, and a general help around the farm, as there was no task she wouldn't undertake. Her presence became even more important as the Haydens discovered in the winter of 1877 that they were once again expecting a child.

If Herbert Hayden had already felt as though he was under tremendous pressure, the imminent arrival of another mouth to feed didn't help. He continued his regular commute back and forth to Madison, taking on as much work as possible, but he was also still borrowing when he could—in fact, Mary Stannard even arranged for Hayden to borrow seventy-five dollars from her half sister, Susan Hawley, a significant sum during that period.

As the spring of 1878 came along, Hayden was a disheartened man with unfulfilled dreams who was struggling mightily to maintain his meager station. He also had a wife who was pregnant, and most likely, because of health difficulties during previous pregnancies, not giving him all the comfort and wifely attention that he may have desired. It's not unrealistic to think that his self-esteem was probably quite low on the night of March 20, 1878.

By the measures of the era, Hayden was considered an attractive man. Solidly built with wavy dark hair and a neatly trimmed goatee, he was well-groomed and known for being generally charming. Rumors had circulated that more than once he had already gone outside of his marriage for intimate female company, and with Rosa in her condition, it wasn't surprising that he would turn his ungentlemanly attention to the convenient—and presumably "easy"—target, Mary Stannard.

The Haydens had been invited to the local parish oyster supper on the night of the 20th, and after arranging for Stannard to watch their children, the aspiring minister and his pregnant spouse went to the nearby social event. After a short time, Hayden claimed he had a headache and left early, saying he was going home to also check on the children—although it appears he was more interested in the babysitter.

Conveniently, Hayden found that the children were fast asleep in their beds and the convivial Mary Stannard was by herself. Like any cheating jerk, Hayden didn't hesitate when he saw his opportunity. According to the later testimony of Stannard's half sister Susan Hawley, this was the first time that Hayden made a sexual advance on Stannard, who tried at first to resist. Hayden persisted in applying his charms on the poor girl, and ultimately, triumphed.

The affair continued for the next few months, with the couple allegedly enjoying a regular nightly rendezvous in the woods between their two properties. They were also often spotted around town, riding together in Hayden's horse-drawn carriage or walking together in the woods.

Like many affairs, the tryst burned brightly and briefly, and when it was over, the two parties went their separate ways in somewhat amicable fashion. Hayden settled back into family life, with his wife Rosa giving birth to their daughter (also named Rosa) in August, while Stannard took her son Willie and went to work in nearby Guilford for Edgar Studley, whose wife and daughters were traveling abroad. All was well . . . for a while.

At the end of August, while working at the Studley home, Stannard started experiencing the symptoms of pregnancy: intense nausea, swollen breasts, and a tight abdomen. She consulted with Edgar's mother Jane Studley, who was also living in the house. The elder Studley seemed to think that even though Stannard was experiencing some menstruation, it was possible that she could still be with child, since it's not uncommon for women to have some spotting early on in the process. Having already been pregnant out of wedlock once—and knowing full well the heartache, emotional turmoil, and public derision that came with it—Stannard immediately began to panic.

If in this situation today, even someone as educationally challenged as Stannard could've easily taken a home pregnancy test to determine her condition, but that option wasn't available in the late nineteenth century. To be properly examined by a doctor was well beyond what the simple woman could afford, so rather than even go through the whole determination procedure, she decided that it would be best to just take the steps to abort the baby altogether. Unfortunately, she also chose to turn to her former lover—who would turn out to be a bigger jerk than she ever could've imagined—for help.

On August 31, Stannard's situation went from bad to worse: The pious Edgar Studley learned of her potential condition from his mother and told Stannard that he would not allow such an immoral situation to continue under his roof. He fired Stannard and insisted that she and her son Willie leave at once. He brought them back to Rockland the next day, and during the ride, Studley later claimed that Stannard confessed to him that she believed she was pregnant with Reverend Hayden's child, and that it was going "to be taken care of." Stannard asked him not to tell her father Charlie of her situation; Studley complied, furnishing the excuse that he let Mary go because he couldn't tolerate her young son at his house any longer.

When Mary Stannard got home, she shared her situation with her half sister Susan and her sister-in-law Mary, and then decided that she should tell the reverend. On September 2, she went to the Haydens' house three times to see her former lover, except the first two times, he wasn't there. The third time, however, while visiting under the pretext of needing to borrow a hay rake, she was able to catch Hayden at home, and confronted him.

Stannard's half sister Susan Hawley would later testify that Mary had been successful in getting Hayden to go to the barn alone—an event witnessed by multiple neighbors, although Hayden and his wife would deny it under oath. According to Hawley, Stannard said that she had explained the state of affairs to Hayden, who had told her that he would go as soon as possible to Middletown to see a doctor to get some medicine to "take care" of the problem.

Back in her home, Stannard expressed great relief to her sister-in-law. Hayden, on the other hand, had just had the final straw placed on his already tenuous load. Between his heavy financial obligations, overwhelming family situation, and failing clerical career, potentially fathering a bastard child—and thus destroying any hope of becoming a minister, let alone the other considerations—was more than he could handle. A better man probably never would've gotten himself into such a quandary in the first place, but only a true jerk would react like Hayden did.

The next day, Tuesday, September 3, 1878—Mary Stannard's twenty-second birthday, and her last day alive—started off simply enough. Stannard woke up early, tended to her chores, including going to the local grocery for the food that would be her last meal. On the way back, she stopped at the Hayden's house, but Reverend Hayden was not home. He had told his wife that he needed to go to Durham for oats. Nonetheless, Stannard stayed and visited with Rosa Hayden for an hour before asking if she could take the older Hayden children back to her house to play with her son Willie.

One would think that while on the way back to her house with the Hayden children, she most likely would've been encouraged at the prospect of Hayden acting so quickly to solve their problem.

Stannard wouldn't have been so happy if she had known Hayden's solution.

Obviously, Hayden hadn't gone to Durham as he had told his wife, but instead to Middletown, where his first stop was at the home of an acquaintance who was supposed to have made some tools for him—a trip that may have been nothing more than an alibi for being in Middletown. The acquaintance wasn't home, so Hayden continued to Tyler's Drug Store, where he made a fateful purchase: an ounce of arsenic. (He told the clerk it was "for rats," but if that was the case, he should've ingested it himself!)

Upon exiting the drug store, he ran into Dr. Leonard Bailey, who had attended to Rosa Hayden during her pregnancy with their first child. According to Dr. Bailey, Hayden asked him hypothetical questions as to whether his wife could be pregnant so soon after the birth of their third child, and if so, if there was medicine that could be prescribed to undo that. Taken aback that a supposedly religious man would ask such questions about abortion, Dr. Bailey told Hayden that there was no such medicine. The men parted.

Apparently discouraged by his meeting with Dr. Bailey, Hayden returned to Rockland, ready to solve his problem without the aid of medicinal remedies.

The first place Hayden went upon his return was to the Stannard home, ostensibly for a glass of water after his long ride—never mind that there was a natural cold spring just a little farther down the road. His real purpose most likely was to meet with Mary and arrange a time when they could be alone and he could give her the "medicine" he had procured in Middletown. He was probably startled to see his children at the Stannard residence when he arrived, but was able to maintain his composure and indicate to Mary that he wanted to chat in private.

Conveniently, Mary Stannard left to get a pail of water from the aforementioned spring. After making small talk with Charlie Stannard, Hayden took his children back toward their home and "fortuitously" encountered Mary on the way. Again, according to Susan Hawley's in-court testimony, Stannard said it was during this meeting that Hayden told her that he had obtained the abortion medicine and that she should meet him later that afternoon, about an hour after the midday meal, at the big rock in the woods between their properties. When Stannard asked why Hayden couldn't just give it to her there to take, he told her that he wanted to be with her in case there were any problems after she ingested it . . .

Like her staying alive.

Both families enjoyed their midday meals. Shortly afterward, around two o'clock, Mary Stannard announced to her family that she was going off by herself for the afternoon to pick blackberries; at the same time in the Hayden home, the good reverend told his wife that he needed to go to their woodlot to "throw out" some wood. Both left their respective homes at approximately the same time, heading to the same general area.

What exactly happened over the next fours hours on September 3, 1878, will only ever be known for sure by two people: Mary Stannard and the person who murdered her. All the forensic evidence and witness testimony, however, very strongly suggests that person was Herbert Hayden.

At six o'clock, Stannard was found dead by her father Charlie, who had gone looking for her when she hadn't returned from picking blackberries. He discovered his murdered daughter's body by the big rock in the woods near their house, laid out on the ground. Her own bonnet had been propped under her head like a pillow, and her hands were folded on her abdomen as if she was just taking a nap. The scene was a parent's worst nightmare.

Stannard's assailant had made a poor attempt to stage the scene as if the young woman—possibly distraught over having been pregnant out of wedlock, yet again—had committed suicide. The problem with that scenario was there was a large wound on her head where she had been struck with a blunt object (most likely a hefty stick or log) and her jugular vein, carotid artery, and larynx all had been cut despite no knife being found anywhere near the body, making suicide even less probable. No blood was found on the dead girl's hands either, which there certainly would've been if she had slit her own throat.

The neighbors and local authorities were notified, and a group of men—including Herbert Hayden, who had just gotten back to his house after his day supposedly chopping wood—brought Stannard's body back to her family home, where it was autopsied (for the first time) by the local medical examiner.

During the flurry of activity following the discovery of the murder, Hayden seemed to be near the center of it, either providing information about Stannard's health that only her sister Susan, sister-in-law Mary, and the Studleys would've known, or trying to suggest to others that the Stannards had a significant family history of insanity. He also allegedly asked more than one person if the authorities had a suspect in mind, although he never asked anyone who they thought it might be.

As it turns out, the Rev. Herbert H. Hayden was the first person questioned by the inquest jury on the day after the murder. He claimed that he had spent the entire afternoon at the woodlot by himself, and then returned straight home when he was done. He never saw Stannard until later that night when he went to the murder scene with the other men to retrieve her body.

Mary Stannard was laid to rest—temporarily, as she would be subsequently exhumed three times—on Thursday, September

5, in a simple ceremony attended by all of Rockland. The next day, Hayden was arrested for her murder, with his knife being impounded as evidence.

For the people who lived in Rockland, it seemed like a pretty open-and-shut case, but unfortunately for Mary Stannard, the case wasn't tried in Rockland. The first trial in the Justice Court was held in Madison and was officiated over by Henry B. Wilcox, a justice of the peace who had no trial law experience, and who, when asked to sign his friend Hayden's arrest warrant, had replied that he would rather sign his own death warrant!

Unlike today, where judges are supposed to be impartial arbiters or recuse themselves if they have a personal interest in a case, courts during the Victorian era relied more on personal interpretations of justice. Wilcox let it be known right up front that he sincerely doubted that Hayden, a civilized, educated man of the cloth, could be capable of murder. He also showed an extreme prejudice that was all too common at the time, dismissing out of hand the testimony of Susan Hawley and Charlie Stannard. In his opinion, they were uneducated and poor, so therefore, they couldn't possibly be telling the truth.

Hayden, for his part, was indignant at the charge and smugly played the role of wronged victim, charming officials, smoking cigars, and acting a bit too casual considering the circumstances. Despite the glaring inconsistencies in his testimony, he spoke confidently, employing the communication skills he had honed in the pulpit.

As impressive as the reverend was, what really clinched his case was the performance of his wife Rosa, who testified from a rocking chair because of her physical ailments. She often broke down on the stand, crying throughout her seemingly well-rehearsed statements and descriptions, which conveniently matched her husband's story nearly word for word.

The hearing was over in a few days and not surprisingly, Wilcox found Hayden innocent because he literally didn't think that Hayden had acted guilty. He also indicated that a "good" woman like Rosa Hayden couldn't have possibly lied to protect her husband, and that there was no evidence that Hayden was even close to Stannard! Hayden was freed from jail immediately.

The decision was celebrated by Hayden's congregation in Madison and in the press, both of whom shared many of the same prejudices as Wilcox. Hayden publicly reveled in a well-attended church service on September 29, where he self-servingly quoted scripture that spoke of how "the truth shall make you free." The "poor" reverend was even heralded by his congregation for acquitting himself so well during his ordeal.

Hayden's freedom was brief.

The second of the four autopsies that were performed on Mary Stannard's body had revealed the presence of ninety granules of arsenic in her body, which scientific investigation proved had been part of the same batch of poison purchased by Hayden at Tyler's Drug Store on the day of the murder. Human blood had also been found deep in the grooves of Hayden's knife.

Ironically, it was also during this examination that it was found that Stannard hadn't been pregnant at all, but was suffering from a cyst on one of her ovaries. The symptoms of the malady had only mimicked pregnancy.

On October 8, 1878, Herbert Hayden was arrested for a second time. He spent the next thirteen months in prison, apparently having a grand old time, eating well, receiving visitors, enjoying cigars, and penning most of his aforementioned autobiography. Meanwhile, his wife was forced to sell off their personal items for cash and rely on the charity of neighbors to feed the family.

While Hayden was savoring his time in jail, his defense team went on the offensive, claiming the arsenic had been planted and suggesting that other suspects—some outlandish—were guilty of the murder. A pro-Hayden group called "The Friends of Justice" even went around campaigning for Hayden's innocence.

The "Great Hayden Trial" started with much ado on October 7, 1879, and like the previous inquest, much was made of the character of the witnesses. The "ignorant" Susan Hawley and Charlie Stannard were belittled and badgered in court, their testimony discredited mainly based on their social standing. The more cultured Herbert Hayden, and, more importantly, his faithful, sickly wife Rosa, were treated with respect by the judge and attorneys. Ultimately, they came across more favorably—especially Rosa, whose tour-de-force as the innocent wife was particularly powerful, even though it was rehearsed and clearly fabricated in places.

A large part of the prosecution's case was spent establishing how the arsenic discovered in Mary Stannard was the same arsenic obtained by Hayden in Middletown; in retrospect, it was a brilliant scientific presentation of forensic evidence that had never been seen before in a Connecticut courtroom, and way ahead of its time. Although in this age of regular television courtroom dramas and forensic police shows, such scientific proof would be critical to a case, in the nineteenth century, it was essentially unheard of, and thus didn't carry the same weight.

Instead, realizing that the actual evidence was incontrovertible, the defense, given wide leeway by the judge, instead attacked the four different expert witnesses (some of them respected Yale University professors and scientists) who testified about the arsenic, disputing their every statement and frustrating them repeatedly on the stand. The blood on Hayden's knife, which was also human—although the DNA testing to prove it Stannard's was not available yet—was also similarly discredited.

Even with the overwhelming physical evidence against Hayden, it came down to who the jury liked better: the coarse, unseemly relatives of a dead woman who had a bastard child and wasn't around to testify for herself, or the appealing, sophisticated man of the cloth and his agonizing, reputable wife.

When it came time for deliberations, eleven of the jurors voted for acquittal, but one, David B. Hotchkiss, held out for murder in the second degree. The jury deliberated for eighty-two hours and held fifteen ballots, but Hotchkiss refused to give in—apparently, he was the only one who based his vote on the indisputable facts and believed that the reverend and his wife were capable of lying. The other jurors, however, said afterward that they voted for acquittal despite the overwhelming evidence against Herbert Hayden because they believed Rosa Hayden and were hesitant to sentence such "a beautiful woman" to a life of widowhood. (But an innocent victim like Mary Stannard was okay to lie in a cold grave with no justice, evidently.)

In the end, a mistrial was declared, which was as good as an acquittal because the state decided not to retry the case. Hayden was set free, although that was a relative term. He was banned from ever preaching again, and in fighting the charges, had incurred great debt. The family was also forced to move to New Haven, where Hayden toiled in relative obscurity for the next twenty-seven years. He died May 13, 1907, after a prolonged illness.

So what happened on that fateful day in 1878? The best guess is that at the rendezvous in the woods by the big rock, Hayden gave Stannard the special "medicine" to abort the phantom pregnancy. Implicitly trusting Hayden, Stannard unwittingly ingested it all . . . except arsenic is a very slow-acting poison. Probably realizing that something was very, very wrong, Stannard most likely tried to flee, which is most likely when Hayden struck her on the head with a log or rock.

Possibly worried that he hadn't given his victim enough arsenic to be lethal, or panicking that she was dying too slowly and he wouldn't be able to get back home without arousing suspicion, Hayden decided to speed the process—and ensure that Stannard couldn't tell anyone about his actions—by slitting her throat.

From his years working in his parents' store and on the farm, Hayden knew how to slaughter an animal quickly, mercifully, and, most importantly, without getting any blood on himself. He dispatched Stannard with his knife and then tried to stage the body so that it appeared that the young woman had cut her own throat.

The major flaw in Hayden's plan had been using his own knife, which he undoubtedly hadn't planned on and obviously couldn't leave behind. Perhaps he thought he could get back and plant one at the murder scene, but Charlie Stannard discovered his daughter's body before Hayden could return, and then it was too late.

Of course, that's all speculation and guesswork. There's no doubt, however, that Rev. Herbert H. Hayden was a jerk.

CHAPTER 14

Salvatore
"Midge Renault" Annunziato:
A "Made" Jerk

In the iconic mobster film *Goodfellas,* the main character Henry Hill talks about the fraternity of organized crime, saying:

> *You know, we always called each other good fellas. Like you said to somebody, 'You're gonna like this guy. He's all right. He's a good fella. He's one of us.' You understand? We were good fellas. Wiseguys. But Jimmy and I could never be made because we had Irish blood. It didn't even matter that my mother was Sicilian. To become a member of a crew you've got to be one hundred per cent Italian so they can trace all your relatives back to the old country. See, it's the highest honor they can give you. It means you belong to a family and crew. It means that nobody can fuck around with you. It also means you could fuck around with anybody just as long as they aren't also a member. It's like a license to steal. It's a license to do anything . . .*

In a story that almost sounds like it was scripted in Hollywood, Salvatore Annunziato would rise up from a poor, scrappy kid to become an organized crime boss of New Haven and a "good fella" who lived as though he believed that he could do almost anything and get away with it. His life was an unruly, violent ride fueled by broken bones, booze, and bullets, punctuated by bar scrapes and prison bars, and ultimately coming to an end that was as mysterious as it was abrupt.

*Salvatore "Midge Renault" Annunziato (left) leaves court
with his attorney on a snowy day in March 1971*
NEW HAVEN JOURNAL-COURIER

Connecticut may have had more powerful and famous gangsters, but few were more beloved, hated, and colorful than Annunziato. Essentially a real-life version of Joe Pesci's iconic *Goodfellas* Tommy DeVito character—right down to his short stature—the volatile man who was known to almost everyone as "Midge," was at turns vicious and charismatic. In one moment, he could be buying drinks for everyone in a restaurant, and in the next, he might be smashing up the place, or even shooting the bartender. An allegedly "made" member of the Mafia and a successful amateur boxer, Annunziato loved kids, but also never shied away from an opportunity to intimidate rivals, shake down business owners, influence politicians, or corrupt law enforcement officers. If he wasn't actively causing trouble, he was certainly near it at any given moment, and because of his connections, didn't seem to care who knew about it.

In short, Annunziato was a jerk, and proud of it.

Before he would rise to infamy as "Midge Renault," however, Salvatore Anthony Annunziato was born on December 24, 1919, in the Fair Haven section of New Haven. The son of an abusive bootlegger, he was one of ten children in a poor home, a rough-and-tumble brood who were constantly at odds with the law—his five older brothers were mostly juvenile delinquents, either ending up in jail or reform school before their teen years. Although Salvatore was supposedly the "smartest" of his siblings, he wouldn't be mistaken for a teacher's pet by any stretch. He stole, shot dice, and often hit other students, including girls. Following family tradition, he was arrested before his tenth birthday.

A few years later when his mother died from rheumatic fever, the already troubled thirteen-year-old Salvatore went into a deeper tailspin. He was repeatedly involved in illegal incidents, including one time when he stole a car and ran over another kid who was riding a bicycle. He soon ended up in reform school with a few of his older brothers.

Following another path established by his siblings, Salvatore became interested in boxing, and the naturally combative boy soon excelled at the sport. His older brother Fortunato had been fighting under the moniker "Jack Renault," so the five-foot-three Salvatore decided to be a chip off the ol' family block, adopting the ring name "Midget Renault." The nickname was eventually shortened to "Midge," and it would stick with him for the rest of his life.

In 1936, at age sixteen, Midge Renault won the Connecticut amateur flyweight title, and seemed to be headed for a successful run in the ring. Over the next three years, despite fighting multiple times a month and winning more than a few bouts, the hard-charging brawler never again reached the same level of success. It also didn't help his boxing career that one of his brothers punched out the state athletic commissioner who had suspended Midge for slugging an opponent who was down.

By 1940, Annunziato was out of organized boxing and trying to find a new vocation. He flirted with a number of legitimate professions—shoe repair, manufacturing, furniture upholstery—but never really settled into any of them, instead getting into street fights and drifting in and out of jail.

World War II came along, and like many young men, Annunziato was drafted in 1942. Unlike most of them, however, he chose to get out of his obligation by starting a brawl in the recruitment center with police officers. While he was at the police station being booked, he then allegedly stood on a chair and challenged anybody in the place to fight for fifty dollars. He was declared unfit for service and spent the next two months in jail.

Although he wasn't ready to make a commitment to the military, Annunziato was prepared to take on a significant one in his personal life. He met and married Louise Corraro, and the young couple soon welcomed two sons: Francisco (who would be called "Frank") in 1943, and Anthony, in 1945. Later on, the couple would add two daughters to the brood.

Meanwhile, back on the street, Annunziato became a player in the wartime gas-rationing racket, dealing in counterfeit and stolen gas ration coupons. It turned out to be a lucrative enterprise, and it also helped him make connections in the criminal underworld. After the war ended—and with it, the fraudulent coupon business—Annunziato and a few accomplices started holding up illegal card games. After one such robbery in November 1945, he was caught by police and sent to prison for the next four years.

Ever working the angles, the gregarious Annunziato took full advantage of what could have been a bad situation and used his prison time as an opportunity to network with other criminals. During his incarceration, he connected with Ralph Mele, who purportedly ran the Connecticut territory for renowned New York mob boss Frank Costello (of the infamous Luciano crime family network). He also met Charles "Charlie the Blade" Tourine, another notorious gangster who would mentor Annunziato and show him the ropes, as well as bats, brass knuckles, black jacks, and other tools of intimidation.

Annunziato was released from prison in 1949, and the thirty-year-old former fighter began his organized crime career in earnest, settling easily into Mele's gang. He was allegedly involved in everything from participating in simple shake downs and extortion, to running floating craps games and illegal lotteries, to conducting protection schemes and loan sharking—all the mob classics.

As it turns out, many of the traits that would qualify Annunziato as a jerk—such as his quick temper, willingness to engage in fisticuffs, dishonest nature, and general disregard of legal authority—were also key attributes for a successful career in organized crime, and soon he was moving up the ranks. Business was also going well for his boss Ralph Mele, who, without getting approval from the top levels of the Mafia, had pushed his efforts into other territories. Unfortunately for Mele, the crime families in those areas pushed back, and in March 1951, he was found dead near East Rock in New Haven with five bullets in his head.

Although no one is certain because such things aren't always openly discussed, it is believed that soon after Mele's demise Annunziato became a "made man," meaning that he was officially inducted into the Mafia. Most likely the highly regarded "Charlie the Blade" Tourine was his sponsor, and as such, would have played a key role in the secret initiation ceremony. Once a full Mafia soldier, Annunziato would have special responsibilities and privileges, including all the far-reaching and potent influence that the mob could muster. He just needed to stay loyal, make sure that the upper hierarchy of the family got their regular cut of all profits, and do what was of asked of him without question.

Annunziato eagerly complied.

The early 1950s were the last days of the Golden Age of the Mafia. For reasons still not exactly clear, J. Edgar Hoover, the feared director of the Federal Bureau of Investigation, had taken the official position that the Mafia did not exist. Some claim that mob bosses had some compromising personal information about Hoover's alleged homosexuality and were blackmailing him; others suggest that the director was a compulsive gambler and had gotten in over his head, so he was forced to ignore the Mafia's activities to erase his debts. Whatever the reason, the FBI wasn't investigating organized crime at this point, and it was prospering accordingly.

Now that Mele was gone, his New Haven territory was allegedly divided between Annunziato and another thug, Ralph "Whitey" Tropiano. Although they despised each other, the two wise guys forged a reluctant truce that allowed them to work together to take control of most of the illegal activities in the Elm City. As partners, Tropiano and Annunziato successfully ran the local numbers racket (an illicit unsanctioned lottery), which was a very lucrative venture; on his own, Annunziato focused on soliciting protection money from dining establishments and other businesses, as well as managing various gambling activities.

These doings well under his control, Annunziato moved into another money-making arena: union management. In 1952, he became the business agent for the New Haven chapter of the International Brotherhood of Operating Engineers, Local 478, which was mostly comprised of operators of heavy construction equipment. With the backing of "Charlie the Blade" Tourine, Annunziato soon gained control of the union, and with it, was able to exert a heavy-handed influence over every construction project from New Haven to Greenwich. In addition to demanding four-figure bribes for his personal approval of projects, he leaned on construction companies to hire superfluous workers, and to significantly overpay for gratuitous items such as tickets to union dinners or advertisements in the union newsletter. He also generously accepted unauthorized cash gifts to look the other way if safety rules or labor laws needed to be bent so that a project could be expedited or completed at a cheaper cost.

As a union boss, Annunziato wasn't a complete jerk, however. He routinely took care of his friends and relatives, often getting them cushy, high-paying jobs with almost no responsibilities. He even sponsored a youth football team, called the Fair Haven Midgets, of course.

The timing of Annunziato's ascension to union boss was particularly fortuitous. In 1953, Richard C. Lee became mayor of New Haven and ushered in grand plans to revitalize the city. Lee procured millions of dollars in federal construction grants as part of the effort to create Interstate 95, including the building of the Pearl Harbor Memorial Bridge that would straddle the Quinnipiac River and New Haven harbor. In turn, this money found its way into the union's coffers and Annunziato's pockets.

Annunziato's wealth and union connections also brought him political power. He had public servants and elected officials in the palm of his hand, often getting them to take care of everything for him from parking tickets to criminal charges. In 1954, after Annunziato was arrested for running over a man and then assaulting him, US Representative Albert W. Cretella of New Haven bailed his "friend" out of trouble, fixing the charges so that all Annunziato received was a slap-on-the-wrist fine.

With everything going so well, Annunziato seemed to feel that he was invulnerable. He made a show of carousing and throwing his weight around, buying drinks for everyone, telling off police officers, and generally behaving irresponsibly. Still as physically aggressive as ever, he got in numerous fights, often doling out savage beatings without any fear of reprisal because of his mob ties. People across the greater New Haven area knew who Sal "Midge" Annunziato was and, more importantly, for whom he worked. Most were also very reluctant to step forward to officially complain about it.

On separate nights in 1955, while out with his brother Angelo and two "associates" at the Red Lobster restaurant in Milford, and then at the Double Beach House in Branford, Annunziato initiated riots—possibly as part of a plan to intimidate the respective owners into selling him their businesses—resulting in both eateries being trashed. The police were called in to break up both fracases, and Annunziato was charged with numerous infractions. When he went to court, however, no witness would testify against him, so the majority of the charges against him had to be dropped, resulting in a conviction that garnered only a one-year sentence. The case was appealed, giving him a temporary reprieve.

By 1957, things were starting to change for the Mafia in New Haven, and across the country. The pressure from the public had increased, and law enforcement—including Hoover's FBI—was finally forced to deal with the problem. The bureau started taking a deeper look into Annunziato's activities, compiling a sizable file on him and other area mobsters. The local authorities also started cracking down on organized crime-related doings, so when Annunziato's conviction from the 1955 restaurants case came before the Connecticut State Supreme Court in March 1958, it was upheld. He had to serve his one-year sentence and was remanded to prison.

Annunziato was not completely out of the political sway, however. Rather than being sent to a state penitentiary, he was incarcerated in New Haven at a local jail on Whalley Avenue, which he soon made his home away from home. After generously paying off the guards, he was allowed the run of the facility, spending very little time in his cell. In addition to controlling all the illegal activities on site—gambling, prostitution, alcohol and drug distribution, etc.—he supposedly dined on fine food brought to him from the outside and did union business like he was in his own office.

The year went by quickly and easily for Annunziato, but it wasn't all peaches and cream when he was released in 1959. Because of the growing public tide against the mob and pressure from the FBI, he was unceremoniously relieved of his duties as union boss.

Midge's personal life was going through a rough patch, too. Although still married to Louise and living in a nice East Haven home, he had picked up a mistress a few years earlier, an older divorcée with whom he openly stayed half the time. He took care of the woman, furnishing her house in the identical way as his other home so that he could be comfortable in both places. Louise knew of the situation and didn't like it, but Annunziato, being a jerk, didn't really care. He tried to spend time with his children, however, giving extra attention to his sons.

For the most part, Annunziato's boys hadn't fallen far from the jerk tree, often skipping school, fighting with other kids, and causing trouble. On the evening of December 31, 1959, however, tragedy struck—Annunziato's younger son, Anthony, was accidentally hit by a car and died from his injuries two days later. Annunziato was devastated, and subsequently worked hard to bring his other son, Frank, closer to him and his way of life.

Before Frank was old enough to join the family business, Annunziato had other serious issues. The FBI and the New Haven police had ratcheted up their efforts to shut down the mob, and in the process, made Annunziato's criminal life miserable. In 1960, Annunziato was arrested on what seemed like, for him, a petty offense—accepting $350 in payments and bonuses from a construction company involved with the Interstate 95 project. Considering the thousands he had collected in illegal kickbacks and bribes, it was small potatoes, but just as the infamous mobster Al Capone was taken down by simple tax evasion, the authorities were looking for any excuse to thwart organized crime and get those who were involved behind bars.

It worked. Despite a two-year appeal process, Annunziato was incarcerated again, except this time he was sent to the Federal Correctional Institution in Milan, Michigan. Although a medium-security facility, it was nothing like the vacation he had experienced when he had served his previous sentence in New Haven four years earlier. He did his time without incident, was freed, and returned to Connecticut.

Within a year of being released, Annunziato was arrested five times, each incident more violent than the next. He led a racial attack in Fair Haven; incited a clash at an East Haven social event; tried to ram an East Haven police officer with a car after a chase; and savagely attacked a loan collector with a baseball bat. In short, Annunziato was still the same jerk he always was, if not worse.

The most violent incident, however, came in November 1963 when he was at a New Haven bar. While drinking heavily—possibly because he was on trial for the aforementioned offenses—Annunziato got into a heated argument with a fellow hoodlum by the name of Lawrence Zernitz. Things quickly escalated, and before anyone realized what was happening, Annunziato drew a revolver and shot Zernitz in the stomach.

This time there was no calling in political favors to lessen the charges. Annunziato was first found guilty on charges related to the loan collector assault, for which the judge sentenced him to five to ten years. While serving that time, he then underwent the trial for the shooting incident, which turned out to be a farce. Evidently, some of Annunziato's mob "acquaintances" got to the prosecution's witnesses before the trial, so once those witnesses reached the stand, many of them conveniently claimed that they could not recall the details of the night in question. Even more remarkably, when it came time to testify under oath and for the record, Lawrence Zernitz—the man whom Annunziato had shot at point-blank range—suddenly couldn't identify his assailant!

Despite the glaring lack of witness testimony, the jury declared Annunziato guilty, and he was sentenced to an additional five years in prison. He was serving his time when in 1966, his conviction was overturned on a technicality. "Luckily" for Annunziato, Zernitz had overdosed on heroin—some say suspiciously— and was no longer around to (not) testify, so the state's attorney dropped the case. Annunziato made parole after four-and-a-half years served, and was once again a free man.

Thanks to the aforementioned Mafia-busting efforts by local police and the FBI, the New Haven-area mob had changed dramatically by the time the forty-eight-year-old Annunziato was again prowling the back streets, seedy bars, and dark alleys of the Elm City in June 1968. The cachet of being a mobster wasn't quite as glamorous as it once had been, and there was constant law enforcement surveillance, which made criminal operations even more difficult. The New Haven territory was also now fractured, split among a few different organized crime groups, all of whom were vying to be the top crew.

When he was first released, Annunziato attempted to get into a few different legitimate businesses, including an industrial laundry, a restaurant, and a concrete company, but none of those efforts panned out. Within months, he was back to his old jerk ways, causing trouble and mixing it up with the new heavies who had come along during his prison-induced absence. Before long, he was warring with a number of New Haven gangsters, including Edward Devlin.

This time, however, Annunziato had a new ally—his son Frank, who was now twenty-five and seemingly ready to join the mob. A proud father, Annunziato was more than enthusiastic to have his progeny follow in his footsteps, although there was some question whether Frank was fully on board with the idea or had the *cojones* for the job. It would eventually turn out to be a bad decision all around.

In the midst of the ongoing disputes and sometimes violent skirmishes between Annunziato and the other members of local organized crime factions, Annunziato allegedly got word that one of his soldiers, Edward Gould, was planning on going to work for his rival Devlin. That didn't sit well with Annunziato, for whom loyalty meant everything.

Some people would have had a talk with someone about to jump ship; other less sophisticated folk might have roughed up a potential defector. But Annunziato was an ill-tempered, violent jerk—he ordered his son Frank and another member of his gang to "whack" Gould, as they like to say.

According to court testimony, late in the evening on August 10, 1968, Francisco "Frank" Annunziato and Richard Biondi met up with Gould on Grand Avenue in New Haven and asked for a ride. Gould obliged; the three got into the car and set off. According to Gould, he looked up in the rearview mirror and saw Annunziato raising a gun, and quickly realizing what was going down, hit the brakes. He jumped out and fled, but not before Annunziato and Biondi managed to shoot him in the shoulder and foot.

The police wasted no time getting involved, although it would be two-and-a-half years before both Salvatore and Frank Annunziato would simultaneously stand trial for the attempted murder of Edward Gould. (Before he could get his day in court, Richard Biondi was machine-gunned down in his own apartment on December 23, 1968, supposedly on Devlin's orders.) In the interim, the elder Annunziato continued his usual business, regularly getting in and out of trouble—and jail.

After numerous legal delays, the trial began in February 1971, and over the course of two weeks, the inglorious career of Salvatore "Midge Renault" Annunziato was in the headlines. In addition to witness testimony from numerous unsavory characters, the jury heard a litany of Annunziato's criminal activities and other transgressions, including how, after the botched hit, he allegedly admonished his son, "Frankie, you can't do nothing right."

After absorbing all the gritty details of Annunziato's checkered history, the jury went into deliberation on March 3, 1971. Five hours later they came back with a verdict: guilty.

"That's the most vicious verdict in the world!" Annunziato shouted in court, but it stood nonetheless. Although he wasn't in the car or at the scene, he was still sentenced by Judge Herbert S. MacDonald to nine to fourteen years in prison, while son (and trigger man) Frank got five to ten years.

Annunziato's lawyers tried to work the appeals process, but in 1972, the proud career criminal and lifetime jerk was back in prison yet again. This time, he would serve almost six years of hard time before getting sprung yet again on a technicality—

apparently his well-paid (and very active) attorneys were better at their work than Annunziato was at staying out of trouble.

As before, as soon as he was released in 1978, Annunziato went back to his old ways. The fifty-nine-year-old former fighter and union boss returned to running illegal gambling enterprises, shaking down legitimate business owners, and working his old union connections for bribes. He was also drinking heavily, spending the majority of his daylight hours in bars, and had become more surly than ever—he even threatened newspaper reporters with "cement shoes" when they asked too many questions. His chaotic life came to a head when he was arrested after allegedly shooting at two men on Putnam Street outside the home of his longtime mistress, hitting one of them in the leg.

If that wasn't bad enough, he was also still on the FBI's radar. Even if "Midge" Annunziato wasn't the organized crime kingpin he had been back in the 1950s, the bureau had continued its surveillance of his activities, and had been successful in recording him on videotape receiving a $500 kickback for operating an illegal gambling casino at a union Christmas party in December 1978. He was formally charged for that as well as labor racketeering, embezzlement, and conspiracy in April 1979, and between that and the shooting, Annunziato—out of jail temporarily on $30,000 bond—was surely headed back to prison, this time for an extended stay.

Unfortunately, Annunziato had even bigger problems. The bosses of New York's Genovese crime family supposedly had grown tired of Annunziato's public antics, and after the charges, had summoned him to New York City to tell him that they were "displeased." One rumor suggested that afterward, they even placed a contract on his life. Either way, he was a marked man, and his time was running out.

On June 19, 1979, an old Genovese crime family acquaintance, Tommy "The Blond" Vastano, arrived at the Annunziato's East Haven home for a visit along with Pasquale "Shaggy Dog" Amendola, another reputed gang member. At about 8:40 p.m., all three men decided to go out "for a ride" in two cars. Annunziato and Vastano were in one car, Amendola in another. After a short distance, Amendola was instructed by Annunziato to "go home," which he did.

Salvatore "Midge Renault" Annunziato would never be seen again.

Nine days later, Annunziato's lawyer officially reported to police that his client was missing, touching off a massive manhunt involving local, state, and federal law enforcement. The front-page headline of the *New Haven Register* proclaimed "Cops Believe 'Midge' May Have Been Slain." His long-suffering wife Louise would testify that Annunziato never came home that night, and that she hadn't heard from him since.

The usual suspects were quickly rounded up—everyone who knew Annunziato was interviewed, criminals and cohorts were brought in and questioned. Leads were followed by the FBI from Aruba to London, all to no avail. Annunziato was gone, and no one seemed to know what had happened. And if anyone did know, they weren't talking—or were being stopped before they could.

In the wee hours of January 28, 1980, six months after Annunziato's disappearance and before he could testify before a grand jury looking into what had happened, Tommy Vastano—the last person who had seen Annunziato alive—was brutally shot to death in his Stratford driveway. No one witnessed the crime, and it appears no one was ever charged for it, either. Vastano was one of numerous Genovese crime family members to either go missing or end up dead over a short period that year.

Speculation about Annunziato's fate was as creative as it was unsubstantiated. One newspaper story suggested that Annunziato had been under the care of a plastic surgeon shortly before his disappearance, and had taken thousands of dollars in cash with him that night he went for the ride. Another rumor alleged that he surreptitiously had been sent "out west on the farm," a cushy retirement home of sorts for gangsters, where former made men would go to live out their lives in anonymity and peace—a great concept although no such place has ever been found to exist. It also seems very unlikely that an organization such as the Mafia would leave loose ends just lying around basking in the California sun.

Other stories told to the police by criminal informants and anonymous tipsters painted a less rosy—and more probable—ending for Annunziato. Most suggested that he had, in fact, been executed by the mob; one supposed witness claimed that Annunziato was murdered the night of his disappearance, his body weighted with an anchor and then dumped off a bridge into Bridgeport harbor.

As part of a 1991 FBI investigation, agents discovered the remains of three men who had been buried under a Hamden garage, one of whom had been five foot three, the same height as Annunziato. DNA tests at the time weren't conclusive, and even though the process has improved since then, Annunziato's daughters (his remaining blood relatives, as son Frank died in 1983) have stated they are not interested in pursuing the case.

Like the case of renowned fellow union organizer Jimmy Hoffa, it seems rather improbable that after so many decades Annunziato's disappearance will ever be solved. Chances are that he met his death in the violent manner that had become so familiar to him and that had befallen so many of his gangster brethren— including Joe Pesci's Tommy DeVito—courtesy of a bullet he never saw coming.

To some, Salvatore "Midge" Annunziato was a "good fella." To others, he was just a jerk.

CHAPTER 15

William Stuart:
The (Allegedly) Most Celebrated Jerk in Connecticut History

Sometimes trying to determine if the label of jerk can be applied to someone can be tricky. Then other times, it's as simple as reading the title of their autobiography. To wit: *Sketches of the Life of William Stuart, The First and Most Celebrated Counterfeiter of Connecticut—As Given by Himself.*

As demonstrated throughout this book, jerks come in all different varieties, from cruel murderers and hypocritical holy men to arrogant blowhards and eccentric characters. As one of the state's "most celebrated" criminals, William Stuart falls somewhere between the last two groups—by his own admission, he was an adventurous, wicked, devil-may-care troublemaker and confirmed rogue (in the truest sense of the word) who never met an opportunity that he didn't like to heartily frolic or take improper advantage of a situation.

Unlike some other jerks, Stuart was an incorrigible character and inveterate storyteller whom most would welcome on the bar stool next to them—for the cost of a mug of ale, a more entertaining night full of ripping yarns and tales of derring do would not be found. He was a man who unapologetically reveled in his own bad behavior.

Following are some snippets from the introduction of his very entertaining autobiography, which he wrote at the age of sixty-six in 1854:

> *If I am the hero of my own story, my heroism was displayed in distinct opposition to the laws of the land.*

For a series of years, I was perpetually involving myself, my connectors, and the community in troubles and losses. These are calamities incident to an unjustifiable attack upon the institutions and laws of the land, and if in the course of events I became the sufferer, I have only to aver that the necessities of order and justice required my punishment.

I give this outline to the world, to warn men inclined to criminal courses, of the unmitigated evils attendant upon a willful disregard of honesty, public morals and legal enactments.

It seems pretty straightforward that this braggart was a man who harbored no illusions as to the magnitude of his jerkiness. As his autobiography is the prime source for his many alleged misdeeds, we have to take ol' Bill Stuart at his "repentant" scoundrel's word (although it would be wise to keep in mind those "B. S." initials). Then again, if Stuart was legitimately guilty of a tenth of the acts for which he takes credit, that's more than enough to convict him of being a jerk in the first degree. Records show that he did spend considerable time incarcerated at the infamous New-Gate Prison in East Granby, so he was obviously no angel.

William Stuart was born on May 23, 1789, in Wilton. His father owned a farm and, apparently, a good number of belts and leather straps that could be used for corporal punishment as Stuart claimed his youthful waywardness earned him repeated floggings. He was a mischievous child who had "a rare knack" of involving others in trouble yet somehow escaping blame, a trait that he would rely on throughout his life.

Young Bill engaged in boyish pranks, including torturing the local schoolmaster Edward Coburn by dumping his son in "semi-liquid manure," dulling Coburn's new ax, and tarring and feathering his cow. As a teen, Stuart was also arrested after pushing—on a lark—a local "bad" girl by the (working?) name of Poll Rider into a ripped featherbed and then into a fire, which burned off most of her hair; his joke earned him a $200 penalty that he paid with funds from a $3,000 inheritance that had come following his father's death.

Accepting that hard, honest work was not even remotely in his nature, Stuart turned to counterfeiting early, hammering six-pences into shillings and then turning the shillings into quarters. He also fashioned quarters out of melted pewter.

Flush with inheritance and phony money, Stuart couldn't keep himself out of trouble. He spent many nights in the company of "rude men and noisy girls," drinking rum and smoking tobacco until the wee hours, and partaking in all sorts of rabble rousing.

In 1806, when Stuart was seventeen, he went to the wilds of Susquehanna, Pennsylvania, to bring his grandfather back to Wilton to live out his days. While there, he took a shine to one of his cousins, an attraction that had he been allowed to pursue legally, he wistfully claimed, would've changed the course of his life from immoral to honorable. After depositing his grandfather safely in Wilton, the still-quite-infatuated teenager returned to Susquehanna even though he thought the inhabitants there were "a race as debased and corrupt as those who have already entered the Stygian pool."

For all his grumbling, Stuart fit in just fine among the heathens, earning money by day cutting and transporting timber and then spending it by night on whiskey, women, gambling, and other debauchery. He was also involved in constant shenanigans—such as stealing an old woman's honey pot and sharing it with his fellow rowdies—that constantly had him at odds with local authorities.

After a year and a half, Stuart felt the need to move on from the coarseness of Susquehanna, and after a tearful parting with his angelic "blossom of the mountain," he returned to Wilton. Life back in Connecticut wasn't nearly as exciting as it had been in Pennsylvania, and soon he was rambling about the state in pursuit of action. He found it soon enough.

While boisterously drinking at a Norwalk tavern, he and his close lifelong friend Joseph Mills were approached by a stranger

A portrait of William Stuart from his autobiography
SKETCHES OF THE LIFE OF WILLIAM STUART, THE FIRST AND MOST CELEBRATED COUNTERFEITER OF CONNECTICUT—
AS GIVEN BY HIMSELF, WILLIAM STUART

who recognized them as "ambitious and unscrupulous youth." As such, the stranger, who called himself Joseph Sherlock, thought they might not be averse to less-than-legal undertakings.

At the time, there was no official federal paper money—each state had chartered banks that issued their own notes, and the US government wouldn't start printing its own until the Civil War in 1861. Sherlock showed them counterfeit money and explained a simple con: that they could prosper significantly by using phony bills in larger denominations to overpay for purchases and then bank the legitimate change they received. He offered them $100 of counterfeit money for $10 of legitimate cash, explaining that by following his plan, they could each make $50,000 within six months.

"Was not here the golden bait?" Stuart asked himself in his autobiography. "What greater inducement could be laid before the senses of an ambitious and unscrupulous youth?"

Stuart took $300 worth of "Burroughs's money"—notes forged by renowned Canadian counterfeiter Stephen Burroughs based on Albany and Philadelphia banks—for his horse, saddle, and bridle (worth $35), and immediately began changing it at every opportunity. Within two weeks he and Mills had passed it all onto unsuspecting locals, and only had good money left in their pockets. They were hooked.

Next time out, they received more than $1,000 in counterfeit money from Sherlock, who gave them tips in how to properly weather the newly minted phony bills by oiling them, folding them in blotting paper, and then ironing them. Sherlock also gave them the location in Canada where they could get as much fake money as they needed, and offered other strategies for successful counterfeiting.

Stuart and Mills enthusiastically became experts at the practice, traveling across the countryside to visit as many different shops and gatherings of merchants as they could. They bought everything from watches to sheep with fraudulent money and kept the real change. As promised, they got very wealthy very quickly. The savvy Stuart was sure to mix in good money to help keep suspicion at bay.

Still, merchants became aware that there were counterfeiters in the area, and were on the lookout for the Burroughs bills. Trying to stay a step ahead, Stuart started traveling to Slab City—an area that is now near Sherbrooke in Quebec, Canada, just over the Vermont border—to get new counterfeit bills from a different engraving source. By having phony notes made on a different set of banks, yet continuing to trade $10 in true money for every $100 in counterfeit, he was soon able to build quite an estate for himself.

Stuart spent the two years of the end of the decade passing counterfeit bills across the Northeast, from Massachusetts down through New York and Pennsylvania to Maryland, employing the same basic ruse. Communication between law enforcement and civic authorities was hardly what it is today (the telegraph wouldn't even be invented for another quarter century), and the advent of photography and "Wanted" posters were still far off, so as long as the crafty Stuart was careful to keep moving to different towns and "spread the wealth," he was able to evade arrest.

It also helped that Stuart seemed to be especially poised and cunning. One time while in Philadelphia, he met a man of "doubtful reputation" named Smith who intently claimed that he wanted to partake in the counterfeit scam. Stuart resisted at first—he had heard that a reward of $300 was being offered to anyone who was instrumental in capturing a counterfeiter, and thought it might be better to lay low—but after Smith swore an oath of secrecy, Stuart eventually went back to Connecticut for $1,800 in phony bank notes. When he returned to Smith's home, Smith seemed overly eager to see him, which immediately aroused Stuart's suspicions.

Smith asked Stuart to wait in his parlor, and as soon as he was alone, Stuart took all his fake bills and hid them in Smith's desk. Smith returned a few minutes later with two local constables, who went to arrest Stuart for being a counterfeiter. Stuart let the men search him, and after they could find nothing but good money, he told them with "a bold and honest face" that *Smith* was the true counterfeiter and that *he* was using Stuart as an innocent dupe! He then suggested—over Smith's protests—that they search the house; of course, they discovered the bogus money in the desk. Both were hauled off to the judge, and after a brief trial, Stuart was declared innocent and released. Smith, however, was found guilty and sentenced to seven years in the state prison.

Stuart, ever the jerk, laughed all the way to Baltimore.

In Baltimore, he told of how he met a young woman who was "every way fitted as a partner, having all the qualifications to be a perfect rogue." She could cry and lie on command, and was a master of disguise. They managed to pass a lot of counterfeit money together, but then Stuart was caught and jailed. His accomplice helped him break out of jail by passing him black powder through a window, which he used to blow out part of the cell wall. In his eagerness to get out of town, however, he didn't bother to say goodbye or even thanks to the woman. Love 'em and leave 'em!

From Maryland, Stuart headed further south and eventually wound up in South Carolina where he met a free "mulatto" (mixed race) man by the name of Pomp who "looked smart for business." He convinced Pomp to join in him in a devious boondoggle: They would go to various estates where Stuart would make a show of what a skilled and obedient "slave" Pomp was. Having made a good impression, Stuart would "sell" Pomp for a hefty amount and depart. Pomp would then escape as soon as possible and meet Stuart at a predetermined location, where they would divide up the proceeds from the sale and move on to the next mark.

The con worked a few times, earning them a tidy sum, but then came a time when Pomp didn't show up at the rendezvous. Stuart waited a few days, but figured Pomp had been caught in the ruse. Although he claimed he had felt sorry for his partner, Stuart nonetheless went on his merry way, spending the money they had made together.

Stuart headed back to Connecticut, meeting in New York a woman who was elegant, attractive, charming, and, most importantly, "well schooled in roguery." Stuart decided that she was the ideal partner for a new swindle, and they spent the next few months traveling around New England pretending to be wealthy socialites. Moving in high society, they were able to successfully pass counterfeit money on to an entirely new class of unsuspecting victims. Unlike his other partners, however, Stuart parted with this one on good terms, giving her $100 in real money before heading back to the family farm in Wilton.

By 1810 the twenty-one-year-old Stuart hadn't been back to farming for long when he heard that South American provinces were rebelling against Spain and that American privateers were setting sail to capture Spanish merchant ships. Thinking he could cash in big with a jaunt at sea, he joined up. He was on board only a few weeks before he grew tired of nautical life, which coincided directly with being ordered to scrape barnacles off the hull of the ship while anchored in Savannah harbor.

In the course of protesting, he ran afoul of one of the officers—an agitated Stuart doused him with a bucket full of "brine and filth."

The defiant act would've earned him five hundred lashes, but rather than wait around to be punished, he managed to jump ship (another crime) by quickly going ashore with a landing party and pretending to be suffering from severe intestinal discomfort. After slipping off for "privacy," he ran all the way to Connecticut without looking back.

Then again, maybe he didn't totally escape punishment. Upon his return to Wilton, Stuart was besieged by his cousin to get married to a friend, and although he and his impending bride were "reluctant," they eventually were talked into a union. Despite lavishly praising his wife for her devotion, trustworthiness, resourcefulness, kindness, and for possessing good sense and infinite patience (she often bailed him out of trouble), and for simply being "one of the best women that was ever created," he never mentions her name—or those of his children—anywhere in his autobiography. Considering that Stuart drops the names of everyone from his old schoolmaster, to passing rubes he swindled, to those he was imprisoned with, it's either a significant slight or a chivalrous attempt to protect her reputation. (According to other sources, her name was Sally, and she stayed with him until her death in 1849 at the age of fifty-six.)

Anyway, claiming that after taking a wife he was interested in settling down and "abandoning roguery forever," Stuart moved to Bridgewater to avoid contact with his former cohorts. They soon found him anyway, and applied what appeared to be modest pressure. In less than three months, he was back to his old ways.

Stuart continued working his most successful scheme—paying for something with counterfeit notes and keeping the good change—while also causing general mischief. One of his proud pranks was going around town with a nervous mare that was prone to kicking and then getting her to intentionally wreck buildings, knock down fences, and batter hapless people who crossed him.

Stuart also became more creative in the ways he cheated people, coming up with events like horse and dog fights—events "that threw men off their accustomed watchfulness" by causing chaos and drunken revelry—which allowed him to fleece tavern keepers and pass even larger amounts of phony money.

Even though Stuart hadn't actually been caught trading counterfeit cash up to this point, some members of the community were becoming suspicious of his activities, and tried to snare him in the act. In pursuit of a $300 bounty for catching a counterfeiter, one local merchant by the name of Tilley W. Reed apparently tried to convince Stuart that he wanted to go into business with him. After vetting Reed and making him swear all sorts of oaths of allegiance, Stuart bought one of Reed's horses for $300 in forged bills, but immediately regretted it and tried to get the fake money back. Reed resisted, and after Stuart offered $100 in genuine script, Reed insisted on $300 and the return of the horse. Quite vexed at being double-crossed, Stuart offered Reed a few mugs of cider—spiked with opium. After Reed passed out, Stuart took back the counterfeit money and burned it, then took Reed's horse and sold it for $95.

"I have told this tale perhaps a thousand times," wrote a pleased Stuart, "and have never seen the man who did not acknowledge that exact justice was done to Reed."

The War of 1812 broke out and twenty-three-year-old Bill Stuart found his "great purpose was to profit by the excitement." He volunteered as an enlisting agent, using the opportunity to get new recruits drunk and exchange their good currency with counterfeit. He was also able to get his bad money used to pay soldiers, and generously volunteered to serve as an inspector for questionable bills, which was like putting a rooster in charge of the hen house.

The societal and financial unrest caused by the war also provided ample novel ways for Stuart and his cohorts to expand their fraudulent ways. A large number of new banks were springing up, and as quickly as Stuart could get his hands on any notes from one of these fledgling institutions, he sent them to his engraver in Canada. The phonies were forged so well and so rapidly that Stuart was able to spread them faster than the real notes, and thus, they were believed to be the genuine article, causing untold headaches for the banks.

Stuart also used the war as an excuse to pillage the locals around New London, where he was stationed. He "kept up a perpetual series of frolics" and passed thousands of counterfeit dollars before hostilities ended in 1815 and he was discharged.

Following the war, he picked up where he left off, routinely traveling to Canada to get counterfeit money and then coming back to distribute it across the Northeast. He had a few close calls, including when he was forced to eat a phony bill in Danbury. That particular effort didn't quite fool authorities, and he was jailed.

While incarcerated, Stuart scammed the jailer out of copious amounts of alcohol. Having been promised a gill of rum (about a quarter pint) for every rat he caught while in his cell, Stuart caught one, collected his drink, and then pretended to dispose of it. In reality, he kept the rodent hidden and presented it as a new one day after day, thus repeatedly collecting the rum reward until the creature finally escaped.

After serving his sentence, Stuart returned to Bridgewater and for the next year, continued to be a nuisance, distributing fake bills and annoying all with his shenanigans. On the spur of the moment during a visit to New York, he decided to enlist in the army "to fight Indians." While training, Stuart was made a sergeant, and—as he had done in his prior military stint—used the position to profit. Rather than just pass counterfeit money (which he did in large amounts, as always), he concocted a swindle where he would repeatedly get men to "desert" and then "recapture" them, earning a sizable reward each time.

As in other instances, when it came time to follow through on a commitment—and actually fight Indians—Stuart chose discretion over valor and deserted. He high-tailed it back to Connecticut but was forced to hide out as a wanted man. Unhappy with this low-profile situation, he put together a plan to go abroad and live free in Europe.

Stuart joined the crew of a ship bound for France, but deserted yet again before leaving North American waters. This time, he got off in Georgia and spent three months there with an attractive widow who "was ripe for almost every enterprise, and was willing to engage in any object that promised a golden reward." Before going back to Connecticut, he promised her that he would return with counterfeit money so that they could profit together. Obviously quite smitten, he didn't mention his liaison to anyone after getting home. He checked in briefly on his wife and family, and then went to Canada to get the fraudulent funds he needed for an extended stay in Georgia.

While making some final preparations for his trip, Stuart was in Ridgefield when he went to buy a handkerchief and accidentally paid with a bad five-dollar note. He was arrested and brought to court in Danbury where he had already done jail time for counterfeiting.

This time Stuart was not so lucky—he couldn't bamboozle the court or devise a daring escape. In November of 1817, Bill Stuart, then twenty-eight, was sentenced to five years in East Granby's infamous New-Gate Prison. He didn't send word to his Georgia peach letting her know about his situation, which was probably just fine by his wife and children in Bridgewater.

Stuart claims that just before he was shipped off to New-Gate, he was approached by officials of the court and offered a shorter sentence (only a month!) if he were to divulge the name of his associates in the counterfeiting scheme. He informed them that he was a one-man operation. "They knew I lied, and I knew it," he wrote, "but before I would entrap others to secure myself, I would be hanged on the nearest tree."

Stuart was a firm believer of honor among thieves—and jerks, apparently.

Four weeks later he was on his way to join a prison full of both. In the early part of the nineteenth century, New-Gate Prison was a foul place filled with criminals, reprobates, and all manner of ne'er-do-wells. A former copper mine that was crudely converted for use as a long-term jail, it was the first official prison in the United States; previously, those guilty of serious crimes were either dispatched immediately (usually at the end of a rope), or were inflicted with severe corporal punishment (whipping, branding, etc.). In New-Gate's storied history, many inmates attempted to break out, some successful, some not so much. More than one ended up crushed under tons of rocks after an ill-devised escape tunnel collapsed.

Stuart's impression of the place? While suggesting that "the poverty of language is such that no description, however faithfully wrought, can ever approach the truth," he still painted a colorful picture:

> *Loathsomeness and putridity, united with billions of ento-mological living specimens, shock the senses of a man uninured to filth, and he instinctively feels that in such cases nothing but fire can act successfully as a purifier and health preserver . . . armies of fleas, lice and bed bugs nightly covered every inch of this polluted prison, and would skip, hop and crawl away to avoid being trampled in the mire upon the floors like the grasshoppers of a meadow in the month of August.*

In short, it was nasty. But Stuart admitted that he had it coming for all his roguery, and resolved that once his time was done, he would pursue an honest existence. The problem was that he still had five years to be a jerk.

The first thing Stuart went about doing was to make life miserable for the prison keeper, Captain Elam Tuller. He constantly defied Tuller, arguing about the lack and quality of food rations, as well as standing up for what he believed were his rights.

While serving their sentences, inmates would learn trades so that they could make products that could be sold to help offset the cost of running the prison; prisoners were also allowed to earn money for themselves, which could be used to buy rations or be put toward their freedom. Stuart decided to become a cooper and learned to make barrels, a skill that he claims he mastered immediately. Although he could make two whiskey barrels a day, Tuller insisted that he make three. Stuart resisted this suggestion, which only caused more trouble.

In the meantime, Stuart couldn't resist falling back on his previous skill set. He pressed twenty-five-cent pieces into the chalk he was given to make barrel hoops adhere to wood, and by placing them between two boards, was able to create a crude mold. Using pewter that he melted down from the buttons of the other prisoners, he was soon able to mint his own coins, which he passed onto the unsuspecting visitors who came to New-Gate to buy barrels and other wares.

Tuller eventually caught the industrious cheat with a pocket full of phony silver pieces, and when called on it, the sharp-witted Stuart replied, "I was sent here for counterfeiting, and I shall lose my skill unless I do a little at the business." Tuller simply responded, "Stuart, I believe that you are the devil," and walked away amused.

Stuart and many of the other prisoners preferred to stay in the tunnels of the old copper mine whenever it was possible. Since it was some fifty feet straight down into the earth, the mine would stay the same somewhat comfortable temperature year round (between fifty and sixty degrees Fahrenheit), and although it was damp, there was relief from the bed bugs underground. The guards would seal the four-foot-wide vertical shaft entrance at night, and left to their own devices, prisoners would gamble, fiddle, and dance the hours away.

Stuart would also spend a portion of the evening devising plans to secure his premature liberty. At one point, he and a few cohorts spent ten nights digging an escape tunnel, only to have an outgoing inmate spill the beans. Tuller punished them by revoking their privilege to stay underground.

Meanwhile, Stuart's obstinate resistance to Tuller's insistence about increasing his barrel production continued to irritate the jail keeper. Tuller eventually transferred Stuart out of the cooper shop and into the nail block. Making nails was a fairly menial and tedious job, and was considered the lowest of prison tasks—each week, a prisoner would be given fifty-six pounds of iron, and in turn, would be expected to produce eight pounds of nails a day.

Of course, rather than take his punishment gracefully, Stuart decided to further annoy Tuller in a manner only a true jerk could conceive. After his transfer into the nail shop, Stuart noticed a sign up on the wall that declared any prisoner who was new to the black-smith's business would have six months to learn the trade, after which they would be expected to produce the eight pounds of nails.

On his initial attempt, Stuart proved to be a natural-born nail maker, impressing Tuller and the prison blacksmith with his skill. However, when Tuller suggested Stuart would now be expected to hammer out the daily allotment of nails, Stuart pointed out that he was sent there "by the operation of law," and according to the official prison rules, he had a full six months to keep learning how to make nails before he was obliged to meet the goal. Thus, he literally sat on his anvil each day—to Tuller's ever-growing ire—and watched the others work.

During this time, Stuart was able to convince one of the guards to give him a quart of rum, which he immediately imbibed. Tuller noticed Stuart was drunk and wanted to know from where Stuart got the alcohol; Stuart declined to tell him, and after a week, the exasperated Tuller put him in the "dungeon," chaining him to a rock deep in the mine and giving him only bread and water.

Tuller would have had more success getting a leopard to change its spots than getting a stubborn jerk like Stuart to reform his behavior. Stuart survived the extreme punishment, and decid-ing that he needed to teach Tuller a lesson, started plotting a pris-oner rebellion. When it came to revolt, however, only Stuart and three other prisoners acted, with disastrous results. Stuart bore the brunt of the guards' retaliation, receiving numerous lacera-tions, a wound on his head from a red hot iron bar, and a musket ball fired into his groin, which would remain lodged there for the rest of his life.

Despite the seriousness of his wounds, it appears Stuart survived almost completely out of spite for Tuller. He eventu-ally healed, although he pretended to be lame to avoid doing any work throughout the remainder of his sentence, which had been extended due to his part in the insurrection. In May 1825, Stuart finally went to Tuller, and playing upon his sympathies ("My fam-ily has suffered," "I am lame for life"), was able to negotiate his own release for twenty-two dollars, which he borrowed from the other inmates.

When Stuart was finally free, he threw down his crutches and walked out of New-Gate and into the tavern next door, where he drank and taunted his former captor. Tuller told him that had he known Stuart was faking his injuries, he would've kept him imprisoned "as long as the grass grows and water runs."

Thus a reformed man, Stuart returned once again to his family in Bridgewater, and vowed to live the rest of his life on the straight and narrow. Some of his former associates tried to involve him in various criminal shenanigans, but Stuart claims he was able to resist and focused on an honest life of farming. He still had "seasons of wildness," in large part due to his dependence on rum (no one is perfect!), yet he never again passed any counterfeit currency, nor did he participate in any illegal acts.

Or so he says.

Stuart died on January 19, 1868, at the age of seventy-eight, an apparently quiet end to a wild and adventure-filled life.

According to Stuart, the intent of chronicling the stories of his life was to serve as "a shining example" of how living the life of unadulterated jerk will only result in misery. Yet throughout his autobiography, he seemed to take great delight in sharing his wicked deeds, never wanting for modesty when recounting his own ingenuity.

An honest attempt at reform, or one everlasting con from a hopeless jerk?

Bibliography

INTRODUCTION

Casablanca, Ted, "Christian Takes on Sex, Violence, Underwear and Horse Manure," *E! Online,* April 2000.

Icon Group International, *Jerks: Webster's Quotations, Facts and Phrases,* 2009.

Sachse, Nancy Davis, *Born Among the Hills: The Sleeping Giant Story,* The Sleeping Giant Park Association, 1997.

CHAPTER 1: BENEDICT ARNOLD

Arnold, Benedict, "To the Inhabitants of America," New York, October 7, 1780, found at www.earlyamerica.com.

Brandt, Clare, *The Man in the Mirror: A Life of Benedict Arnold,* Random House, New York, 1994.

"Died: In England—Brigadier-General Benedict Arnold," *Columbian Centinel,* Aug. 1, 1801, found at www.earlyamerica.com.

Randall, Willard Sterne, *Benedict Arnold: Patriot and Traitor,* William Morrow and Co., New York, 1990.

CHAPTER 2: GEORGE METESKY

"Bomb Blast in Macy's," *New York Times,* July 25, 1956.

"'Bomber' Ordered to State Hospital," *New York Times,* April 19, 1957.

Brussel, James A., *Casebook of a Crime Psychiatrist,* Grove Press, New York, 1968.

"Crime: George Did It," *Time,* February 4, 1957.

Greenburg, Michael M., *The Mad Bomber of New York: The Extraordinary True Story of the Manhunt that Paralyzed a City,* Union Square Press, New York, 2011.

"Hunt for Bomber Covers 16 Years," *New York Times,* December 25, 1956.

"'I'm Glad I Did It,' Bomber States," *Springfield Union,* January 23, 1957.

Madden, Melissa Ann, "George Metesky: New York's Mad Bomber," "TruTV Crime Library," www.trutv.com.

CHAPTER 3: LYDIA SHERMAN

"The Derby Poisoner," *New York Times,* January 11, 1873.

McCain, Diana Ross, "A Poisonous Woman," *Connecticut Magazine,* September 1988, pp. 145–149.

"The Modern Borgia," *New York World,* July 2, 1871.

Schechter, Harold, *Fatal: The Poisonous Life of a Female Serial Killer,* Pocket Star, 2003.

Sherman, Lydia, *Lydia Sherman: Confession of the Arch Murderess of Connecticut,* T. R. Callender & Co., Philadelphia, 1873.

"Trial of Mrs. Sherman," *New York Times,* April 17, 1872.

CHAPTER 4: JULIUS SCHACKNOW

The Anointed, *God Is Alive,* 1972, www.popsike.com/THE-ANOINTED-LP-72-BROTHER-JULIUS-Cult-Xian-Folk-Psych/130506466065.html.

Cawley, Peter, "God's Little Acres," *Connecticut Magazine,* October 1979, pp. 35–39.

"Cult leader Brother Julius dies at 71," *New Haven Register,* July 30, 1996.

Gaines, Judith, "Connecticut Cult Leader One of Many 'Messiahs,'" *Globe Newspaper,* May 23, 1993.

Leavenworth, Jesse, "'Prophets' of Doom Challenge Area Clergy," *Hartford Courant,* February 15, 2003.

Monagan, Charles, "Disciples Gather Around Julius, 'the Son of God,'" *Meriden Journal,* April 1974, p. 1.

————, "Julius' Backers Weigh Legal Action," *Meriden Journal,* April 1974, p. 1.

————, "Julius Has 'Total Control over the Kids,'" *Meriden Journal,* April 1974, p. 1.

————, "Local Reactions to Julius Mixed," *Meriden Journal,* April 1974, p. 1.

Renner, Gerald, "Cult Leader's Problems Grow as Following Shrinks," *Hartford Courant,* June 1, 1993, p. 1.

"Who Is Brother Julius?," New England Cable News, producers Alan Cohn and David Roach, originally broadcast 1993. (In four parts on YouTube.com.)

CHAPTER 5: UNCAS

Oberg, Michael Leroy, *Uncas: First of the Mohegans,* Cornell University Press, 2003.

Phillips, David E., *Legendary Connecticut: Traditional Tales from the Nutmeg State,* Curbstone Press, 1992.

"Uncas: Sachem and Statesman," www.mohegan.nsn.us/heritage/ SachemUncas.aspx.

CHAPTER 6: REV. SAMUEL A. PETERS

Cohen, Sheldon S., *Connecticut's Loyalist Gadfly: The Reverend Samuel Andrew Peters,* The American Revolution Bicentennial Commission of Connecticut, The Waverly Printing Co., Hartford, 1976.

Patterson, Alan Owen, "Spotlight: Connecticut's Blue Laws," *Hog River Journal,* Winter 2008/2009, Vol. 7, No. 1, pp. 50–51.

Peters, Rev. Samuel A., *A General History of Connecticut,* sold by J. Bew, 1781.

Trumbull, J. Hammond, *The True-Blue Laws of Connecticut and New Haven, and the False Blue Laws Invented by the Rev. Samuel Peters,* American Publishing Co., Hartford 1876.

CHAPTER 7: ANASTASE A. VONSIATSKY

Bisbort, Alan, "Dreams of Glory," *Connecticut Magazine,* March 2000, pp. 44–49, 107–109.

"Famous Cases & Criminals: Vonsiatsky Espionage," www.fbi.com.

"Guide to the Anastase A. Vonsiatsky and Marion B. Ream Papers," http://library.providence.edu.

"Mme. Mouromsky Waits," *New York Times,* May 17, 1922.

Stephan, John J., *The Russian Fascists: Tragedy and Farce in Exile 1925–1945,* Harper & Row, New York, 1978.

CHAPTER 8: AMY ARCHER-GILLIGAN

Bovsun, Mara, "True Crime Story Behind Classic Comedy 'Arsenic and Old Lace,'" *New York Daily News,* January 17, 2010.

"Dig Up More Bodies in Hunt for Poison," *New York Times,* May 12, 1916.

Phelps, M. William, *The Devil's Rooming House: The True Story of America's Deadliest Female Serial Killer,* Lyons Press, Guilford, 2010.

CHAPTER 9: P. T. BARNUM

Barnum, P. T., "The Art of Money Getting, or Golden Rules of Making Money," 1880.

———, *The Life of P. T. Barnum, Written by Himself,* Redfield, New York, 1855.

"P. T. Barnum in Jail—What the Great Showman Did Over 50 Years Ago," *New York Times,* November 22, 1883.

Saxon, A. H., *P. T. Barnum: The Legend and the Man,* Columbia University Press, New York, 1989.

CHAPTER 10: PHILIP MUSICA

"Accuse Musica & Son of Big Bank Frauds," *New York Times,* March 18, 1913.

Clikeman, Paul M., *Called to Account: Fourteen Financial Frauds That Shaped the American Accounting Profession,* Routledge, 2009.

"The Coster Case," *Connecticut Circle,* January 1939, pp. 14–15.

"Head of Old Drug Firm Commits Suicide after Fantastic 15-Year Hoax," *Life,* December 26, 1938, pp. 18–19.

"Musica Confesses to $600,000 Thefts," *New York Times,* April 12, 1913.

"Musica: The Documentary," www.philipmusica.com.

Shaplen, Robert, "Annals of Crime: The Metamorphosis of Philip Musica-I," *The New Yorker,* October 22, 1955.

———, "Annals of Crime: The Metamorphosis of Philip Musica-II," *The New Yorker,* October 29, 1955.

"Trade: My God, Daddy!," *Time,* Dec. 26, 1938.

CHAPTER 11: SAMUEL COLT

Edwards, William B., *The Story of Colt's Revolver: The Biography of Col. Samuel Colt,* The Stackpole Company, Harrisburg, PA, 1953.

Grant, Ellsworth S., *The Colt Legacy: The Colt Armory in Hartford,* Mowbray Company, Providence, RI, 1982.

Hosley, William, *Colt: The Making of an American Legend,* University of Massachusetts Press, Amherst, 1996.

Simon, Kenneth A., "Colt: Legend & Legacy," Connecticut Public Television, www.simonpure.com, original broadcast 1997.

CHAPTER 12: HANNAH HOVEY

Coffey, Edward N., *A Glimpse of Old Monroe,* Monroe Sesquicentennial Commission, 1974.

Cortesi, Lawrence, "Was Mercy Desborough in League with The Devil?," *Connecticut Magazine,* October 1972, p. 27.

"Hannah Cranna, The Witch of Old Monroe," www.monroe historicsociety.org/hannacranna.html.

Philips, David E., *Legendary Connecticut,* Curbstone Press, Connecticut, 1992.

Taylor, John M., *The Witchcraft Delusion in Colonial Connecticut 1647–1697,* The Grafton Press, 1908.

"The Story of the Witch of Monroe," *Connecticut Post,* November 1, 2007.

CHAPTER 13: REV. HERBERT H. HAYDEN

Ethier, Bryan, *True Crime: Connecticut,* Stackpole Books, Mechanicsburg, PA, 2009, pp. 19–35.

Hayden, Rev. Herbert H., *The Rev. Herbert H. Hayden, An Autobiography,* Press of the Plimpton Mfg. Co., Hartford, 1880.

McConnell, Virginia A., *Arsenic Under the Elms: Murder in Victorian New Haven,* Praeger Publishers, Westport, 1999.

CHAPTER 14: SALVATORE ANNUNZIATO

"Annunziatos Hope to Get Bail Reduced," *New Haven Register,* March 4, 1971, p. 1.

Fisher, Stanley, "Ex-Annunziato Friend Tells of Shooting Aftermath," *New Haven Register,* Feb. 24, 1971, p. 64.

———, "Police Tell of Finding Two with Gunshot Wounds," *New Haven Register,* Feb. 19, 1971, p. 44.

Hoffman, Christopher, "Midge Renault and the Heyday of the Mob," *New Haven Independent,* Aug. 25, 2009.

———, "Operation Richmart," *New Haven Independent,* Sept. 28, 2009.

———, "Pinnochio," *New Haven Independent,* Sept. 21, 2009.

———, "Top Hoodlum," *New Haven Independent,* Sept. 7, 2009.

————, "Whitey," *New Haven Independent,* Aug. 31, 2009.

Kochakian, Charles, "Cops Believe 'Midge' May Have Been Slain," *New Haven Register,* June 29, 1979, p. 1.

————, "Midge Associate Is Shot to Death," *New Haven Register,* Jan. 28, 1980, p. 1.

Mattia, Thomas, "Security Tight as Trial of Union Aide Begins," *Bridgeport Telegram,* Sept. 26, 1979, p. 24.

Pileggi, Nicholas, *Goodfellas,* Warner Bros. Pictures, U.S.A., 1990.

Quinn, John, "Over the Underworld," *Elm City Clarion,* May 26, 2002.

Schwartz, Leland, "Annunziatos Convicted of Murder Plot," *New Haven Journal-Courier,* Mar. 4, 1971, pp. 1–2.

CHAPTER 15: WILLIAM STUART

Orcutt, Samuel, *History of the Towns of New Milford and Bridgewater, Connecticut, 1703–1882,* The Case, Lockwood and Brainard Co., Hartford, 1882, pp. 411–412.

Peterson, Karin E., "Connecticut's First & Most Celebrated Counterfeiter," *Hog River Journal,* Winter 2008/2009, Vol. 7, No. 1, pp. 32–39.

————, "Escape from New-Gate Prison," *Hog River Journal,* Summer 2006, Vol. 4, No. 3, pp. 32–37.

Stuart, William, *Sketches of the Life of William Stuart: The First and Most Celebrated Counterfeiter of Connecticut—As Given by Himself,* self-published, 1854.

Index

A

All Russian Fascist Party (RFP), 99
All Russian National Revolutionary Party (VNRP), 99
Allen, Ethan, 4–5
Andre, Major John, 10, 12, 13
Andrews, Franklin, 117, 118–19
Annunziato, Frank, 192, 197, 199–200
Annunziato, Salvatore "Midge Renault," 189–203
    avoiding military draft, 192
    birth and troubled childhood, 191
    boxing career, 191–92
    "Charlie the Blade" Tourine and, 193, 194
    children of, 192. *See also* Annunziato, Frank
    death of son, 197
    disappearance of, 201–3
    gas-rationing racket, 192–93
    Goodfellas and, 189, 191
    Gould hit and, 199–200
    initiating riots, 196
    keeping mistress, 197
    as "made man," 193–94
    marriage, 192
    numbers and protection rackets, 194
    photograph, 190
    political power, 195
    pressure on Mafia and, 196–97
    prison time, 193, 196, 197–98, 200–201
    Ralph Mele and, 193
    shooting fellow hoodlum, 198
    starting crime career, 192–93
    summary of jerkiness, 189–91
    technicalities reprieving, 198, 200–201
    throwing weight around, 195–96
    union boss, 194–95
    "Whitey" Tropiano and, 194
    wife Louise and, 192, 197, 202
Archer, James, 110, 112, 117
Archer-Gilligan, Amy, 107–20
    abuse charges, 110
    arrest and trials, 118–20
    Arsenic and Old Lace and, 107
    birth and early life, 107–9
    Dr. Howard King and, 111, 113, 115, 116, 117
    drug addiction gambit, 119–20
    dysfunctional family life, 107
    exhumed bodies telling story, 116–18
    fatal flaw in business plan, 113–14
    going on offense against accusers, 112–13, 118
    having victims buy arsenic, 111
    insanity defense, 120
    investigation into murders, 115–18
    James Archer and, 110, 112, 117
    killing husbands, 110, 115
    killing "inmates" of home, 110–15, 116
    later years and death, 120
    marriage to James Archer, 109
    marriage to Michael Gilligan, 114
    medical examiner bought by. *See* Dr. Howard King and
    Michael Gilligan and, 114–15, 117
    murderous spree, 110–16
    opening old folks home, 109
    playing sympathetic figure, 112
    portrait, 108
    public image, 109–10, 112, 113–14
    sentences for murders, 119, 120
    suspicions about, 110–11, 112–13, 115
Arnold, Benedict, 1–16
    aligning with Loyalists, 10–11
    apothecary business, 3
    attacking own country, 14–15
    betraying country, 11–15
    birth and early life, 1–3
    characteristics and traits, 1, 3
    children of, 4
    courtmartials, 6, 11
    death and obituary, 16
    duel at sea, 4
    eluding capture, 12–13
    end of military career, 15–16
    engraving of, 2
    Ethan Allen and, 4–5
    events leading to betrayal, 5–11
    financial problems, 10–11
    flaunting/justifying betrayal, 13–14
    Fort Ticonderoga and, 4–5, 7
    George Washington and, 5, 7, 9, 11, 12–13, 14
    heroism, 6, 8–9
    John Andre and, 10, 12, 13
    joining Sons of Liberty, 4
    later years, 16
    leg injuries, 5, 9
    loyalty oath, 9
    marriage to Margaret Mansfield, 4
    marriage to Peggy Shippen, 10
    promotion to major general, 6–7
    Rev. Samuel A. Peters and, 4, 83, 85
    squabbles with fellow officers, 4–6, 7–8
    summary of jerkiness, 1
    synonymous with "traitor," 1

travel and seafaring life, 3–4
    West Point command, 11
Arnold, Benedict III, 1, 3
Arnold, Hannah (sister), 3
Arnold, Hannah Waterman King (mother),
    1, 3
arsenic
    Amy Archer-Gilligan killing with,
        110–16
    Lydia Sherman killing with, 37,
        38–39, 41, 43, 44–45, 46–47
    Mary Stannard murder and, 182–83,
        186, 187, 188
    murderess having victims buy, 111
    symptoms, 37, 111

B
Bailey, Dr. Leonard, 182
Bailey, James, 133
Barnum, P. T., 121–34
    bankruptcy then prosperity, 129–30
    birth and early life, 122
    books by, 129
    Bunker Siamese twins and, 128
    Cardiff Giant hoaxes, 131
    circus of, 132, 133–34
    death and legacy, 134
    death of wife, 132
    duping for money, 126–27
    final hoax, 134
    James Bailey and, 133
    Jumbo the elephant and, 133
    learning to profit by lying, 124–25
    libel conviction and jail release
        celebration, 124
    marriages and children, 122, 132
    mermaid fraud, 126–27
    money-making insights, 129–30
    newspaper of, 122–24
    obituary before death, 133–34
    political career, 130
    portrait, 123
    quotes attributed to, 121–22, 130
    selling "humbug," 125
    summary of jerkiness, 121–22
    "Swedish Nightingale" and, 128
    Tom Thumb hoax, 127–28
    Universalism religion and, 122,
        133, 134
Barnum's American Museum, 125–28, 129
Barnum's Grand Scientific and Musical
    Theater, 125
Beardsley, Dr. J. C., 44–45
Beville, Elsie, 49
Biondi, Richard, 200
Birdseye, Mary, 79
Boston Tea Party, 80–81

Brother Julius. *See* Schacknow, Julius
Brotherhood of Russian Truth, 99
Brussel, Dr. James A., 26–27, 28–29, 30, 31
Bunker, Chang and Eng, 128
Burroughs, Stephen, 208

C
Cardiff Giant hoaxes, 131
Cassacinamon, Robin, 72–73
Clinton, General Henry, 14
Colt, Samuel, 150–63
    birth and early life, 150–51
    building Coltsville, 158–59
    children and sibling deaths, 160
    Civil War, guns and, 160–62
    death, legacy, rumors, and
        speculation, 162–63
    dream mansion, 159–60
    gun development/business, 151–52,
        153–59, 160–62
    laughing gas demos, 152–53
    living high life, 157
    meeting/marrying Elizabeth, 157, 159
    nephew/son of, 163
    questionable business practices, 158
    sketch, 152
    summary of jerkiness, 150
    underwater mines, 151, 154
    waterproof cable company, 154
    year at sea, 151
Costello, Frank, 193
Coster, F. Donald. *See* Musica, Philip
counterfeit scams. *See* Stuart, William
cult leader. *See* Schacknow, Julius
Curtiss, James, 40

D
Desborough, Mercy, 164

E
Easton, Colonel James, 5

F
Fashist magazine (Vonsiatsky), 98, 100,
    101, 102–3, 104
Finney, Howard E., 26, 28, 29
Fort Griswold, 15
Fort Stanwix, 7
Fort Ticonderoga, 4–5, 7

G
Gage, General Thomas, 84
Gates, General Horatio, 7–8
A General History of Connecticut (Peters),
    77, 86–89, 90
Gilbert, Abigail, 79

Gilligan, Michael, 114–15, 117
God is Alive (album), 53–54
Goslee, Carlan, 112, 115, 117–18
Gould, Edward, 199–200
Gowdy, Alice, 117
gun development/business, 151–52, 153–59, 160–62

H
hair company scam, 138–40
Hallett, Charity, 122, 132
Hawley, Susan, 179–80, 181, 183, 186
Hayden, Rev. Herbert H., 175–88
    autobiography, 175–76
    birth and early life, 176
    career and income challenges, 177–78
    children of, 177, 178, 180
    day of Stannard murder and, 182–84, 188
    forced to higher calling, 176–77
    marriage to Rosa, 177
    murder trials and acquittal, 185–88
    murdering nanny. *See* Stannard, Mary
    portrait, 174
    prison time, 186
    summary of jerkiness, 175–76
Hayden, Rosa Shaw, 177, 178, 179, 180, 182, 185–86, 187–88
Henshaw, Caroline, 163
Herald of Freedom and Truth, 122–24
Heth, Joyce, 124
Hill, Henry, 189
"Historical Discourse at New Haven" (Kingsley), 90–91
Hitler, Adolf, Vonsiatsky and, 99, 100, 101, 102, 103, 104
Hoover, J. Edgar, 194
Hotchkiss, David B., 187
Hovey, Captain Joseph, 165–66
Hovey, Hannah (Hannah Cranna), 164–73
    birth, 165
    Connecticut witchcraft and, 164–65
    death and funeral legend, 171–73
    entitlement attitude, 168, 170
    fisherman jinx story, 168
    ghost of, 173
    gravestone, 167, 173
    hay wagon hex story, 169
    house of, 167–68, 172, 173
    husband's death and, 165–66
    pie hex story, 168–69
    rooster of, 168, 171
    saving crops lore, 169–70
    witchcraft charges, 170
    witchcraft image and legends, 166–73
Hubbard, Carol Jenkins, 141–42
Hubbard, Edward, 141–42
Hurlburt, Old (Dennis), 40–42, 45

J
Johnson, Mary, 164

K
Kennedy, John F., 106
Kennedy, Stephen P., 25–26
King, Dr. Howard, 111, 113, 115, 116, 117
King, Hannah Waterman, 1, 3
King Philip's War, 74–75
Koresh, David, 59
Kuhn, Fritz, 101–2
Kunze, Wilhelm, 102, 103–4

L
Lathrop, Daniel and Joshua, 3
Ledyard, Colonel William, 15
Lee, Richard C., 195
Lydia Sherman: Confession of the Arch Murderess of Connecticut (Sherman), 33
Lynch, Maude, 117

M
Mad Bomber. *See* Metesky, George
Mafia
    Golden Age of, 194
    J. Edgar Hoover and, 194
    pressure mounting on, 196–97
    Ralph Mele and, 193, 194
    See also Annunziato, Salvatore "Midge Renault"
Mansfield (Arnold), Margaret, 4, 5
Mason, Captain John, 66–67, 71, 74
McKesson & Robbins, 143–44, 145–48, 149
Mele, Ralph, 193
mermaid fraud, 126–27
Metesky, George, 17–32
    admitting to bombings, 31
    arrest of, 18, 30–31
    birth and early life, 17
    bomb traits, 21, 22
    bombing spree, 21–26
    charges filed, 31
    Con Edison battle, 19–21, 22–23, 25, 26–27, 29, 30
    concerted manhunt for, 25–31
    disabled and fired, 19–20
    Dr. James Brussel and, 26–27, 28–29, 30, 31
    "fateful day," 19
    first bomb "unit," 20–21
    later years and death, 32
    letters leading to undoing, 21, 22–23
    lung-damaging accident, 19
    as "Mad Bomber," 17
    mental illness, 31–32
    military service, 17
    newspaper aiding in arrest, 29, 30
    parents and siblings, 17, 27–28

photo of arrest, 18
post-military life, 17–19
psychiatric profile, 26–29, 30
public awareness of, 23–24, 25
released from custody, 32
summary of jerkiness, 17
tips leading to arrest, 29–31
trial and sentence, 31
tuberculosis plaguing, 19, 31, 32
wartime bombing truce, 21
Mills, Joseph, 206–8
Montgomery, Richard, 5
Mouromsky, Liobouv, 94–95, 96–97
Musica, Philip (aka Donald F. Coster), 135–49
  arrests, 136, 138, 140, 148
  birth and immigration from Italy, 135–37
  bogus *Who's Who* biography, 142
  bootlegging business, 141–43
  charitable work, 144–45
  F. Donald Coster alias, 142–49
  family participating with, 137, 138, 139–40, 142–43
  final minutes and suicide, 148–49
  Frank D. Costa alias, 141–42
  hair company scam, 138–40
  jailed and pardoned, 138
  jailhouse snitch and spy recruiter, 140
  Julian Thompson and, 143, 144, 145, 147
  living high life, 139
  marrying Carol Jenkins Hubbard, 141–42
  McKesson & Robbins and, 143–44, 145–48, 149
  photograph, 136
  summary of jerkiness, 135
  waterfront crime, 137–38
  William Johnson alias, 140–41
  wrecking marriage to get wife, 141–42

N

Narragansett tribe, 62, 63, 65, 66–70, 71, 73–75
Nazis. *See* Vonsiatsky, Anastase A.
Nineteenth Hole, 97

O

Owen, Hannah, 79

P

Pequot tribe, 64, 65–67, 69, 72–73
Peters, Rev. Samuel A., 77–91
  affinity for England, 78, 80
  appealing to British general, 84
  beating Loyalist drums, 81, 83–84
  Benedict Arnold and, 4, 83, 85
  birth and early life, 78
  Boston Tea Party and, 80–81
  bounty on, 84
  calling patriots traitors, then retracting, 81, 82
  casting aspersions from afar, 85–86
  children of, 79
  death of wives and children, 79
  economic and professional success, 79
  exile in England, 85–90
  A General History of Connecticut, 77, 86–89, 90
  Gov. Jonathan Trumbull and, 80, 82–83, 86
  later years and death, 90
  marriage to/death of three wives, 79
  oath and resolves for America, 81
  ordination, 78
  perspective of childhood friend, 90–91
  pseudomania (abhorrence of truth) of, 91
  returning to America, 89–90
  seeking refuge, 83
  slandering Blue Laws, 87–89, 90
  smallpox bout, 78
  Sons of Liberty and, 80–82, 83, 84
  souring on England, 90
  summary of jerkiness, 77–78

Q

Quinnatisset Farm and Country Club, 97

R

Ream, Marion Buckingham, 95–98, 105–6
Rev. Herbert H. Hayden: An Autobiography (Hayden), 175–76
Royster, Priscilla, 105
Russian fascism. *See* Vonsiatsky, Anastase A.

S

Schacknow, Julius, 48–60
  abuse charges, 55, 56–57, 59
  birth and early life, 48–49
  David Koresh vs., 59
  death and legacy, 59–60
  downfall, 57
  fading into background, 56
  gathering followers, 49–50, 52–53, 54
  as God's only son, 51
  guidance from God, 49, 51
  Joanne and, 50, 51–52, 55, 56
  lawsuits and charges, 56–57
  messianic cult leader, 51–56, 58–59
  military service, 49

music business (TAMPCO) and
albums, 53–55
Oh God! movie and, 59
photograph, 50
preaching at IT&T job, 50
preying on weak and young, 52–53
as prophet, 50–51
real estate and construction
businesses, 54–56, 57
reorganizing his flock, 54–55
self-proclaimed divinity, 48, 59, 60
separating followers from money, 53,
55–56
summary of jerkiness, 48
swapping wives, 51–52
as "the sinning Jesus," 51
threatening departing members, 58
wives, divorces, and children, 49,
51–52, 59–60
womanizing and sexual focus/abuse,
49, 51, 54, 55, 56–57, 59–60
Schuyler, General Philip, 7
Seeley, Deacon Seth, 122–24
serial killers. *See* Archer-Gilligan, Amy;
Sherman, Lydia
Sherlock, Joseph, 207–8
Sherman, Horatio N., 42–44
Sherman, Lydia, 33–47
arrest and trial, 45
bestselling confession book, 33
biopsy implicating, 45
birth and early life, 33–35
children of, 35–36, 38–39
confession of murders, 46
description of, 35
Edward Struck and, 35–37
Horatio Sherman and, 42–44
inheriting fortune, 41–42
James Curtiss and, 40
killing children, 38–39, 43
killing husbands, 37, 41, 44
life sentence and death, 46
marriage #1, 35
marriage #2, 41
marriage #3, 42
as nurse, 39, 40
Old (Dennis) Hurlburt and, 40–42
poem about, 46–47
portrait, 34
religious awakening, 46
summary of jerkiness, 33
suspicions about, 39–40
tribulations leading to first murder,
35–37
Shippen (Arnold), Peggy, 10, 16
Siamese twins, 128
slave sale scam, 210
Smith, Charles, 117

Smith, Mary, 49
Sons of Liberty
Benedict Arnold and, 4
Samuel Peters and, 80–82, 83, 84, 85
Stannard, Charlie, 181, 183–84, 185,
186, 188
Stannard, Mary
affair with Hayden, 179–80
background and vulnerability, 178
funeral and exhumations, 185–86
hired as Hayden nanny, 178
murder of, 175, 182–84, 188
suspected pregnancy and responses,
180–81, 186
trials for murder of, 185–88
Stephens, Redmond, 95
Stratton, Charles Sherwood, 127–28
Struck, Edward S., 35–37
Stuart, William, 204–18
annoying/playing prison keeper, 215,
216–18
attraction to cousin, 206
autobiography, 204–5, 207, 218
bilking widow, 213–14
birth and boyhood pranks, 205–6
counterfeiting scams, 206, 207–9, 210,
211–12, 213, 214, 216
death of, 218
impression of prison, 215
jail/prison time, 209, 213, 214–18
joining/deserting army, 213
Joseph Mills, Joseph Sherlock and,
206–8
lame for life, 217–18
marriage, 211
nautical adventures, 210–11, 213
negotiating freedom, 217–18
other scams, 211, 213
in perpetual trouble, 206, 211
portrait, 207
reformation of, 218
scamming potential snitches,
209, 212
slave sale scam, 210
summary of jerkiness, 204–5
war/military profits, 212–13
women accomplices, 209, 210
Studley, Edgar and Jane, 180–81
"Swedish Nightingale," 128
Sweetman, Minnie, 52
Sweetman, Paul and Joanne, 51–52, 56

T

Tatobem, 64, 65
Thayer, Robert, 113, 118
Thompson, Julian, 143, 144, 145, 147
Tourine, "Charlie the Blade," 193, 194
Tropiano, Ralph "Whitey," 194

The True-Blue Laws of Connecticut and New Haven, and the False Blue Laws Forged by Peters (Trumbull), 90
Trumbull, Governor Jonathan, 80, 82–83, 86
Trumbull, James Hammond, 90–91
Trumbull, Reverend Dr., 90–91
Tuller, Captain Elam, 215, 216–18

U

Uncas, 61–76
  assassination attempt, 73
  befriending and destroying Miantonomi and the Narragansett, 63, 67–71
  birth and heritage, 62
  Captain John Mason and, 66–67, 71, 74
  consolidating power, 67–68
  currying favor with English, 68–69, 70, 73, 75
  death of, 75
  death of son (Attawanhood) and, 75
  destiny as leader, 62–64
  eating flesh of Miantonomi, 70
  English withdrawing support, 74, 76
  erosion of/rebuilding power, 73–75
  European explorer arrival and, 64
  harassing colonists and Pequot, 72–73
  illustration of, 63
  King Philip's War and, 74–75
  Last of the Mohicans and, 61, 76
  Narragansett revenge against, 71, 73
  overrunning/exterminating Pequot people, 65–67
  Owaneco (father) and, 62, 64
  Owaneco (son) and, 74, 75
  peace treaties and, 68, 71
  Podunk staged raid and execution, 73
  shrewdness of, 67
  summary of jerkiness, 61–62
  taking wives, 64, 67–68
  Tatobem and, 64, 65
  Winthrop, Cassacinamon and, 72–73
underwater mines, 151, 154

V

Vastano, Tommy "The Blond," 201–2
Vonsiatsky, Anastase A., 92–106
  annulment of marriage, 97
  as bigamist, 92, 96

birth and early life in Russia, 93–94
as "Count Annie," 97
death of parents and siblings, 94
devotion to Romanovs and fascism, 98
emigration to United States, 96
espionage indictment, trial, imprisonment, 104–5
Fashist magazine, 98, 100, 101, 102–3, 104
FBI searching and seizing property, 104
FBI tracking, 100–101, 103, 104
Fritz Kuhn and, 101–2
Hitler and, 99, 100, 101, 102, 103, 104
later years and death, 106
life after prison, 105–6
Liobouv Mouromsky and, 94–95, 96–97
living high/fast life, 97–98
Marion Ream and, 95–98, 105–6
marriages, 94–95, 96, 105
pursuing fascist agenda, 98–104
Russian military service, 94, 95
separating self from Hitler's party, 102–3
son of, 105, 106
summary of jerkiness, 92
using women and womanizing, 92, 95–96, 97–98
Wilhelm Kunze and, 102, 103–4
Vserossiyskaya Fashistskaya Organizatsiya, 99

W

Walker, Capt. Samuel H., 155
Washington, George
  Arnold, Benedict and, 5, 7, 9, 11, 12–13, 14
  purported nurse of, 124, 129
waterproof cable company, 154
Winthrop, John, Jr., 72–73
witchcraft. *See* Hovey, Hannah (Hannah Cranna)

Y

Young, Alse, 164

Z

Zernitz, Lawrence, 198

About the Author

For more than a decade, Ray Bendici has been an editor and award-winning writer at *Connecticut Magazine.* He has also edited *Connecticut Curiosities, 3rd Edition,* for Globe Pequot Press, and runs DamnedCT.com, a website dedicated to everything unusual, weird, and extraordinary in the state, from supposedly haunted places and UFO sightings to quirky characters and mysterious legends. He resides in Shelton with his wife and two sons. Visit him at raybendici.com.